RAISED BY COMMITTEE

By

Carollyne Haynes

Order this book online at www.trafford.com
or email orders@trafford.com

Most Trafford titles are also available at major online book retailers.

Note for Librarians: A cataloguing record for this book is available from Library and Archives Canada at www.collectionscanada.ca/amicus/index-e.html

Printed in Victoria, BC, Canada.

ISBN: 978-1-4269-2144-5 (sc)

ISBN: 978-1-4269-2234-3 (dj)

Library of Congress Control Number 2009940586

Our mission is to efficiently provide the world's finest, most comprehensive book publishing service, enabling every author to experience success. To find out how to publish your book, your way, and have it available worldwide, visit us online at www.trafford.com

Trafford rev. 12/15/2009

 www.trafford.com

North America & international
toll-free: 1 888 232 4444 (USA & Canada)
phone: 250 383 6864 ♦ fax: 812 355 4082

To the memory of Miss Lillian Hopkins,
known to many simply as Nurse,
and all the Aunties, social workers and others who made up the
Children's Committee.

To my husband, Jim
for giving me the courage and space to tell my story.

And for my children, Alex, Toby and Malonie -
for teaching me the meaning of unconditional love
I hope you had a very happy time of it indeed ...

PREFACE

Memory is a nebulous thing at best, and mine is no exception. *Raised by Committee* would not be possible without the meticulous notes made by a myriad of social workers, child care workers and others concerning the rather turbulent events of my adolescent life. I am indebted to them. I am also indebted to Caroline Hitchcock of the Devon County Council for retrieving my file from the bowels of City Hall and photocopying the more than five hundred pages it contained.

My appreciation is also extended to Joyce White, my writing tutor, for her encouragement and support in telling my story; my friends, Maxine Macgillivray, Patti Sloan, and Carol Stewart for reading the various drafts; and, Pearl Luke for reviewing the completed manuscript. And finally, my loving appreciation to my husband, Jim, who helped me realize that the real story was about what happened after. So now I offer up to you the story of what happened - after the police came.

CHAPTER ONE

**Excerpt Of Report To The County Of
Devon Children's Committee**

I have been investigating an application for these
children to be received into care, the mother having
deserted. Family have been known to the department
for some time because the mother often left home.
I visited Mrs. Puddicombe in her bed-sitting room
in Exeter. She was only interested in [her youngest
daughter] Jane. Said that Mr. Puddicombe had been
getting into bed with her eldest daughter, Gail. Mrs.
Puddicombe was advised to tell the police. She was
not willing to do this.

Police informed on 15.2.63.

Gail is nearly thirteen, with fair hair and slight
build. She has been attending the grammar school
at Riverton, though while she should be of grammar
school ability her work has suffered through her
family responsibilities. Her mother admits that she
has always been more of a sister than mother to her

daughter and Gail has been in the habit of going with her mother to night clubs, etc. She has also been the victim of indecent assault by her father for some years. With her mother's absence from the home she has also had to take more than usual responsibility for her younger brother and sister.

This combination of circumstances has given her a maturity and knowledge beyond her years in some aspects. She is rather highly strung and excitable and liable to outbursts of temper. Her feelings for her parents are ambivalent and in some ways protective.

She has been anxious about her break in education, and would like to continue her music lessons. She also likes sport.

Respectfully submitted
Miss Jean Stinson
Child Care Officer

The doors of the black Mariah slammed shut, sealing us inside. My mother, grandmother and aunt stood huddled on the pavement, their collars pulled high against the cold night air. They waved and blew kisses at us, calling out 'bye, bye'. Nanny always said it was important to put on a good face, just in case the neighbours were watching – which, of course, they were. Peaking out from behind their curtains, they might have guessed we were going on an outing. But children don't usually go on outings in black Mariah's, especially not at night, in the dead of winter. Mum struck a match and lit a cigarette, casting an eerie glow over my grandmother and aunt as they stood beside her. I smiled back at them from inside the van and waved with more enthusiasm than I felt.

My brother, Justin, sat beside me, wide-eyed with excitement. He had just turned eight, and had no idea what was really happening. My baby sister, Jane, clambered up on the seat and watched as the figures huddled on the pavement faded into the darkness, then burst into tears.

"Mummy!" she wailed, her little hand clawing towards the rear window, as if trying to pull her back into view.

"You'll see her later," I tried to console her, hoping it was true.

Mum had been gone for weeks this time, only reappearing that afternoon outside my school accompanied by a policeman. I had been in my classroom packing my homework books when Janet burst in looking for me. I was often the last one to leave, delaying the inevitable return home to a cold and empty house. Dad wouldn't get home from work until five o'clock, and Justin and Jane would be at the babysitters. Dad would start up the fire when he got home, or else he'd put a few shillings in the meter and turn on the electric fire.

"Gail, you'll never guess what," Janet announced, her eyes glistening with excitement. "You're mum's outside looking for you, and she has a policeman with her."

Janet was the class know-it-all who made everyone's business her own.

So Mum had come back, just like I told myself she would. I knew she couldn't leave me with Dad, not knowing what he was doing to me like she did. She couldn't let it go on much longer - it had already gone on too long. I buckled my canvas satchel closed and headed towards the door. I'd been saving the money Dad gave me to buy a real leather satchel but I didn't have enough yet. Mum had bought me a canvas satchel as a reward for getting into grammar school but I had had my heart set on a real leather one. I'd tried to hide my disappointment but Mum had seen the look that crossed my face and had threatened to take it back if I wasn't more grateful than that. Didn't I know they weren't made of money, she'd said. Like I hadn't worked that out already!

Mum was standing at the end of the school driveway, leaning against one of the stone gate pillars smoking a cigarette. She was tall, slim, and beautiful, her short blond hair sporting a recent home perm.

"Hello, Mum," I said, not sure of how to react under the circumstances.

"Ah, there you are," she said, "I've been waiting here for ages. The police want to talk to you about what's been going on at home. You know, with your father and all."

She ground her cigarette butt out with the toe of her high-heeled shoe.

The sense of relief that had washed over me when I saw she was back was short-lived. I stared at her, a sense of panic washing over me. Dad had made me promise never, ever, to tell anyone. He told me, time and time again, that I would be in dire trouble if I ever told anyone. It was our little secret, he'd said. And now, here was Mum telling me I had to talk to the police about it. I wasn't sure I could do that. I just wanted her to come home and keep me safe at night.

A small cluster of students watched as Mum and I climbed into the back seat of the police car. I avoided their gazes, trying to hide the humiliation I felt. I wanted to tell them to get lost and mind their own bloody business. As the car pulled away, I stuck my tongue out at them. Let them talk about that.

"I've told the police my side of the story about your Dad," Mum said. "Now they want to hear your side."

I shifted uncomfortably in my seat. Didn't she understand that I didn't want to tell them my side of the story? I just wanted it to end. I didn't want anyone to know what an ugly, sordid life I'd been living. They might think it was my fault, or that I had somehow wanted Dad to do the things he did. And what would happen if I did tell? Would they take him away? Would Mum come home and look after us if they did?

At the police station we were shown into an interrogation room on the second floor. Sgt. Salter would be right with us, the policeman said. And then we were left alone. The room was large with two windows at one end. They had bars on them. There was a large desk close to the windows with two straight-back wooden chairs facing it. We sat down and waited, in silence.

My initial joy at seeing my mother had quickly evaporated. I was angry at her for leaving us. She'd gone to a New Year's Eve party and never bothered to come home. She'd even joked as she was leaving that she wouldn't see us until next year. I'd thought she meant it and got upset and asked to go with her. But she said she was only joking - didn't I know it was New Year's Eve and next year was only tomorrow? Didn't she know that tomorrow was a life time away, when I had to live through another night in the house alone with Dad? But in the end at least he hadn't left us, like she had. As much as I feared Dad at night, I knew he would be there for us in the morning.

The door opened abruptly and Sgt. Salter came in. He seated himself behind the desk, took out a fresh pad of lined paper, and picked up his pen.

"Right then," he said glancing between my mother and me, "you better tell us what's been going on at home, Gail."

His manner was direct but his tone of voice was gentle. He waited for me to speak, but I couldn't. No words would come out. I didn't know where to begin. I took a deep breath and started talking, slowly at first then faster and faster, the words falling over each other in a nervous tangle. I said I was doing my best to help look after the younger children, and trying to get Justin to school on time, but sometimes he was late because he wouldn't hurry up, and how Dad took Jane to the babysitter, but Graham didn't even help because he was always up at Nanny's house, and I wasn't very good at cooking but I was trying to learn, but Dad was usually home in time to make dinner and put Jane to bed, and that I put Justin to bed after I finished my homework because he was allowed to stay up until eight, and Dad had usually gone to the pub by then and didn't get home until late. My voice trailed away. I sat there staring at my hands, picking at my cuticles until they bled.

"And?" Sgt. Salter prodded.

I shrugged, unsure of where to go from there.

"It's alright Gail. You can tell him what happens," my mother coaxed.

"I can't," I whispered. "Dad made me promise."

"What happens when your father gets home from the pub, Gail?" Sgt. Salter asked after a few moments.

I started biting on my cuticles, tearing away strips of skin with my teeth. I could taste the blood but was oblivious to the pain. I was used to ignoring pain. My mother slapped my hand away from my mouth.

"Stop doing that, for crying out loud. Just tell Sgt. Salter what's been going on and everything will be alright."

I burst into tears. Alright for whom, I wondered. Certainly not alright for me, if my ugly secret got out. Certainly not alright for

Dad, if people found out what he'd been doing. And certainly not alright for Justin and Jane if they took their Dad away. Dad was all we had since Mum had gone.

Mum reached over and gently put her hand on my arm in a rare act of compassion. "It's alright you can tell the sergeant all about it. He isn't going to hurt you."

I cried ever harder.

"But what will they do to Dad? And what will Dad do to me, if he finds out I told?" I felt like a trapped animal, with no way out.

It was getting dark outside as the weak February light faded. I hated the nights worst of all. I stared at the lone light bulb hanging from the centre of the ceiling, its green metal shade coated in a layer of dust. The light made kaleidoscope patterns through my tears. I took a deep breath and forced myself to stop crying. Crying never did any good. Babies cry and I wasn't a baby, I had no time for that nonsense.

"What happens when your father gets home from the pub, Gail?" Sgt. Salter asked again, once I had calmed myself.

"He does things," I whispered.

"What sort of things," he asked.

"You know. Grown up sorts of things." I couldn't speak.

I started scratching at my arms, distractedly picking at the pimples till they were red and bleeding. As long as I never told anyone what was going on, I could pretend it never happened. I could carry on as if everything was alright. Everyone seemed to love my father, except my grandparents that is.

Dad's stage name was Rex Royston, and people raved about his trombone playing and the bands he put together. Everyone told me how lucky I was, to have a father like him. I'd seen dance halls full of people clapping and cheering as he played Moonlight Serenade, and pretty women would have tears in their eyes as the sweet melody washed over them. I'd be so proud to say that he was my Dad - until we got home, that is. And now I was being told to push Humpty Dumpty off the wall which would surely crack the shell of Dad's public image. I was afraid that all the king's horses and all the king's men wouldn't be able to put him back together again.

And what if they didn't believe me? What if, after I told them everything, they made me go home to Rex's house anyway? What then? Who would protect me then? Would Mum come home? Her violent temper outbursts were almost harder to bear than what Dad did. At least Dad never beat us like Mum did, except once he spanked Justin for breaking a neighbour's window. But he'd never raised his hand to me, at least not in the daytime, or yelled at us or called us names or pulled us into the house by our hair because he wanted help with something, or slapped us so hard across our ear that we heard ringing sounds for ages afterwards, just because we were making too much noise. I loved my father, most of the time, and I didn't want them to hurt him. I just wanted him to stop doing those grown up things to me.

"Would you like something to drink?" Sgt. Salter asked, after a few moments silence.

I nodded and gave him a watery smile.

Once we were alone, my mother turned on me.

"What's your problem, why won't you tell them what's been happening?"

"You've known about this for ages," I hissed back at her, "why have you waited until now to do anything about it. Why didn't you stop him before?"

I dug my fingernails into the flesh on my arms, reliving the utter despair I'd felt when I realized that my mother knew what was happening, but wasn't willing to stop it. I was eleven at the time. I'd come into the kitchen as my older brother, Graham, was asking for a shilling. He wanted to go to the pictures with his friends. Mum told him she didn't have any money. Dad's daytime job as a postman didn't leave much money left over for treats. We relied on his band jobs for the extras. Graham had grumbled, obviously feeling hard done by. He was two years older than me, with a healthy sense of his own entitlements.

"How come Gail always has money?" he'd asked petulantly.

"Because she's a prostitute," my mother said, not realizing I was in the room. "You're father gives it to her."

I'd gasped, unable to believe what I was hearing. She'd looked up from her ironing when she heard me.

"You know about it?" I asked, incredulous. "If you know about it, why don't you make him stop? Why d'you let him do those things to me?"

For a moment I dared to believe the nightmare might be over. If my own mother knew about it, surely she would make him stop.

"Keeps him off my back," she said, shrugging nonchalantly before turning her attention back to her ironing.

A chill ran down my spine. I was drowning in a sea of torment. I realized in that moment that my own mother was holding a life raft that she had no intention of throwing me. The one person in the world that I should have been able to count on had forsaken me. Almost a year had passed since then, and now she was throwing me that life raft. I guessed it was probably full of holes by now.

Sgt. Salter came back into the room and handed me a glass of milk and some biscuits. When I'd finished I looked up to find him smiling at me.

"Well I hope that makes you feel better." He picked up his pen. "Now do you feel like telling me what happens, when your father gets home from the pub?"

I looked into Sgt. Salter's eyes and saw compassion without judgment so, taking a deep breath, I began.

"Mostly when he gets home, I'm asleep in bed already. But then he comes into my room, and shakes me till I wake up, and he whispers my name and tells me to come downstairs, and he stinks of beer and cigarettes and if I pretend not to wake up he gets mad, and one time he dragged me out of bed by my arm, and it's like he's a different person at night than the dad I know in the day time, and he scares me when he's like that." I paused, unsure of how to continue. I sat there, opening and closing my mouth, like a fish out of water, unable to make the words come out. They were stuck in my throat, choking me. I stared intently at the floor, willing myself to continue.

"He puts his penis in my mouth and then he makes me give him horsey rides up the stairs," I finally blurted out.

There, I'd said it. I'd spoken the unspeakable. The secret I'd been living with for almost two years was finally out. I expected a thunderbolt to strike me dead on the spot, or to hear a booming voice from above chiding me to 'honour thy mother and father'. But instead there was just an ominous silence. I glanced up at my mother.

She nodded imperceptibly as if to say 'go on'. My shame was almost palpable and I hung my head, unable to look at Sgt. Salter. Tears dripped onto my hands clenched on my lap, and a thin trickle of snot escaped from my nose. I wiped it on my sleeve, watching as the glistening trail soaked into the wool of my school blazer, leaving a dark stain behind.

"How long has this been going on?" Sgt. Salter asked after a few moments.

"Since I was eleven."

"And how old are you now?"

"Nearly thirteen."

"And you were aware of this, Mrs. Puddicombe?"

She shrugged, defensively.

Sgt. Salter's jaw set into a hard line, as he slowly shook his head.

"Excuse me one moment," he said, and left the room once more.

When he returned he had a police woman with him.

"Gail, I want you to tell this nice police woman everything you can remember about what's been going on. She's going to write it down and when you're finished she'll read it back to you. Once you agree it's accurate, we'll ask you to sign it. Her name is Constable Jones."

I spent the next hour and a half talking as if I would never stop. The floodgates had been opened, and the pain and torment of the last two years came gushing out. Occasionally I'd break down in tears, only to start talking again faster than before.

Eventually I ran out of things to say, and the energy to say them with. Constable Jones read back my statement and I weakly nodded my assent. But there was so much more to say. I wanted to tell them that even though Dad was the bogey man at night, he was my daddy by day. I wanted them to know that I loved him, and that he loved his children. He'd stayed and looked after us, even if Mum hadn't, and now I hoped he would be okay. At last it was over. I signed my statement.

Sgt. Salter explained that I needed to be examined by Dr. Foster and that Constable Jones would accompany us in the police car.

It was raining, hard, and the alley leading to Dr. Foster's office was dark. Very dark. The sign at the entrance to the alley, with the hand pointing the way, swayed on its hinges. It was chipped and faded, but it didn't really matter. Everyone in town knew where the doctor's surgery was, and what days he was available, and how many babies he'd delivered, and who he was treating for what. Such information was passed on during hushed conversations over tea in the café down by the monument.

Constable Jones rapped sharply on the door. Regular surgery hours were long since finished. The door was opened almost immediately. A pool of light fell into the alley, lighting up raindrops like fireflies. We were hustled inside.

"Please remove her clothing below the waist," Dr. Foster told Mum, once we were in the examining room, "and get her to sit up on the table. There's a sheet here to cover her with. I'll be right back."

I scrambled out of my clothes and stood shivering in my bare feet, wearing only my petticoat and blouse. I climbed onto the table and pulled the sheet up under my chin in an attempt to keep warm, but I couldn't stop the shivering.

There was a light tap on the door. Dr. Foster came in and asked my mother to wait outside. I felt very small in that room, alone with the doctor I had known all my life but never before been alone with. Mum was always with me, talking about me as though I wasn't even there, except for the occasional 'isn't that right, dear?' One time she'd been describing, in graphic detail, a nasty sinus infection which was troubling me. Dr. Foster had looked down at me from his towering six-foot height, and placed his index finger over one nostril, thereby closing it off. He then instructed me to 'Blow!' It seemed a strange request, given the nature of my ailment, but I did it anyway. As I blew, an accumulation of thick green mucus was propelled from my nostril onto the doctor's hand. As I lay shivering on the examining table I wondered if he too remembered the incident and, if so, whether he was the type of man to bear a grudge.

Dr. Foster had known me all my life. He was the first human to touch my flesh, as I entered this world kicking and screaming from my mother's womb. He had cut the umbilical cord which joined me to my mother, and now he was going to 'examine' me. What part of me didn't he know? He pulled on a pair of rubber gloves, snapping them around his wrists. Then he picked up a scary looking instrument and turned to face me, all the while talking and trying to calm me. But I wasn't listening. I was too intent on watching. Watching to see what he would do next.

"I want you to lie back and put your feet in the stirrups,' he said. And as he speaks, he gently guides my feet into the cold metal stirrups, which feel like ice on such a dark and rainy night. My petticoat slips down my thighs and bunches on my hips. I thrust it between my legs and strain to pull my knees together to cover my private parts. I don't want anyone looking at me down there. I'm tired of being treated like a piece of meat, like I don't even own this body I'm in. I feel so small, so unable to shield myself from yet another man probing my body. I start to cry. Silently, like I've learned to do. I bite my lip to stop myself from crying out. I hear the doctor talking, soothingly, telling me it won't hurt. But it does hurt. It hurts far more than he or my father can ever know. It hurts to the very core of my being.

I withdraw inside myself where it's safe, where I can no longer feel the pain or humiliation. Inside where there is only a gentle rocking, and a soft wailing that blends with my soul and becomes me. I become numb. And nothing on the outside matters because I can't feel it, it can't hurt me anymore.

But I can feel the cold metal entering my body. I tense, instinctively, and it hurts more.

"Relax, relax. It's alright. It'll only take a minute. It won't hurt if you relax." And so Dr. Foster drones on, for what seems like an eternity. Then I feel the pressure easing, cold metal sliding out of me, a reassuring pat on the knees, the sheet being pulled down over me, to quell the shivering which is wracking my skinny body.

"You can get dressed now, Gail," he tells me, as he walks towards the door. He leaves it ajar, and says to come out when I'm done. As I reach for my tunic and knickers I hear him talking. Words drift into the room in disjointed whispers '... violated ...' '... ruptured hymen...' '... very tense, nervous child...'. The tears start flowing again. I hate being talked about in this way. I've become Exhibit A in a police file.

As I listen to their muffled talk, I worry about what people will say if they find out. I'll have to deal with the humiliation and shame of it all, which will almost be worse than the abuse itself. Then I could just leave my body, rise up into the far corner of the room, and watch what was happening from there. That way it didn't seem so bad. I could pretend it was someone else down there and I was just watching, like a show on TV. Except it made me cry a lot. And I got angry a lot. And I couldn't do anything about it, unless you count the time I bit Dad's penis as hard as I could. I'd heard him cry out and I'd tasted his blood in my mouth in that instant before his hand came crashing down across the side of my head in a blind fury, knocking me to the floor. But even that didn't stop him; it just gave him a taste for a bit of violence.

When we got back to the car the driver was talking on his radio. He turned to Constable Jones.

"It's all clear over at Hamsmoor now. I'm to drop you off there, so you can pick up the other children and a few of their things. They'll send the police van over to bring you all back to the station. A child care worker will meet you there."

"Oh no," I wailed, dangerously close to hysteria. "I can't go back home to Hamsmoor now. Dad will see me. He'll kill me for telling. He made me promise never to tell, and if he sees me with the police he'll know I told."

"It's okay, Gail. They've taken your dad to the police station to talk to him," the police officer said. "And we've arranged for you and your little brother and sister to stay somewhere else for a couple of nights."

"What about Graham? Isn't he coming with us?" I asked, anxious to have the protection of a big brother.

"He's going to stay with Nanny," Mum said. "But Nanny doesn't have room for the rest of you lot."

"But Justin and Jane haven't done anything wrong!" I protested, "Can't they stay home with Dad."

"You haven't done anything wrong either, Gail," Constable Jones said. "But we need to find a safe place for all of you to stay, until we get things sorted out. It's for the best, you'll see."

As the police car pulled up in front of our house the neighbour's front room curtains twitched. Nothing went unnoticed in Hamsmoor. Word would spread like wildfire that the police were at the Puddicombe's.

We walked around to the back of the house and went in the kitchen door. The dinner table had been set. A knife and fork lay untouched at my place. There was a half-eaten plate of sausages, fried eggs, chips, and beans where my father sat. Grease had congealed around the edge of the cold plate. Dad's knife and fork were laid across the rim of the plate, waiting for him to come back and finish his meal. He must have put them there as he got up to answer the door when the police came for him. He hadn't known that as he sat eating his dinner and worrying about why I wasn't home yet, I was at the police station speaking the unspeakable. It had just been another rainy Tuesday to him, until that knock on the door.

"Don't just stand there gawking," my mother chided, jolting me back to reality. "Go upstairs and get some clothes to take with you. We haven't got all night."

"You may want to bring some of your favorite things too," Constable Jones added, in an attempt to take the sting out of my mother's words.

As I climbed the flight of lino-covered stairs, I shuddered at the memory of what had happened there on countless nights. Straining to lift my father's weight on my back and carry him up the stairs. He called them horsey rides. He liked to masturbate on my back as I mounted the steps. I'd cried and begged him to stop, to let me go back to bed, but he wouldn't. My legs would buckle under the weight of him at first. But over the years my legs had grown stronger and now I was a rising star on the school sprinting team. Every cloud has a silver lining, it seems.

I put what few pieces of clothing I had in a brown paper carrier bag. There wasn't much money for clothing in our family budget. I put my black high-heeled shoes in the bag too, along with my nylons and suspender belt. They were birthday presents from my mother when I turned twelve. She wanted me to look grown up when she took me to the night clubs where her boyfriend was playing piano. At twelve years old I had glimpsed a world my friends knew nothing of. Dark, smoky nightclubs where everyone stank of booze and smoked cigarettes, where women draped themselves over men and men smiled at me as if I was a woman, even though I was only a child. My mother would giggle when men admired her 'beautiful sister'. One man, who was old enough to be my father, bought me a drink and sat too close. He started talking to me in that tone of voice my father used when he was telling me to take my panties off, and tears had spilled out of my eyes. The man had taken a closer look at me then. He was shocked when he realized how young I was, and had backed away a little. He had a daughter my age, he told me. He said something to my mother about how she should be ashamed of herself, bringing a child into a place like this. My mother had told him to fuck off - it was none of his business.

I pulled my chemistry set off the shelf and carefully placed it on top of my clothes, so as not to spill any chemicals out of the rows of glass vials. It had been a Christmas present from Dad, 'suitable for a smart young girl in grammar school', he'd said. Then I ran downstairs and grabbed the sheet music for Fur Elise off the piano, carefully sliding it down the side of the brown paper bag. I had been working on it for weeks and was due to sit my music exam soon. I didn't think I would pass though because I'd missed a lot of lessons since Mum had been gone. But maybe there would be a piano for me to practice on wherever we were going.

When I got back to the kitchen Nanny and Aunty Barbara were there with Justin and Jane. Dad's dinner plate had been scraped clean and was sitting in the sink waiting to be washed. Mum was smoking a cigarette with one hand and holding Jane on her lap with the other. Nanny looked very worried. They were talking in hushed tones when I came into the room. Aunty Barbara, only ten years my senior, jumped up and gave me a hug and told me not to worry, everything would be okay. I hoped she was right.

Constable Jones stood up.

"If you're all done we can get going. The van is here to take us back to the police station."

Justin looked up from the comic book he had been reading.

"Why are we going there?" he asked, pushing his National Health wire rim glasses onto the bridge of his nose. "It's bed time."

Constable Jones squatted down and put her hand gently on his shoulder.

"You and your sisters are going to stay somewhere else for a couple of days. It's a nice place and you'll be fine there."

"Do I get to go in the police van?" he asked, obviously worried. In our world only the bad guys got to go in a black Mariah.

"Yes, you do. You get to ride all the way to Torquay in it. Good people get to go in police cars too sometimes. Ready?"

Mum turned off the kitchen light and locked the door behind us. I hoped Dad had his key to get back in.

The rain had stopped, but the clouds still hung heavy and low. A black Mariah was waiting for us at the curb. Justin, Jane and I climbed into the back of the van and sat along the bench seats. Our meager collection of possessions was stowed under the seat. First Mum, then Aunty Barbara, and then Nanny, leaned in and gave each of us a kiss goodbye. Nanny thrust a half crown piece in my hand and told me to buy us some sweets when we got to Torquay. She reminded us to remember our manners, and we promised we would. I knew this must be very important, because she had tears in her eyes when she said it.

When we got to the police station we were told to come inside until the child care officer arrived. As I walked through the main door I came face to face with my father. He was sandwiched between two policemen, his hands cuffed behind him. I gasped and turn to run, but collided with Constable Jones. There was a sudden flurry of activity as the officers, realizing what had happened, hustled my father into a side office. He kept straining to look at me over his shoulder as he was hustled along.

"Oh Gail, my beauty, I'm so sorry, so sorry," he kept calling, over and over, his voice reverberating along the corridor. Tears were streaming down his face. "I didn't mean to hurt you, my beauty. I'm so sorry."

I burst into tears, dying a million deaths to see my father, the great Rex Royston, trombonist and band leader extraordinaire, handcuffed, and humiliated in this way. Had I done this to him? Was this the price I had to pay, to end my nightmare?

CHAPTER TWO

The drive to Torquay took over an hour. Miss Stinson, a child care officer with the Children's Department of the Devon County Council, came with us. She told us she would be handling our file. I wondered what file she was talking about, but was too tired to ask. Instead I sat in silence, watching the windshield wipers slapping back and forth.

Justin's anxiety had given way to excitement and eventually exhaustion. He now sat quietly staring out the window, only occasionally looking over at me as if to reassure himself that I was still there. Jane was curled up on the seat beside me, fast asleep. She'd only stopped crying when I showed her the half crown Nanny had given me and I'd promised to buy her some sweets as soon as we found a sweet shop. I told her there would be loads of sweet shops where we were going.

The black Mariah eventually slowed and turned into a driveway flanked by two large stone pillars. An enormous Victorian house came into view. It was bigger than the biggest house I had ever seen in Riverton. There was a peaked roof over the front entranceway and a porch which wrapped itself around the front of the building. The place was in darkness. It looked like a haunted house from one of my brother's comic books.

The porch light suddenly came on, bathing us all in a harsh light and casting ghostly shadows all around. The front door opened and we were hustled inside along with our meager belongings. A tired looking woman, with dark hair and pinched features, eyed us up and down as if assessing our suitability for admission. Jane, roused from her sleep took one look around and started crying, loudly. Justin stood motionless, staring at the austere surroundings. In the dim light the house looked even more foreboding on the inside than outside. I was jigging Jane up and down on my hip trying to console her. Her wails reverberated along the dark corridors which lead who knows where. The tight lipped woman was obviously displeased. A younger woman suddenly appeared from one of the darkened corridors, tying a belt around her robe as she hurried towards us.

"Ah, they've arrived, Matron," she said. "Here, let me take her, dear" she said to me as she reached out her hands to Jane. Jane stopped crying almost immediately. "My name is Aunty Linda, but most of the children call me Aunt Liddy. Come along with me, children, and I'll show you where you're to sleep."

Aunt Liddy took us upstairs, leaving Miss Stinson with the matron. She showed us where the dormitories were, all the while talking in a whisper and making a game out of being as quiet as mice so as not to wake the other children. Justin was given a bed in the boys' dormitory. Jane and I were shown to the girls' dormitory on the other side of the corridor. We were given two beds side by side. There were six other beds in the room, five of which were occupied. At the end of the corridor were two large bathrooms, one for the boys and one for the girls.

"Wash up and get your night clothes on, then come downstairs to the kitchen for a bedtime snack. The kitchen is along the corridor to the right of the front door," Aunt Liddy said.

Justin looked scared when we left him in his dormitory to change, with only the light from the hallway spilling into the room. My heart went out to him, standing there alone in the semi darkness. He was trying so hard to be brave.

"I'll be just next door," I whispered to him. "Wait for me at the top of the stairs when you're done."

Jane toddled along behind me, clinging onto my skirt. We quickly changed into our night dresses and went to the bathroom. Just as we were finishing, the matron came in and started making clucking sounds with her mouth.

"You obviously don't know how to take care of yourselves," she chided. "Now come over here and wash your hands and face properly, with soap and water, and brush your teeth and hair."

I looked down at my hands, as if seeing them for the first time. They were a bit grubby I suppose, but I didn't see how that would stop me from sleeping. And sleep was all I wanted at that moment.

"Come along, some of us want to get back to bed."

I could see Justin waiting for us at the top of the stairs. He was wearing a pair of pyjamas which Graham had long since grown out of, but which Justin had yet to grow into. I hurriedly did as I was told while the matron helped Jane wash her hands and face. Justin, seeing what was happening, suddenly disappeared. I heard the sound of water running in the boys' bathroom next door. Justin was a survivor, I reassured myself. He'd be alright.

Aunt Liddy had warm milk and biscuits waiting for us when we got downstairs.

"I'll get them tucked into bed when they're done, Matron," she said.

"Thank you, Linda. Call me if you need me." Matron turned to us. "Welcome to Languard House, children. If you behave yourselves, you'll be quite comfortable here. Goodnight."

When we were done, Aunt Liddy took us back upstairs and put us to bed. I lay there in the darkness, listening to the sounds of the other girls breathing, and wondered what was happening to Dad. Was he in jail or had they let him go? What was going to happen to us now? I thought of Justin lying alone in the dormitory across the hall. He always became quiet when he was scared. He was only eight and none of this was his fault and now here he was in what looked like a haunted house, alone in the dark. I wanted to go and check on him but thought better of it. I didn't want to get into trouble with the matron and, if truth be known, I was scared too. I pulled the blankets over my head and curled up into a tight ball. But I couldn't sleep, the events of the past few hours had left me emotionally drained. I let the tears flow. I knew how to cry without making a sound, my shoulders heaving, fists clenched, tears and snot drenching my pillow.

I doubted I would ever be able to stop crying now. I felt a small, soft hand on my arm. Jane was standing by my bed, patting me.

"Don't cry. Daddy home soon," she whispered, echoing the words she had heard me say to her so many times in the past. As she spoke, she clambered up onto my bed and crawled under the blankets with me. Within minutes we were both sound asleep.

At 7 a.m. we were abruptly awakened as the harsh dormitory lights were turned on.

"Rise and shine, girls. No time to waste. Breakfast will be ready in half an hour. Get yourselves washed and dressed and don't forget to make your beds."

Before I could even open my eyes the owner of the voice was gone. I heard the same message being delivered in the boys' dormitory. The lumps in the other beds started squirming as the occupants woke up. One girl after another climbed out of bed and scurried off to the bathroom. I shook Jane awake and we followed the exodus.

I helped Jane get dressed then sat her on my bed while I dressed myself. She was still half asleep and seemed entranced by all the activity. The other girls were fully awake now and the noise level was steadily increasing. A couple of girls came over to our bed.

"Oh isn't she sweet," one of them said, as she fondled Jane's dark, curly hair.

"What's your name," the other asked, in that sing-song voice adults often use with babies.

"That's Jane. She's my sister. She's four," I told them. "My brother, Justin, is over with the boys. He just turned eight. I'm Gail."

I turned my attention back to getting dressed. I wasn't really much in the mood for conversation. I was tired and anxious and not terribly sure I liked this place.

As I put my school uniform back on I wondered what Maureen would think when she called for me this morning. She always called for me at half past eight on her way to school. No one would have told her not to call for me today. I imagined her standing at my back door, knocking and knocking, thinking I had overslept again. I'd been doing that a lot lately but she always waited for me, no matter how late we were. I hoped she wouldn't wait too long, and get into trouble at school. It would have been nice if I could have told her not to call for me today, to warn her somehow. I wondered how long it would be before we were allowed to go back home.

Jane and I waited at the top of the stairs for Justin. When he finally appeared he was wearing odd socks, his shirt was buttoned up askew, and his blond, curly hair had obviously not seen a comb. But he was smiling very proudly as he introduced me to Jeffrey, his new friend. I re-buttoned his shirt and ran my fingers through his hair to smooth it down. The socks would have to do.

Breakfast was served in the dining room, a large rectangular room with rows of tables and benches. A hatch along one side revealed a kitchen. The noise level was considerable, as almost twenty children of various ages took their places. We found a table just inside the door where the three of us could sit together. Jeffrey joined us and kept up a running dialogue of who was who, which boys were the bullies and which girls were the cry babies, and who his favorite aunties were. The smell of porridge was wafting from the kitchen, and we waited eagerly for our food. Aunt Liddy saw us and came over.

"I'll show you around after breakfast and go over some of the house rules," she said.

Just then Matron came in and the noise level dropped dramatically. She looked far less austere in the daylight, due mainly to the ample application of lipstick and rouge. Her hair was swept up into a bun and she wore horn-rimmed glasses shaped like the wings of a bird. She may have been beautiful once. When the noise level was under control, Matron said grace.

The word 'amen' was barely past our lips before the stampede began. Children grabbed their bowls, clambered over the benches, and made their way to the kitchen hatch, where the cook was ladelling out lukewarm, watery porridge.

"Come on," said Jeffrey, "or there won't be any left."

We didn't need to be told twice. I grabbed my bowl, gave Jane hers, and joined the stampede. Plates of cold toast were put on the tables and our glasses were filled with milk. There was no jam. This was to be our breakfast every day at Languard House, except for Sundays when we were given a boiled egg and toast with jam.

After breakfast, Aunt Liddy showed us around. There was a large conservatory to the left of the main entrance, with shelves full of books and games. An old piano sat gathering dust at one end of the room. I was glad I'd brought my music with me, maybe I could practice Fur Elise here.

"You'll be given clean clothes every Wednesday and Saturday, and bed sheets get changed every Monday," Aunt Liddy explained, as she led the way up the main stairs. "And I don't want to catch you jumping on the beds or sliding down the banister," she warned us, as Justin eyed the long, curving banister of the central staircase with a twinkle in his eye.

"The older children are expected to help strip down the beds and put the sheets in the laundry chute, just outside the bathroom. You're to make your beds before you come down for breakfast." Aunt Liddy surveyed the crumpled blankets on my bed. "Let me show you how we like the beds made here at Languard House," she said, stripping the bedding off to reveal a lumpy mattress with a thick rubber sheet tucked across the middle, to protect it from 'accidents'.

"Matron's husband, Mr. Kaye, gives out your spending money on Saturday mornings," Aunt Liddy told us, as we finished re-making our beds, "provided you haven't misbehaved during the week, of course."

Justin's eyes lit up at the prospect of having his own spending money. I could almost hear him thinking that maybe this place wasn't going to be so bad after all.

"And, of course, there are chores to be done, just like at home," Aunt Liddy said.

"But we're only going to be here for a little while," I said, sounding as grown up as I could, "so we don't really need to know all these things. Our Mum will come and get us as soon as everything gets sorted out. It's just that she doesn't have room for us all at the moment, so we had to come here last night."

Aunt Liddy put her arm around my shoulder and gave me a hug. "Let's hope so, dear, but meanwhile you might as well make yourselves comfortable. Sometimes these things take time to sort out."

On Sunday Mum came to see us. She brought her boyfriend,

Norman Brooks, with her. She kept Jane on her lap the whole time, only shifting her from one side to the other to light her cigarettes.

"Norman just got a gig at this really snazzy joint in Exeter," she said, exhaling clouds of cigarette smoke as she spoke. "You wouldn't believe the people who go there, all dressed up to the nines. And they just love his music, always making requests and getting up and dancing."

She shifted Jane to her other hip.

"D'you kids need anything here?"

I shook my head.

"No, not really. We're only going to be here a little while, aren't we?"

She side stepped the question.

"Well, let me know if you think of anything in the meantime."

But in my heart I suspected she couldn't give me what I needed most of all, which was her love and protection.

It seemed like an eternity before Miss Stinson, our child care worker, came back to see us.

"I hope you're all settling in nicely, and getting to find your way around," she said.

"Yes, we're fine thank you," I said. "But I was wondering how long we have to stay here. We've been here over a week already."

"I can't tell you for certain," Miss Stinson said. "We'll have to see what the courts decide. There's a hearing scheduled for March 1, which is only a few days from now. We'll know more once that's over."

As the days slowly ticked by my anxiety rose. I was horrified to think we now had to go to court, like a bunch of common criminals. My anxiety translated itself into anger and hatred, for myself mostly. I wanted to lash out and scream 'Why is this happening? What have I done? Leave us alone.' But instead I retreated into a sullen silence. If only I hadn't told the police about Dad, we wouldn't be here. We would still be in Riverton with our friends and going to Nanny's house whenever we wanted.

My grandparents lived two streets over from us and I was in the habit of spending as much time as I could at their house. As the nights closed in Granddad would send me packing, grumbling that I should be home in bed already and where was my bloody mother anyhow? Why wasn't she home where she belonged, looking after her kids? I was afraid it would break his heart when he found out why I never wanted to go home when Mum wasn't there.

On our second Sunday at Languard House my grandparents came to visit. They brought my cousin, Sherry, with them so she could say goodbye. We'd grown up together but now she and her family were emmigrating to New Zealand. I took Sherry on a tour of Languard House, making light of the fact that her future seemed so exciting, while mine seemed so bleak. We promised to write.

When we got back downstairs, Mum was sitting in the conservatory talking with Nanny. She was wearing a new dress with matching jacket, and very high heeled shoes which showed off her long legs. She kept giggling like a love-sick teenager, telling Nanny what a great fellow her boyfriend was. She said he was going to be a famous jazz pianist one day and buy her diamonds and fast cars. She said he might be getting a job in a famous night club in Manchester, and that would just be the beginning. This man was going places, she said, not like my deadbeat father who only played in pubs and dance halls around Devon. Her words stung and I felt a need to jump to Dad's defense. I said I liked Dad's music.

Granddad had gone to wait in his car when my mother arrived. When visiting hours were over we congregated on the front steps to say our goodbyes. Mum came out holding Jane on her hip and a cigarette in the other hand. My grandfather's car was parked to one side of the steps.

"Isn't he going to come and say hello?" Mum asked Nanny.

Nanny just shrugged. "He's having a hard time with all this you know, Peggy." I could hear a note of accusation in Nanny's voice.

I walked over to Granddad's car to say goodbye. My mother followed.

"Hello, Dad," she said into the open window.

Granddad stared at her, barely masking his anger.

"Don't you 'hello Dad' me!" he hissed. "Look what you've done to these poor kids. I hope you're bloody satisfied." He turned away, unable to say more. There were tears in his eyes.

My mother mumbled something under her breath, like the petulant child she had always been, and went back to Norman's car.

At the court hearing on March 1, 1963 my two brothers, sister and I were made temporary wards of the court, pending a complete review and investigation of the circumstances. We were to remain at Languard House until March 29, at which time we would be told the court's decision about our futures. We could only wait until then.

As the weeks went by I started to worry about the amount of school I was missing. I wondered if I would ever be able to catch up. My marks had been suffering as it was, and missing weeks of school certainly wasn't going to help.

"There really isn't any point you starting a new grammar school before we hear what the courts decide," Miss Stinson told me when I grumbled to her. "We have no way of knowing where you might end up living. Languard House is only a temporary home for children awaiting placement. The courts will want to find you a more settled, permanent home."

"Will we all get to stay together?" I asked.

"The courts usually try to keep families together, wherever possible," Miss Stinson tried to reassure me. "We'll just have to wait and see."

I felt like I was living on an emotional roller coaster—longing for home with the familiar sights and sounds one moment, yet dreading the prospect of being sent back the next. I filled my days with reading, practicing the piano and going for long walks. While school wasn't a practical option for me, some of the children at Languard House did go to local schools and eventually, much to his dismay, Justin was sent to the local elementary school.

As the days and weeks went by, Justin started being as naughty as he could be. He'd slide down the well-polished wooden banister with great whoops of delight, inevitably attracting the attention of one aunty or another. They would promptly march him off to Matron's office for a good telling off and warnings of forfeited spending money. But even this didn't deter him. He seemed to relish the attention.

Jane meanwhile took to following me around everywhere, pulling at my skirt and whining to be picked up. My patience with her grew thin. I had my own demons to deal with.

Mum arranged to take Jane with her for a few days. She and Norman Brooks picked her up next day. As they drove away, Justin and I stood on the front porch waving goodbye, silently wondering why we were being left behind. Justin started to misbehave even more and I sank deeper into despair.

I started spending as much time as I could by myself, seeking out alcoves and corners in the rambling Victorian house where I could be alone. I discovered that the dining room was usually empty between meals, and took to spending time in there. I started to write. It was easier to write about the hurt and shame than it was to talk about it. Words I dared not utter spewed out of my pen in a torrent of angry, hateful words. I wrote about how my father made me give him horsey rides while he masturbated on my back. I wrote about the smell of his semen, and how it felt sticky on my skin, and how much I hated it when he put his penis in my mouth. I wrote about how he had used the red Christmas candle, which sat on the mantle above the fireplace in the sitting room, to see if he could make me bigger 'down there'. I had cried and asked him to stop, but he'd kept doing it, saying it was what you had to do to become a woman. But I didn't want to become a woman; I was just a little girl, and I wanted to stay that way.

I wrote quickly, the words spilling out of me, until my hand cramped into a ball. And I cried. I cried for the child I had been before all this began. I cried for the father I had known and loved and for the mother whose protection I had needed, but never got. And when I couldn't write anymore, I'd hide the pages behind the books on a shelf in the dining room, retrieving them next day to continue my silent venting.

But on Monday when I went to retrieve my writing, it was gone. As I frantically searched along the shelf I heard Matron's voice behind me.

"Looking for something, young lady," she asked.

I spun around, red faced. Matron was standing in the doorway, clutching my writing pad. She asked me to accompany her to the office, where she and her husband, Mr. Kaye, proceeded to berate me about what I had written.

"This is disgusting," she fumed. "What on earth were you thinking to write something like this and then leave it around where anyone could find it? What if one of the children had found it, don't you know how upsetting it could have been for them?"

But I am one of the children, I wanted to scream. I'm only twelve and I didn't want to know any of this stuff myself, but I do. It's my reality and it's festering inside me, like a boil ready to burst. If I didn't get my feelings out, I felt I would explode. Maybe if I put the words on paper they would be out of my head forever, and I wouldn't wake up at night with a scream choking the back of my throat, afraid that he was coming for me again. Perhaps if I could just say how ugly and dirty I felt, now that Daddy had touched me in that way and how guilty I felt for letting it happen. But my shame silenced me. Seeing the words on paper I could pretend it was just a story I had read about someone else. It hadn't happened to me at all. I could keep up the pretense of being the pretty twelve year old daughter of Rex Royston, the band leader and trombone player that everybody loved. Everybody except Mum, that is. But now I had a terrible sinking feeling inside me as Matron glared at me, demanding an explanation. I couldn't offer any. I didn't have the words to explain the turmoil broiling inside me.

A few days later, I was told to go upstairs to the consulting room. A Dr. Penner wanted to talk with me. He introduced himself as the Deputy County Educational Psychologist. He asked me to look at a series of ink blots and tell him what I saw.

"Ink blots," I answered sullenly. He had obviously heard this answer before and failed to see the humor or be put off by my response. He gently encouraged me to try again.

After the ink blots, Dr. Penner arranged some cut-out cardboard people on the desk. He said they represented members of my immediate family. He handed me a series of cards with statement such as 'this person cares for me more than anyone else', or 'I wish this person would care for me more than for anybody else', and asked me to place them beside the person they most represented.

I was still smarting from the bollicking I'd received for my writing, and was anxious to give the 'correct' answers. I didn't realize there was no right or wrong answers. They were just trying to assess how I was coping with the trauma of the last few years.

Dr. Penner later reported to the court that I had placed the card 'this person cares for me more than for anybody else' in my mother's slot. He told the Court he believed this response was simply the expression of a wish, as in reality he had found no evidence to support this statement. I hoped he was wrong. Dr. Penner's report also said that 'the mother likes obedient girls'. I could have told him that without looking at any ink blots. He ended his report by noting that there was no hatred of the father. I'm not sure which ink blot told him that, but it was true. I didn't hate Dad; I just hated the things he did to me. Mostly I hated my mother, for letting it happen. For not caring enough about me to protect me from the bogey man, even when she knew he was coming into my room at night while she was out with her boyfriend.

The March 29 court date was fast approaching. I became very tense. We'd seen a few children leave Languard House over the weeks we'd been there. They'd get dressed in their best clothes, pack their few belongings in a tattered suitcase, and wait at the foot of the stairs for their new family to come and get them. The new foster parents would gush superlatives about what a lovely life they were going to have together, and how the child was going to be such wonderful company for their little Johnny or Susie. Matron would stand there, handing them off with instructions about minding their manners and listening to their new parents, and how she didn't want to see them back here inside a fortnight because they weren't doing as they were told. And the child would stand between them, clutching a favorite teddy bear or doll or dinky toy, wondering how long this home would last. I hoped the courts wouldn't make me go to a foster home. I didn't think I could sleep in a house where there was a man who might wake up in the night and confuse me with his wife.

Miss Stinson drove us to Riverton for the court hearing.

"Your father is expected to attend Court today," Miss Stinson warned me. "I know it might be difficult for you to see him again but I'll be with you."

"He hasn't been to see us at all since we went to Languard House, but he wrote to say he was thinking of us," I said. "Part of me really wants to see him again, to make sure he's okay, but part of me is really scared. Do you know if he's mad at me?"

"I can't imagine why he would be," Miss Stinson said. "I think he should be more worried about how you might be feeling towards him."

I couldn't answer. I didn't know how I felt about him.

When we got to the Court House Mum was waiting on the front steps with Nanny, Granddad and Graham. There was no sign of Dad. When Mum had finished her cigarette, we went inside. We were told to sit on benches along the wall in the corridor until we were called. Miss Stinson went into the Courtroom first to give her report. Then they called my mother in. I sat between my grandparents, with Jane on my lap. I heard footsteps coming up the stairs and looked up to see my father standing there. I felt my grandfather stiffen and I shrank back into my seat, hoping Dad wouldn't see me. I had betrayed him. I had tried so hard to honour my mother and father, just like I had been taught in Sunday school, but they had made it so hard for me to do. I thought there should be an eleventh commandment which said honor thy children. Maybe then we wouldn't be in this mess.

The court room door opened and my mother came out. She looked just like she did when she walked off the stage after a piano performance.

"Oh, you made it then," she said to my father, when she saw him standing at the top of the stairs.

"He should be ashamed to show his face," my grandfather grumbled.

"Don't you start," my mother snapped at him, "they're his bloody kids too, you know."

Nanny put her hand on Granddad's arm to calm him.

"I'm going out for a smoke," Mum announced. "You coming?" she asked my father as she edged past him.

Dad shook his head, but said nothing.

The court room door opened again. My father was asked to go in. After a few minutes he came out and Miss Stinson was asked to bring the four of us children into the courtroom. Inside there was a long wooden table around which sat a judge, a stenographer and a court clerk. The judge, who was introduced as Lady Ashcroft, smiled kindly at us but I was too nervous to smile back.

"The purpose of this court," she explained, "is to ensure your safety and find suitable homes for each of you. Unfortunately, neither of your parents appears to be in a position to provide any of you with a safe home at this time and nor do I feel this would be appropriate, given the circumstances."

I shifted uncomfortably in my seat as I struggled to understand what was being said.

"I want to ensure that each of you has a secure environment to live in, rather than risk prolonging what has undoubtedly been a traumatic experience for all of you. Therefore, the decision of this Court is that each of you be placed in protective custody under the auspices of the Devon County Council's Children's Committee, until such time as each of you reaches the age of eighteen."

She paused, looking at each of us in turn.

"I understand your grandparents have agreed to take custody of you, Graham, as you are already living with them and appear quite settled there. Gail, Justin and Jane, you will be returned to Languard House until suitable homes can be found for you. Your mother has indicated that she may be in a position to offer two of you a home at some point in the future, but that will have to be decided by the Courts at a later time."

I wondered which two she would pick.

As we were about to leave the courtroom, Lady Ashcroft called me over.

"I understand it's your birthday soon," she said.

I nodded, unsure of how to address such an important person. The Ashcroft's lived in the manor house just outside Riverton. I had often crawled under the fence of their estate in search of daffodils and snowdrops, which I'd sell for sixpence a bunch to our neighbours.

Lady Ashcroft reached down beside her chair and took a small package out of her bag.

"Well I hope you have a very happy birthday," she said as she handed me the package.

I stared at it, speechless.

"Aren't you going to open it?" she asked.

I forgot my nervousness and eagerly tore the brightly coloured wrapping paper off. Inside was a real, honest to goodness genuine leather writing case with a zipper to keep it closed. It was the most beautiful thing I had ever owned, and I held it up to my nose, reveling in the smell of it. I loved the smell of real leather.

"Thank you," I mumbled shyly, "it's beautiful. I shall keep it forever."

CHAPTER THREE

A week after our court appearance, Miss Stinson came to Languard House to see me.

"The Children's Committee is concerned about the amount of school you're missing," she told me, "so finding you a home where you can settle has become a priority. There is, however, the issue of what type of school you should go to."

"Can't I just go to a grammar school, like I did in Riverton?"

"We'll have to see. I met with the headmaster at Riverton Grammar and he feels that, given settled conditions, you might be up to grammar school standards," Miss Stinson explained. "Apparently they were thinking of transferring you to the secondary modern school as you were having trouble keeping up. It seems your marks had dropped off and you weren't doing well last term."

"But I did alright in first form," I said, jumping to my own defense. "It's just that with Mum gone I was busy with Justin and Jane, so I hardly had time to do any homework. And during class I found it hard to stay awake some days."

I was devastated at the prospect of being taken out of grammar school. Passing the eleven plus entrance exam to grammar school had been a huge feather in my cap, and I was eager to keep it there. Only a handful of students from the council estate where I lived managed to get into grammar school and I saw it as my ticket out of there.

But without a grammar school education my life seemed completely predictable: leave school at fifteen, get a job in the local factory, find a boyfriend, get pregnant, get married, (usually in that order), have a baby every couple of years, go to the pub Saturday nights and watch telly the rest of the week. Not my idea of an exciting life.

Miss Stinson could see the disappointment in my eyes. "Well, we'll have to see what we can do," she said, giving me a reassuring smile. "I'll ask the Committee to consider you for grammar school if that's what you want and are willing to work hard to catch up. But I can't make any promises, I can only make recommendations."

The following Friday, Mr. Kaye summoned me to the consultation room again.

'What now,' I thought to myself, as I trudged up the stairs behind him. I was getting awfully tired of being tested and prodded by doctors, psychologists, and social workers. I just wanted to be left alone and allowed to live a normal life, whatever that might be.

"I'm going to give you a skills test," Mr. Kaye informed me once I was seated, "so that the Children's Committee can make a decision about which type of school you should go to."

"What! Today! But that's not fair," I said, my temper ignited by a sudden attack of nerves. "I haven't had a chance to swot or anything. Can't I do it next week?"

"I'm afraid not. The Children's Committee meets on Monday to review your file, and they want the results of this test by then."

He handed me a sheaf of papers and a pencil. A sea of numbers and geometric diagrams danced across the pages in front of me. I'd been out of school for more than a month, and the only math I'd done in that time was to add up my change at the shops. I threw the sheets down in frustration. The pencil bounced off the desk and hit the floor, breaking the nib. Mr. Kaye seemed unperturbed by my outburst. He told me to control myself and stop wasting time as he had started the timer already.

By the time I'd retrieved the pencil, sharpened it, and gathered up the test sheets, I'd managed to calm myself. I turned my attention to the task at hand. The first few questions were easy which gave me the confidence to carry on. Soon the excitement of a challenge overtook my anger and I was lost in concentration. Before I knew it the hour was up and Mr. Kaye was asking me to hand in my papers.

I must have done alright because shortly after that Miss Stinson came to see me. She said the Committee had decided to send me to Willowrey Children's Home, where I could attend the local grammar school. It was the best news I had heard in a long time. I was being given a second chance and I was determined I wouldn't blow it.

When I told Justin I'd be leaving Languard House soon a shadow crossed his face.

"What about me?" he asked. "Where do I have to go?"

"I think they're trying to find you a foster home so you can be in a house with a regular mum and dad, just like being at home," I told him. "Only nicer," I added quickly.

"Well I hope it takes them a long time, 'cos Jeffrey and me are building a fort behind the garden shed. It's our secret hiding place and girls aren't allowed."

He ran off in search of Jeffrey.

Jane was hardly old enough to understand what I was telling her but I promised I'd come and see her as often as I could. As the days went by she never left my side, until finally I lost patience with her.

"What will you do when I'm gone?" I yelled at her. "You'll have to learn to get along without me then!"

Her lower lip quivered as she thought about this, then she brightened.

"I'll come with you," she said, obviously pleased with her solution.

I sat down on the floor cross legged, so that my face was level with hers.

"I'm sorry, baby girl, but you can't come with me. They're going to find you a special home with a nice mummy and daddy and, who knows, maybe you'll even have some new sisters and brothers to play with. But I'll come and see you whenever I can. Honest."

There were tears in Jane's big brown eyes.

"But I don't want a new mummy and daddy. I want my own mummy and daddy. And I want you too. Why can't I come with you?"

"Because you can't, sweetheart, you just can't. I'm going to a home for big girls. Maybe when you're big, like me, you can come there too. But for now you have to go where they send you. There's nothing I can do about it."

The thought of starting my new life was exciting, yet frightening. How would I explain to my new friends that I lived in a children's home? What if they didn't like me, or I didn't fit in? In Hamsmoor where we lived the streets brimmed with children and it was easy to fit in. You just had to walk out your front door to find friends playing hopscotch, skipping rope, or colouring with chalk on the pavement. We'd all grown up together like a litter of pups – friendship and acceptance were taken for granted.

Council housing estates were being built as fast as the mortar could dry to accommodate the swelling population. When World War II ended the soldiers had come home, married their sweethearts, and started making babies in alarming numbers. They were cheaper by the dozen apparently. The more babies you had, the quicker your name moved up the housing list. We moved into our house in Hamsmoor Council Estate when I was almost five and Mum was pregnant with her third child, Justin. The roads weren't even paved yet and we were one of the first families to move in. My uncle, aunt and three cousins soon moved into the same council estate, followed by my grandparents. My whole family lived within that neighbourhood.

And now I had to start all over again.

"You don't have to mention the problems you had with your father," Miss Stinson reassured me when I expressed my concerns to her. "Just tell your friends that your parents are getting a divorce. Explain that you're living at Willowrey Children's Home so that you can finish grammar school. There's no shame in that."

I thought about this for a while. Perhaps I could pretend that none of this was my fault, that I was just an innocent victim of my parents' quarrel with each other. I would only tell people about the good things, and try to forget the rest. I could tell them how my father was a trombone player and had his own band just like Glenn Miller, and how my mother played the piano sometimes. If they asked I would tell how she had fallen in love with a jazz pianist who was going to be famous one day and they had run off to make beautiful music together. The romanticism of a twelve year old took hold.

"How soon can I go?" I asked, pushing my fears aside.

"I think it will be quite soon. You've already missed a lot of school."

She got up to leave.

"But how long will I have to stay there?" I asked. Her words about living at Willowrey Children's Home so that I could finish school, had finally sunk in. "It will be ages until I finish school, especially if I go on to sixth form."

Miss Stinson sat back down. "You'll probably be there for quite some time," she said.

"But Mum told me that she and Norman are going to get a place soon so that I can go and live with them. She said so, last time she was here."

Miss Stinson gazed at me for several moments, as if lost for words.

"Do you understand what a Fit Person Order is?" she asked.

I shook my head. There had been so much talk of things like moral danger, and indecent assault, and juvenile court, and fit people that it was hard to keep it all straight. I had closed my ears to much of it. It just didn't bear thinking about.

"Riverton Juvenile Court has ordered that you be committed to the care of the Devon County Council until you are eighteen. From now on, the Children's Committee will act as your parents and will be making important decisions on your behalf."

Miss Stinson paused while I digested this piece of information. I wondered who these people were that called themselves the Children's Committee, and how they could possibly make decisions about my life when they didn't even know me.

"But Mum said they'd save up for a caravan and we could all live in that," I persisted, not wanting to believe what I was hearing. "Mum said there are loads of caravan sites around and we can live in one until they can find a proper house. She said so."

"It will probably take your mother a long, long time to save up for a caravan," Miss Stinson said, "so I think it's best that you set your mind on settling into Willowrey for the time being and getting used to your new school. I'll let you know when you're going as soon as I hear back from the Committee."

The days at Languard House seemed longer than ever now that I knew I was leaving. I told Justin he was the big boy now and had to keep an eye on his baby sister. He became naughtier and naughtier as the days went by. I think he just didn't know what else to do. Fortunately, Aunt Liddy seemed to understand what was happening. She spent as much time as she could with them, carrying Jane around on her hip whenever she looked like she needed a hug, which was often, and turning a blind eye to some of Justin's antics.

One week after my thirteenth birthday I moved to Willowrey Children's Home. I packed my paltry possessions in an old suitcase which matron had given me and placed it by the front door, out of sight. I didn't want Justin and Jane to see it. I felt I was abandoning them.

Miss Stinson had arranged to pick me up at ten. I sat with Justin and Jane after breakfast and tried to read them a story while I waited. But Justin kept jumping on the sofa beside us. When I told him to sit still he tried to punch me. I slapped his leg, hard.

"You're not the boss of me," he said defiantly, before running out of the room.

He was still in hiding when Miss Stinson arrived. I refused to leave until we found him and I could say goodbye. We went from room to room looking for him, but he was nowhere to be found. And then I remembered the fort he and Jeffrey were building behind the garden shed. When I found him there he looked like he'd been crying. I promised to visit as soon as I could but in the meantime he had to be a big boy and stay out of trouble. He said he would try, but his lip quivered as he said it.

The drive to Willowrey Children's Home took almost an hour. Miss Stinson seemed to understand my need for silence. Eventually we turned off the main road on to Willowrey Sands Road, which wound its way down to a beach. Half way down the hill we pulled into the driveway of a modern two storey rectangular building. It was painted white and had a flat roof. The house was surrounded by a large lawn which sloped up behind it and around both sides. A tall boxwood hedge lined the perimeter of the property, with only an opening for the driveway.

Miss Stinson went to the front door and rang the bell. The door was opened almost immediately by a white haired woman in her fifties. She stood erect, but not rigid, and had a kind face. I stayed in the car, watching, as she and Miss Stinson exchanged a few words, nodding and looking in my direction from time to time. After a few minutes they came over to the car and opened my door.

"Hello, young lady," the grey haired woman said, "Aren't you going to come in? We won't bite, you know."

I followed them into the house and put my bag just inside the door.

"I'm very pleased to meet you," the grey haired lady said. "I'm the matron here. They call me Nurse."

She had a steady gaze as if she were looking right through me and reading my thoughts. It would be hard to keep secrets from this lady, I realized. My mother had always told me I was useless at telling lies anyway. She said my mouth always twitched on one side when I did.

"And this is Aunty Dawn," Nurse added, pointing to the dark haired woman who had appeared. "She'll show you around and let you know where to put your things. When you're done, come and join us in the sitting room here," she pointed towards the open doorway to the right of the lobby. "We'll have some lunch ready for you. You look like you could do with some fattening up."

I followed Aunty Dawn up a flight of stairs and along a corridor to a bedroom at the end.

"This'll be your room," she said, making a sweeping gesture with her arm. "You'll be sharing with a girl called Maureen Eastwick. She's at school right now so you'll have some time to unpack and settle in before she gets home. This is your bed," she added, "and the top two drawers of the dresser are for you. You can hang your frocks and blouses in the wardrobe here."

She pointed towards a rickety old wardrobe which had seen better days. There were three dresses, a couple of blouses and a jacket hanging there, presumably Maureen's. Judging by the size of them

Maureen was probably older, or bigger, than me. I hoped we would get along.

"Just leave your things here while I show you the rest of the house," she said, turning on her heel and marching along the corridor. I followed obediently behind.

There was a bathroom at the far end of the corridor and a separate toilet at each end. There were three 'girls' rooms, each with three beds in them. Aunty Dawn's room was next to mine, facing the back, and Nurse's room was at the other end of the corridor, facing the front. Nurse's office was downstairs, off the kitchen, facing the front of the house. The dining room, which adjoined the kitchen, had a long rectangular table and about a dozen chairs set around it. In the corner there was an old treadle Singer sewing machine, and at the other end of the room there was an equally old piano. The sitting room had several sofas and armchairs arranged around a fireplace and looked inviting in a spartan sort of way. In the corner of the sitting room there was a small round dining table set for lunch. At the opposite end of the house from the kitchen there was a playroom which had a door leading outside to the back lawn. A shoe rack sat just inside the door with a row of coat hooks along the wall above it. An old record player sat on a side table. I wished I had thought to bring the records Mum had left behind of Frankie Ifield singing 'I Remember You', and Elvis Presley's new hit called 'Are You Lonesome Tonight'.

"Make yourself at home," Aunty Dawn said, as she concluded the tour. "We want you to be happy here. Now go along and unpack your things then come down for lunch."

I hung my dress and two white school blouses in the wardrobe and put my underwear and socks in the second drawer. I carefully laid my chemistry set and sheet of music for Fur Elise in the top drawer, spreading them out to make the drawer look fuller just in case Maureen peaked. I didn't want her to see how little I had. I put my new leather writing case in the drawer of my bedside table, along with my birthday cards and collection of letters I had received.

I needed a few minutes to myself to let it all sink in. Out the window I could see Willowrey Sands Road as it curved its way down towards the beach, disappearing under an enormous viaduct.

As I stood watching, a train went across the viaduct spewing steam and blowing its whistle three times. I could see the ocean over the rooftops and I could smell the salt air. I liked the idea of living so close to the beach, especially with summer just around the corner.

When I went downstairs Miss Stinson was talking to Nurse. I stood nervously by the door, not wanting to interrupt.

"Ah, there you are," Nurse said. "Come and sit down here so I can get a good look at you. We'll have a nice chat after lunch before the rest of my girls get home but Miss Stinson has to get going soon, so we'd better have our lunch now. You found everything alright, did you?"

"Yes thank you," I said, trying to sound confident and grown up, but instead it sounded aloof. I glanced uneasily at Miss Stinson. I didn't like the thought of her leaving me alone with these strangers so soon.

Aunty Dawn appeared with bowls of steaming soup and a plate of sandwiches. We took our places at the table, but I was too nervous to eat much even though I was starving. I felt self-conscious under the penetrating gaze of Nurse and could barely speak above a whisper.

"You'll have to speak up, girl, if you want me to hear you," she coaxed with a chuckle. "My ears aren't as good as they used to be. I suppose it's no wonder really, what with that loud music my girls play on that record player of theirs all the time. I've never heard the likes of it before, all that screaming at the top of their voices and swooning. They call it music, but I have another word for it."

Miss Stinson laughed along with Nurse but gave me a knowing wink. Miss Stinson was in her late twenties and probably enjoyed the wave of pop music that was hitting the charts these days as much as I did, although I couldn't imagine her actually swooning over anything. She was much too sophisticated for that.

After Miss Stinson left Nurse asked me to join her in her office. She told me a little about the other girls who were living there, then went on to explain a few of the house rules. A list of chores would be put up on the bulletin board in the playroom at the beginning of each month. Chores were rotated amongst each of us on a weekly basis so there was no favoritism. Everyone was expected to pitch in and help. Nurse stressed that this was to be my home and I should make every effort to settle in and think of them as family. She had been at Willowrey since it had opened, eight years before, and had run several other homes before coming here. Spending money would be given out each Saturday and there was an expectation that I should save at least some of it. Dinner was at 5:30 p.m., except on Sunday, when we had our main meal at noon and a light tea at dinner time. We would be woken at seven and were to wash, get dressed, and make our beds before breakfast at seven forty five. She estimated it would take approximately twenty minutes to walk to my school so I would have to leave the house no later than ten past eight. She said she would come with me on the first day.

I nodded intently, wondering how I could possibly keep it all straight in my head and not get into trouble. It seemed like an awful lot of rules for a person to live with, especially after I was used to running wild in Hamsmoor with no one there to tell me what to do, or when to do it.

Shortly before four o'clock three of the other girls came home from school. Hope and Charity were twins and went to the Catholic school in Nestleton. Their parents were Italian. Their mother had died giving birth to them, Charity explained, her eyes raised heavenward as she spoke. Their father had done his best to raise them but had fallen on hard times, so the twins had been placed in care until he could get back on his feet. Charity was the older twin, by twenty two minutes, and she took the responsibility very seriously. Hope seemed content to let her sister take the upper hand in most situations and the two of them were never more than an arms length apart. Both girls had thick black shiny hair down to their waist, which they wore wrapped in a bun on the top of their heads.

The other girl was Maureen. She was fourteen and a half, tall with wavy blond hair. She had a twinkle in her eye and I was never quite sure if she was teasing or goading. She had lived in foster homes most of her life before ending up in Willowrey. She told me she had become too much for her last foster mother to handle. She seemed quite proud of this, as if she had won some tug-of-war with life. She was lively and looked like she could be a lot of fun. I was glad I'd be sharing a room with her. The twins seemed nice but they were complete unto themselves and didn't look like they had much time or interest in anyone else.

The fourth girl, Pam, arrived home shortly after five. She was sixteen which made her the eldest. She had short curly hair and a face that looked old before it was ever young. She was cursed with a strong maternal instinct which she inflicted on the rest of us whenever she had the chance.

At five thirty sharp I followed the rest of the girls into the dining room. Nurse sat at the head of the table. Once we were all settled she said grace, which ended with an enthusiastic 'amen' from Hope and Charity. I heard Maureen stifle a giggle beside me. She obviously didn't share the twins' dedication to prayer. During dinner the conversation was light and friendly and I was able to relax enough to fill my empty belly. Maybe this place wouldn't be so bad. It was almost like I imagined a normal family would be, except we had two mums and no dad. I liked that.

After dinner Maureen proudly showed me the pile of teen magazines she and the other girls had been collecting. They were full of pictures of a new group called the Beatles. I said I hoped they could play music better than they could spell, but Charity said it was just a play on the word 'beat', and had nothing to do with insects at all. I felt like a country bumpkin for not knowing that. I was glad I hadn't brought Mum's Frankie Ifield record with me after all. I didn't think these girls would like it much.

At eight thirty Aunty Dawn came and told us it was time to get ready for bed. I hadn't realized how exhausted I was until I climbed into bed. The flannelette sheets were soft and welcoming. I pulled the covers up under my chin and lay there listening to the sounds of my new home. I could hear Nurse talking to the twins at the end of the hall, then she moved to Pam's room in the middle before coming into our room. She walked towards my bed and leaned down towards me. I flinched.

"Don't worry. I'm not going to hurt you," she said, drawing herself back up. "I was just going to tuck you in." She kissed me gently on the forehead.

"Pleasant dreams," she said. "I hope you'll be very happy here."

"Thank you," I said, choking back tears.

I couldn't remember the last time someone had tucked me into bed. Such a simple gesture but it meant so much. It said 'I care about you, I want to keep you safe and warm', it said more than a thousand words could ever say. I hoped Justin and Jane would soon find someone to tuck them into bed at night too.

CHAPTER FOUR

While I'd been at Languard House, Mum had come to see us every Sunday. She even brought my father with her my last Sunday there. Dad and I had greeted each other awkwardly and talked of superficial things like what we had for breakfast, and what the other children were like, and wasn't it fun living in a seaside town even if it was the middle of winter. None of us said anything about what had happened, except Justin kept asking Dad when he was going to take us home. But Dad just tousled Justin's hair and told him not for a while, buster, which was what he always called him.

I had told Mum I was being sent to Willowrey so that I could go to a grammar school nearby. I thought she would be proud of me for that and I desperately wanted her to be proud of me for something. I needed to know that she still loved me, although sometimes I wondered if she had ever loved me. Surely if she really loved me she wouldn't have let Dad do those things to me?

It had started when Mum left home for the first time, just after I turned eleven. I'd come home and found Dad sitting on the sofa, sobbing. He was clutching a note in his hand and I recognized my mother's handwriting. Between sobs he told me she was gone and wasn't coming back. She said she didn't love him anymore. He was heart broken and I didn't know what to do. I had put my arm around his neck and told him not to worry, we were still here. We still loved him. Only I didn't mean it in the way he must have thought I did.

That night he came to me for the first time. I didn't understand what was happening but he said it was alright. He said it was all part of becoming a big girl. And I had to be a big girl, now that Mum was gone. Afterwards he had given me half a crown and made me promise never to tell anyone. He said it was our little secret so I hadn't told anyone, not for a long, long time.

But when Mum came back a few weeks later Dad didn't stop coming to me. He just waited for those nights when she was out with her boyfriend. You could always tell which nights they were going to be. She'd wash her hair in the kitchen sink, put in curlers and keep them in all day until after she'd had a bath. Then she'd put on makeup and her prettiest dress and fuss about finding a pair of stockings without a run in them. She'd carefully pull them up her long, slim legs, being sure to get the seam line perfectly straight before attaching them to the metal toggles on her suspender belt. She'd tell me to watch Justin and Jane till Dad got home and then she'd hurry down the road to catch the bus into Exeter.

She finally left for good on New Year's Eve, 1963. I prayed she'd come back home to look after us, but she never did. Instead she'd turned up at my school with a policeman, and now none of us could ever go home again.

People always made allowances for 'poor Peggy', as my grandmother invariably referred to my mother. She was completely deaf in one ear, with only limited hearing in the other. As a child she'd attended deaf school in Exeter but my grandmother had fetched her home when war broke out and Exeter was being bombed. Somehow, despite her deafness, 'poor Peggy' learnt to play the piano very well. She'd play for the soldiers that Granddad invited home for Sunday dinners. Nanny said it was their contribution to the war effort, and the least she could do was to make those poor soldiers a home-cooked meal once in a while. Everyone was expected to do their bit, Nanny pointed out. Peggy learned to play all the wartime favourites and the invited soldiers would sing along with tears in their eyes.

Mum loved the limelight and never tired of playing. Some said she was a natural. Pianist, that is.

By the time Mum was seventeen she was sneaking out at night to play the piano in dancehalls with some soldier-musicians who were stationed close by. Sidney Puddicombe was the band leader and trombone player. His stage name was Rex Royston and after the dances he'd walk Mum home. Except they didn't always go straight home and before many months had passed Mum was pregnant. Faster than Dad could hum the opening bars of 'Chattanoga Choo Choo', he found himself in a registry office playing the lead role in a shot gun wedding. Mum was eighteen when my brother, Graham, was born. Dad was twenty five. I was born exactly two years later.

Housing in England was very limited after the war, so my parents spent the first few years of their marriage living in the converted attic of my grandparents' rented terrace house. My grandparents and Aunty Barbara, who was only eight when Mum got married, lived on the main floor, and my mother's brother, Roger, and his wife and new baby lived on the second floor. All three families shared one kitchen and an outdoor toilet.

My grandfather made no secret of his disappointment with my mother, or his disapproval of my father. I grew up believing that my grandfather was a mean and nasty old man who was best avoided. My grandmother, or Nanny as we always called her, was as gentle and accommodating as my grandfather was austere and aloof. She would sometimes give us sweets or a sixpenny piece, but always with the proviso that we not tell Granddad. It took a lot of the pleasure out of the treat, not being able to tell about it.

The day after my move to Willowrey, Nurse took me into Nestleton to buy my new school uniform. With the clothing allowance assigned by the Children's Committee she also bought me a pair of Clark's shoes, Wellington boots and a gym strip. Nurse said there was no point buying cheap shoes as they wore out in no time and then you just had to go back for more. And besides, cheap shoes weren't good for growing feet. Better to have the good ones right from the start, she said.

Next day, Thursday, I started Stoneleigh Grammar. My new navy blue pleated skirt came down to my ankles, so I carefully rolled the waistband over and over, until the hem was just above my knees. When Nurse saw it, she told me to lower it to just below my knees. I began to wonder which Ark she had sailed in on.

The summer term had already started and I was told to do my best to catch up. I was handed a formidable pile of textbooks and told to cover them with brown paper, and write my name on the inside cover. It all seemed so new and crisp, so full of promise. I couldn't wait to show my new books and uniform to Mum when she came to visit on Sunday.

But Sunday came and went with no word from my mother.

"She's probably gone to Languard House to see Justin and Jane," Nurse tried to console me as the afternoon wore on. "No doubt she'll be here to see you later."

I sat by the window all afternoon waiting and watching as the clock nudged its way towards five o'clock. When tea was served at five thirty my mother still hadn't appeared. Nor had she called.

I kept to myself all evening, refusing Maureen's invitations to play cards or checkers and shrugging off Charity's attempts to console me. I stayed close to the window watching as car lights approached, hoping against hope they'd turn into our driveway and my mother would get out. But they never did. Eventually I gave up waiting and went to bed early. I cried myself to sleep.

Every day when I got home from school I'd check the platter on the hall table where our mail was laid out, anxious for word from my mother. But there was no word. On Wednesday Miss Stinson came to see how I was settling in at Willowrey. I asked if she had heard from my mother but she hadn't. She added that Mum hadn't been to Languard House to see Justin and Jane either. As the days turned to a week, I became frantic. What could have happened to her? Maybe she was sick or worse yet, dead! Nurse assured me that they would have heard if that was the case, but my imagination knew no bounds.

On Saturday I took the bus to Torquay to visit my brother and sister. By the time I got to Languard House it was two thirty. I found Justin running around the front garden playing cowboys and Indians with some other boys. His friend Jeffrey wasn't with him which was unusual, but maybe he had visitors. When Justin saw me he came running over.

"Pow, pow," he said, pointing his toy gun at me, "you're dead. Pow!" and off he ran.

"Where's Jane," I called after him.

"Dunno," he yelled over his shoulder, as he gave chase to one of the other boys.

"Is Mum here?" I asked.

"Nope," he said, as he shot his toy gun into the air several times more. "Pow! She's dead too!"

I went inside looking for Jane. I found her curled up on a sofa in the conservatory, listening to Aunt Liddy reading a book. When she saw me she squealed with delight, jumped off the sofa and came running towards me.

"Hello poppet," I said, bending down to scoop her into my arms.

She put her hands on the sides of my face and planted a juicy kiss on my lips. I squeezed her tight, wallowing in the wonderful feel and smell of her. I hadn't realized how much I was missing them both.

"Let's go outside and find Justin," I said, setting her back down. I turned to Aunt Liddy. "Is it alright if we go for a walk?"

"Yes, that'll be fine, but stay on the grounds, just in case they get any other visitors."

"Are you expecting anyone else?" I asked. "Have you heard from my mother?"

"I don't believe so. But she usually comes on Sunday, except last week that is. Perhaps she'll come tomorrow."

We went outside and persuaded Justin to give up his game of cowboys and Indians, and come and sit with us. He was restless and obviously confused and upset.

"Where's Jeffrey," I asked.

"Gone," Justin said, pointing his gun at me and firing off a couple more 'pows'.

"Gone where?" I asked.

"Dunno. A man and a lady came and took him away in a car. They looked pretty mean. I think they're his new foster parents."

Justin looked worried. "Do I have to go to a foster home?" he asked, suddenly looking vulnerable and frightened.

"I think so," I said, "but they're going to find you an extra special nice foster home. Nothing but the best for us Puddicombe's," I added, with more bravado than I felt.

"Can I come and live with you," Justin asked.

"Me too," Jane chimed in.

"Maybe," I said, brightening at the prospect. "We'll have to ask Miss Stinson next time we see her."

When it came time to leave Jane clung to me, wrapping her arms tight around my neck. When Aunt Liddy tried to pry her away she screamed and tightened her grip, almost choking me. As quickly as I could loosen her grip with one hand, she'd tighten it with the other.

"I want to come with you," she wailed, tears streaming down her face as she gave full vent to her emotions.

"Why can't we come with you?" Justin asked, dangerously close to crying himself.

Jane wailed even louder as Aunt Liddy finally extracted her from my arms. It took all my energy not to dissolve into tears myself. It wouldn't help to let them see me cry, but inside my heart was breaking. I kissed them both and gave them a hug, before running down the driveway without looking back. I cried all the way back to Willowrey.

When I got home from school the following Tuesday Miss Stinson was waiting for me. She told me she had received a letter from my mother.

"Is she alright," I asked, torn between relief and apprehension. "Why hasn't she been to see us?"

"Apparently, she's gone to live in Birmingham," Miss Stinson said. "She went with Mr. Brooks. It seems he got a job up there."

I couldn't believe my ears. There had to be some mistake.

"She's gone to Birmingham?" I asked, incredulous. "No goodbyes, no nothing! Did she say how long she's gone for?"

"She says they plan on staying up there indefinitely."

There was a pounding in my head, like it was going to burst. I wanted to scream. This couldn't be true.

"How can she be gone," I cried. "What about us. Doesn't she care about us? She can't leave without us. She said she was going to get a house, so we could go and live with her. She promised."

How could she leave us again, without telling us? She hadn't even come to see where I was living. I slumped into the armchair and curled into a ball as a feeling of numbness settled over me.

"Didn't she say anything to you about going?" Miss Stinson asked.

"No," I said in a flat voice. "Did she go and say goodbye to Jane and Justin?"

"No. Apparently she left for Birmingham a couple of weeks ago."

"Your father has asked if he can visit you here," Miss Stinson said after a few moments silence. "How do you feel about that?"

"I dunno," I said, picking at my cuticles. They started to bleed so I sucked the blood off.

"Of course his visits would be chaperoned," Miss Stinson added.

"I guess that would be okay then," I said after a while, "as long as he comes during the day. I don't want to see him in the dark." My voice trailed away. I didn't need to explain.

"Perhaps we could arrange for Justin and Jane to come and visit you here too," Miss Stinson suggested.

"I think they'd like that," I said. "I told them all about this place. They want to live here too. Do you think they could?"

"It's not up to me," Miss Stinson said. "The Children's Committee decides these things. But Willowrey is only for teenage girls, so I don't think they would agree to it."

"But couldn't you at least ask them if it would be okay?" I persisted, eager to draw the remnants of my family close.

"I'll put it in my report that you'd like that, Gail, but don't build your hopes up."

The following Sunday my father came for a visit. He had a lady friend with him to act as chaperone. Her name was Susan. She wore too much makeup and her skirt was too tight. I'd seen a lot of women like her at the dancehalls Dad played at. The weather was warm and sunny so Dad put the top of his Morris Minor convertible down and took us for a drive along the coast. He seemed more interested in impressing his lady friend than in conversing with me. But I didn't mind. I couldn't think of much to say to him anyhow.

Dad parked on Nestleton seafront and bought us each an ice cream cone. We walked along the pier in silence, eating our cones. At the end of the pier we leaned on the railings, watching the gulls dip and swoop around us.

"Your Dad tells me you just started a new school," Susan said, as we watched the gulls. "Are you enjoying it?"

"Yes, I like it a lot. The school is almost brand new and the teachers are very nice," I said. "I missed a lot of school while I was at Languard House, so they're trying to help me catch up. Otherwise I may have to repeat second form, which would be really embarrassing. I'd hate to be a year older than the rest of the class. They'd think I was a moron or something."

"Well, you sound like a smart little cookie to me," Susan said, as she brushed my hair back from my face, "I'm sure you'll catch up. What's your favourite subject?"

"Science, but I really enjoy geography too. I want to travel and see the world when I'm old enough."

"Why would anyone want to leave glorious Devon?" Dad chimed in. "No place in the world can hold a candle to this little piece of paradise."

I laughed. "Oh Dad, how would you know? You've only been away from Devon once, and that was to go to London for a few days. There's a whole world out there and I'm going to see it one day."

When they dropped me off at Willowrey at the end of the afternoon, Dad said he would come again in a couple of weeks; maybe even bring Justin and Jane with him. I said I'd like that.

A few days later I got a letter from my mother. She told me all about the new flat they had and how 'groovy' it was at the nightclub Norman worked at. She asked if I was well and hoped I was enjoying my new school. She didn't seem to realize, or care, how her sudden departure had affected us all. There was no apology, no explanation. I wrote back saying how happy I was to know that she was having a good time in Birmingham, and yes I did like my new school, thank you very much.

My father phoned to say he had received permission to bring Justin and Jane to Willowrey the following Sunday. Susan would be coming too. When they arrived I showed Justin and Jane around. Hope and Charity made a big fuss over Jane, passing her back and forth between them like a doll. Pam shook hands with Justin and said she was pleased to make his acquaintance. Justin just beamed at her, obviously chuffed to be treated in such a grown up manner.

After showing them around Willowrey, the three of us squeezed into the back seat of Dad's car and he drove us to the beach. Dad and Susan sat on deck chairs while Justin, Jane, and I made sandcastles. Then we ate ice cream cones and watched as the incoming tide washed our castles away without a trace. For a few precious hours we were just like any other family, enjoying a Sunday afternoon on the beach. Or so we could pretend. Maybe one day the tides of time would wash over our lives and we'd carry on as if nothing bad had ever really happened.

Half term break was fast approaching. I received a letter from my grandparents inviting me to spend the holidays with them. Nurse said she would have to check with the Children's Committee first. A week later I was informed that the Committee had approved the visit and I should write to my grandparents to let them know that I would be coming.

Faced with the prospect of actually going back to Riverton I began to worry about how much people knew. Since that fateful night when I'd given my statement to the police, no one had spoken a single word to me about what had happened. It was as if the subject were off limits. If we didn't talk about it we could pretend it had never happened, and that seemed to be the way it had to be. Pretend it hadn't happened.

When the time came, Miss Stinson drove me to my grandparents' house. It felt so good to be back in familiar surroundings. I looked around, taking in the sights and smells of this house where I had felt safe as a child. Granddad's rack of pipes with the brass plate saying 'Smoke and Be Happy' was mounted on the wall beside his chair, the rich, sweet smell of tobacco permeating the living room. The kitchen was suffused with the familiar aroma of Typhoo tea, home made strawberry jam and spices. I inhaled it all, the tension melting out of my body for the first time in months. It was like coming home.

I asked Granddad if they had heard from my mother lately. A dark look crossed his face.

"She's no bloody daughter of mine," he grumbled.

I quickly dropped the subject. I had to admit there were times when I wished she was no bloody mother of mine, too. But she was.

While I was in Riverton I went to see my best friend, Trina. We'd been inseparable since kindergarten, even though Trina had born the brunt of my bullying when things had gone bad for me. Trina's home had become a haven from the cold reality of my own home. I ingratiated myself into their home. Trina's mother, Mrs. Thomas, was like a mother hen fussing over her brood. She never put on make up and fancy clothes and went out to nightclubs. And she hardly seemed to notice when I fell into step with her four children and lined up for snacks or drinks on hot summer days, or soup and cocoa on cold winter nights.

Trina wanted to know all about my life at Willowrey. I made it sound as exciting as I could, omitting the bits about how lonely I was or how much I missed being in a real home. The last thing I wanted was Trina feeling sorry for me. I had my pride.

"Wow, fancy that, living by the beach. You're so lucky, Gail."

"Maybe you can come and visit me sometime over the summer. We can go to the beach every day if we like," I bragged.

When I returned to Willowrey I felt more settled. My fears about what people might think of me, back home in Riverton, had been put to rest, at least for the time being. I hadn't been stoned or spat on. Curtains hadn't twitched as I walked by. In fact, people I met who knew me had been warm and welcoming, asking after my brother and sister and wanting to know that we were all well. It seems the tide had done a good job of covering up the scars on the beach, leaving smooth sand in its wake.

After the half-term break I buried myself in school work,

frantically swotting for year-end exams. I was determined not to fail the year. I was beginning to make friends in my class and was keen to keep up. I enjoyed the peace and solitude of studying and would only close my books when Nurse or Aunty Dawn came to tell me it was time for bed.

With my mother so far away, my only regular visitor was my father. He came to see me every other Sunday and sometimes brought Justin and Jane with him. I came to look forward to these visits. They became the umbilical cord which connected me with my real family – warts, dark secrets and all. Like it or not, they were the only family I had. Dad always brought a chaperone with him - that was one of the rules, only they always acted like it was a date or something. Susan, who had come with him on his first two visits, had been replaced by a girl named Carol. She was eighteen years old.

Then, just when I was getting used to his visits, I received a letter from him saying he couldn't make our regular Sunday visit because his car was being repaired. I was so disappointed I flew into a rage. Aunty Dawn tried to console me but I was too distraught to listen. I just wanted a mother and father who loved me and took care of me. Not parents who tried to fit me in between band gigs or boyfriends or car repairs. I tore my father's photo off my locker door, ripped it into tiny pieces and threw it on the floor.

"I hate him," I said through gritted teeth. "I hope he never comes here again. I don't need him."

I vowed never to rely on my parents again. I would stand on my own two feet and make my own way in life, that way they couldn't disappoint me. I would expect nothing from them ever again.

CHAPTER FIVE

As the rains of spring gave way to balmy summer weather, the haunted look in my eyes started to fade. I began to feel alive. I joined the school track team and was picked to represent Stoneleigh Grammar at the area sports day. I ran in the 100 and 400 yard races, as well as the relay team. My legs were strong from all those horsey rides, and I could run fast. My school marks also improved steadily and, much to my relief, I passed easily into third form.

When my new school friends asked me where I lived I alluded to being a 'boarder' at Willowrey. I explained that my parents were divorced and that they were musicians who traveled a lot, so couldn't take me along. I hid my sense of abandonment behind a veil of nonchalance. It was no big deal, really, I told my friends.

During one of my father's Sunday afternoon visits he announced that he and my mother were now divorced. In the same breath he announced that he was getting engaged to Carol. I was stunned. She was only five years older than me! She was tall and skinny with lank, mousey brown hair. She had that look about her, like a dog that's used to being beaten and doesn't have the gumption to keep away from the stick. I could only imagine what my father was doing to her at night. I wanted to scream at her to run as far and as fast as she could, to get away from him. But I doubt she would have listened. She only saw him as Rex Royston, the great bandleader and trombone player. She thought she'd won first prize. I didn't have the heart to tell her it was really only the booby prize.

I grumbled to Nurse and Miss Stinson that I didn't want my father to visit anymore. I couldn't bear to watch him with this girl. But when Sundays rolled around I'd find myself watching for his car coming down Willowrey Sands Road. And when he did come I'd be happy to see him, until I saw Carol waiting in the car. I don't know if it was jealousy or disgust, or perhaps a bit of both. I tried to shrug it off and make light of it. What else could you expect from a musician I asked myself? Women were always throwing themselves at his feet.

Beatlemania was sweeping across England during the summer of 1963, and Willowrey didn't escape the hysteria. We would all huddle around the radio in the playroom, adjusting the dial until we found Radio Luxemburg, and could hear John and Paul sing 'She loves you, yeah, yeah, yeah', or 'Please please me, ooooohhh'. Their music awakened a restlessness in the youth of England that was to reverberate around the world. Maureen's posters of the clean-cut teen idols, Cliff Richards and the Shadows, were soon overwhelmed by the long-haired 'fab four' from Liverpool. Even Elvis, the American dream machine, had to take second billing to John, Paul, George and Ringo.

On Saturday mornings, Hope and Charity always took the bus into Nestleton to visit their father and go to confession. They were devout Catholics. This week, however, their thoughts were on far more earthly things than confession. They had pooled their pocket money for two weeks to buy the newly released Beatles EP. They carried it home to Willowrey like a trophy. We played that record over and over again until we knew every word, every 'yeah, yeah, yeah,' every 'ooooohhh'. It was unlike anything we had ever heard before and we lapped it up.

Shortly after school finished for the summer holidays I got a letter from my mother. She said she was coming to Devon for a holiday in August and planned to stay in Riverton with my grandparents. She said she hoped to see me while she was there.

"Can I go and stay with my grandparents while she's there," I asked Miss Stinson when she came for her regular monthly visit a few days later.

"May I," Miss Stinson said.

"May you what?" I asked, confused.

"It's 'may I', not 'can I'."

"Oh. May I go and stay with my grandparents while my mother's here?" I groaned.

"I'll have to check with the Children's Committee first, but I can't imagine they'll have any objections. Are you looking forward to seeing your mother again?"

I shrugged.

"Of course, she's my mother."

It struck me as a strange question.

The Children's Committee approved a weekend visit to my grandparents. Miss Stinson drove me. She said my mother wanted to discuss a few things with her. While Miss Stinson and Mum talked I went and found my grandfather who was working in his vegetable garden.

"How's my little Einstein?" he asked, when he saw me. I giggled.

"Oh Granddad, don't you know Einstein was a bloke. How can I be Einstein?"

"Well let's hope you can tell the difference between weeds and seedlings," he teased. "I could do with a little help in this garden."

I started pulling chickweed from between the tomato plants, snacking on sun ripened fruit as we worked in companionable silence. Granddad never was much on conversation. Everyone said he was grumpy, but I was learning to love and appreciate him in a way I hadn't thought possible while we lived in Riverton. Behind that grumpy, stern exterior was a caring, compassionate man. He had no patience or tolerance for my mother's antics, and could barely look her in the eye these days. But none of that anger was directed at me. For me, he wanted only the best. I could see it in his eyes. I think he would gladly have killed my father for what he'd done to me - if he'd been the killing sort of person. Granddad became my rock, my anchor, my beacon. He may not have smothered me in kisses, or showered me with gifts, but what he gave me was priceless - a sense of dignity, of self.

When it was time for me to leave Riverton Mum took me downtown and put me on the bus back to Nestleton.

"I'll be in Devon for another week, so I'll come and see you at Willowrey before I go back. I also want to see Jane in her new foster home, and Justin at Languard House. I've got so many things to take care of while I'm here in Devon," she said, an edge of irritation creeping into her voice. "It would make my life a lot easier if they'd kept you all together. I'm going to spend half my time sitting on buses getting from one place to the other. Ah, here comes your bus now. Got your bus fare ready?"

The following Sunday Mum phoned me as I was on my way out to church. Nurse called me into the office to take the call.

"Hello, Gail. I just wanted to let you know we're coming to see you this afternoon. We'll pick Justin up first, then head over your way shortly after two."

"That's great," I said. "I can't wait to show you where I live. See you then."

I told Nurse what had been arranged.

"That's nice," she said, "I'm looking forward to meeting her."

But I could tell by her tone of voice that she wasn't really. Nurse obviously had opinions about mothers who abandoned their children just because they felt like it.

When I got home from church I changed out of my frock and put on shorts and a top. It was a blistering hot day and I hoped Mum would take us to the beach. I was sitting in the playroom with the twins, listening to their growing collection of Beatles records, when Nurse came to tell me my visitors were here. There was something odd about the way she said it, and I hoped she and Mum hadn't gotten off to a bad start.

I followed her out to the lobby, where my mother was waiting. And there, with his arm around her and beaming like a Cheshire cat, was my father. It seemed so natural at first, to see them standing there, together, that it didn't really register. But something was wrong with this picture. They were divorced now, weren't they? Mum was living with Norman Brooks now, wasn't she? They had blown our lives apart, scattering us across Devon like leaves in the wind because Mum didn't love Dad anymore, hadn't they? And now they were here, together, side by side, in the front hall of Willowrey, smiling at me, and saying how lovely it was to see me. I just stood there, staring back at them. I didn't know what to say.

"Aren't you going to say hello?" Mum said. "Cat got your tongue?"

"Hello," I stammered, as I struggled to make sense of what I was seeing. "You didn't tell me Dad was coming too." I looked directly at my father. "Where's your fiancée, Carol?"

Dad flinched. Mum bristled.

"She couldn't make it," Dad said, casting a quick glance at my mother. "Are you ready to go?"

I slipped on my daps and grabbed my beach bag, which was sitting by the door.

"What are your plans?" Nurse asked. Her hands were folded across her midriff to stop them from flapping around, as they sometimes did when she was agitated. "I like my girls to be home by five, in time for tea."

I wondered how my mother would react to me being referred to as one of Nurse's girls, but she said nothing, if she even noticed. Part of me wanted her to protest, to claim ownership of me, but a bigger part of me liked being one of Nurse's girls. It was as though she were casting a protective blanket over me, taking me into her world where I would be safe from the fall-out of my parents' shenanigans. I was beginning to feel at home in Nurse's world. The madness of my parents' lives was more than I could fathom most days.

As we drove to the beach Mum was laughing and carrying on with Dad as if she didn't have a care in the world. I sat in the back seat scowling but Justin seemed chuffed. He was happy to be with his Mum and Dad again on such a sunny day, with the roof of the car down. Just like in the old days.

"What's your problem?" Mum finally snapped at me as we sat on the beach watching Justin and Dad build a sandcastle.

"Nothing," I mumbled.

"Well obviously something's eating you. You haven't said two words since we picked you up."

I picked at my cuticles, making them bleed. I stared at the blood, wondering how long it would take a person to bleed to death.

"I thought you and Dad were divorced," I finally said.

"So what if we are. Can't we still spend some time together?"

"But what about Norman Brooks? I thought you were with him now. And Dad said he was engaged to that drip, Carol. She isn't much older than me. It's disgusting." My voice trailed away.

"Well Norman Brooks isn't here, is he?" Mum said, "And what harm can it do if your dad and I spend a few days together?"

But I wondered about their nights together mostly.

"But what about us?" I blurted out. "Are you and Dad getting back together? Are we all going back to live in Riverton, just like nothing happened?"

I shuddered at the thought. As much as I wanted to live a normal life, in a normal house, with normal parents, I was beginning to realize that it was just a fantasy. My parents didn't do normal. Nurse and Willowrey were now my reality, and I wasn't sure I wanted to give it all up. I had a chance here to do something with my life, to live a semblance of normal even if it wasn't exactly. But they say blood is thicker than water, and honour thy mother and father, and all that stuff. My head hurt from thinking about it all. I felt a need to change the subject.

"How was Jane when you saw her?"

"Oh, she's fine," Mum said, "growing like a weed and as cute as ever. She's getting excited about starting school in September. Don't think much of her foster mother though. Old bag, didn't even crack a smile the whole time we were there. Said she didn't want Jane spending the night with us because it would be too unsettling for her. Can you imagine that, too unsettling to spend a night with her own mother. Who does that woman think she is?"

"But does Jane seem happy there?" I persisted.

"Not really. She kicked up a terrible stink when it was time for us to leave. It nearly broke my heart. Even your dad had tears in his eyes."

When they dropped me off at Willowrey, Mum said she would be around for a few more days and would try to see me again before she left. But I didn't hear from her again until I got a letter a week or so later, saying how much she'd enjoyed her holiday in Devon. I wondered if Dad had enjoyed it too. She went on to say how excited she was about getting Jane back. I read this line over and over, trying to make sense of it.

"Nurse," I said, as I walked into her office holding Mum's letter in my hands, "what do you think my mother means about 'getting Jane back'? Has she gone to Birmingham for a visit?"

Nurse put the papers she was working on aside and turned to face me.

"You better come in and have a seat, dear," she said, motioning to me to close the door.

"While your mother was back in Devon she applied to have the Fit Person Order for Jane revoked."

"What does that mean?" I asked.

"Your mother has applied to the courts, claiming that she's now in a position to provide a safe home for Jane."

"But what about me and Justin?" I asked, tears springing to my eyes. "Isn't she taking us too? Why didn't she at least take Justin too? He needs her more than Jane. Jane already has a foster home but Justin is still at Languard House." Tears choked back my words. The gaping wound of abandonment was still raw inside me, and now the salt of rejection was being poured onto it.

Pain and sadness washed over me. I was a baby again, crying for my mother but she couldn't hear me. Or if she could, she was turning a deaf ear. Had she given any thought to Justin and me? How we might feel about being left behind by her, again. I tried to tell myself I didn't care; I didn't need her. But I did, I did care, I did need her. But mostly I just wanted her to want me.

On Sunday I took the bus to Languard House to see Justin. I guessed he was probably feeling the same way I was about Mum taking Jane back. We didn't talk about it. Neither one of us had the words to describe the sense of abandonment and rejection, or the pain of not being wanted by your own mother. Except this time it was different. This time one of us had been singled out as wanted, and the others rejected. It seemed worse, somehow. Justin and I were on the reject pile and we clung silently to each other to reassure ourselves that we were lovable, even if Mum didn't seem to think so.

"Perhaps you can come and live at Willowrey with me," I told him.

"I keep asking them about it and they haven't said no, so maybe they're still thinking about it."

I needed to keep Justin close. I felt he was all that was left of the crumbling ruin that had once been my family. I wondered if he needed me as much as I needed him. He was becoming more and more introverted as the months went by, and I began to worry about how he was managing to deal with all this. He seemed to be getting lost in the shuffle.

A few weeks later, Nurse called me into her office after dinner.

"The Children's Committee has found a foster home for your brother, Justin," she said, getting straight to the point. "He's going to a home in Kennford, just outside Exeter. It's a nice family with one young boy and a new baby. I'm sure Justin will be happy there."

Nurse paused, giving me time to absorb this information.

"I know you were hoping he'd be able to come and live with us here, but the Committee didn't think this was in Justin's best interest."

"It's probably just as well," I said, after a few moments thought. "It wouldn't have been much of a life for him here, with all us girls."

"He'll be quite close to your grandparents' home, and they'll be able to keep in regular touch with him," Nurse assured me. "They're very concerned that he not be cut off from the family."

Now I would be completely alone, except for my father's visits which had become sporadic at best.

As the summer drew to a close I began to look forward to school. It would be good to start at the beginning of the year and not feel like I was always two steps behind everyone else.

On Sundays we had to go to church. The Children's Committee said we were required to have a religious upbringing and Nurse took this responsibility seriously, despite our varied protests. I'd daydream through most of the service but when it came time for the hymns I'd join in with a gusto which surprised even me. Aunty Dawn suggested I try out for the church choir, which I did. Much to my surprise they accepted me. I was duly fitted for a choir smock and told to attend choir practice Wednesday evenings. The church became a major focus for my life. I signed up for confirmation classes, and went to the Youth Club on Friday evenings. Church offered what I needed most -

unconditional love. Maybe my parents couldn't offer it, but I came to believe that God could.

For the autumn half-term break it was arranged that I go to Birmingham to visit my mother and Jane, who was living with her now. As the train made its way north the rolling hills and red soil of Devon gave way to a dreary, flat countryside. The cities and towns became bigger and dirtier, with factory smoke stacks spewing soot and grime into the air. A light rain was falling by the time I got to Birmingham and it was dark.

Mum and Jane were waiting for me at the station. We took the bus back to Mum's flat in Handsworth.

"My you're getting big," I said to Jane, as I tried to pick her up and twirl her around. "I can hardly lift you anymore. How old are you now?"

"Five," she said, holding up five pudgy fingers.

"Holy camoly, you're nearly all growed up big, just like me," I said tickling her.

"Show Gail your room," Mum told Jane. "You'll have to share Jane's bed of course," she added, turning to me, "but I've emptied the top dresser drawer for you. Get yourself settled. Norman will be home soon, so I have to get his dinner ready. He leaves for work at seven but once he's gone we can snuggle up and watch some telly."

Jane's bedroom was small, with nondescript beige wallpaper peeling around the corners. The window was covered with a sheer lace curtain in a pathetic attempt to hide the sooty bleakness of Birmingham from view. It was the first time I had been in an industrial city, and I hated the acrid smell of factory smoke that seemed to permeate everything. When I blew my nose even my snot was black. I wondered how people survived here, breathing in such filthy air. I missed the clean, salty air of Devon.

When Norman got home he seemed genuinely pleased to see me. He had an easy going manner about him and an endless supply of jokes. Life seemed to be a game for him. He stammered a bit, but that didn't slow him down. I wondered how he managed when he sang on stage but Mum said no one could sing "Yellow Bird" like he did, so I guessed he managed alright.

After dinner we curled up on the couch to watch some television. The light rain had become a full-fledged downpour and we could hear the raindrops splattering on the window panes. Every so often a gust of wind would rattle the window and we'd draw closer together, happy in the comfort and warmth of our little world.

Next day Mum took us out early so that Norman could sleep. Most nights he worked until two in the morning and then slept until noon next day. We took the bus into the centre of Birmingham and looked around the shops. It was crowded and noisy, with cars and buses honking and jostling for position and people crowding the pavements so you could hardly walk. The rain had stopped and a weak sun was struggling to peak through the overcast sky.

That night, after Jane had reluctantly gone to bed and a neighbour arrived to babysit, my mother and I got ready to go to the Blue Lagoon nightclub where Norman was playing. Mum put makeup on me, trying to conceal how young I really was, and loaned me a pair of nylon pantyhose to wear instead of my white knee socks. She said pantyhose were the latest thing. They were so much better than old-fashioned stockings and suspender belts with their metal toggles, which showed lumps on your legs if you wore a tight skirt. I left my hair loose around my shoulders. As we stood side by side in the hallway putting our coats on I caught our reflection in the mirror. We had a striking resemblance to each other and could probably pass for sisters.

We took a taxi to the club and slipped into a booth quite close to the stage. Norman smiled when he saw us and gave a little nod in our direction. A few of the other people turned to look at us, wondering who the pianist was smiling at. I held my head up high, trying to look cool and sophisticated. The club was dimly lit and I hoped no one could tell I was only thirteen and a half.

When Norman started up with the opening bars of 'Yellow Bird' my mother almost swooned. He looked at her across the shiny black top of the grand piano and sang just to her. I shifted uncomfortably in my seat feeling like an intruder in some intimate interlude.

"Isn't he fab," Mum kept saying, much to my annoyance. Did she have to carry on like a love sick teenager? "Doesn't he just send you?"

Send me where, I wasn't quite sure.

"Yeah, he's cool," I said, trying to mimic her enthusiasm. But really

I just wanted to listen to the words and the music. I could identify with that yellow bird, up high in banana tree, who sat all alone like me.

All too soon the holiday was over and Miss Stinson was there to pick me up. Jane helped me pack while Mum and Miss Stinson talked in the living room. Miss Stinson wanted to know how it was going now that Jane was living with them. Mum went to great lengths to assure her that everything was perfect. Jane had settled down and was doing well at school. It seemed to me that Jane was becoming a bit spoilt, throwing tantrums whenever she didn't get her own way, but no one asked my opinion, so I said nothing.

Mum and Jane came to the train station to see us off. Mum said she would come and visit me in Devon, maybe around Christmas time depending on what Norman's work was like. I said I would like that.

It was almost supper time when we arrived at Willowrey. I couldn't help but notice that there was something different about the place. Coming from the sitting room was a ghostly flicker and I could hear voices and music as if the radio was on. I stuck my head around the door and could hardly believe my eyes – we had a television! Willowrey had finally joined the twentieth century.

"Oh cool," I squealed in excitement, "Now we can watch Top of the Pops on Thursdays."

Maureen, hearing my voice, motioned for me to join them on the sofa.

"Quick, come and watch this show with us, before it's time to turn it off."

I plonked myself down on the sofa beside Maureen. It felt good to be back at Willowrey. This was my home now.

Two weeks later, in November, 1963, John F. Kennedy was shot. Nurse called us into the sitting room to watch the news on television. We had never been so connected to world events before and it amazed me that we could sit in Devon and watch what was going on in America almost as soon as it happened. Nurse said it was important to pay attention to world events, but after a while I became restless and went back to my studying. It was less traumatic.

November went by in a blur of school work, choir practices, and church. Before I knew it we were making plans for Christmas. My grandparents invited me to Riverton for part of the holidays. My Aunty Barbara was getting married the weekend after Christmas, and I was to be her bridesmaid.

A few days before Christmas, Nurse called me into her office. She said Miss Stinson would like to speak to me on the phone. I hoped it wasn't to say my visit to my grandparents was cancelled.

"Hello," I said tentatively into the receiver.

"Gail, I thought I should let you know that we've heard from your mother," Miss Stinson said.

"Is everything alright?" I asked, not sure why she was phoning to tell me this, but fearing the worse.

"Your mother and father have just been into the Exeter office, with Jane," she said.

"My father? Do you mean Norman Brooks?" I asked, somewhat confused.

"No, Gail, I mean your father. Apparently he drove up to Birmingham to fetch your mother and Jane, and bring them back to Devon. It seems your mother called him and asked him to come."

I shook my head, trying to make sense of it all.

"They want us to take Jane back into care," she continued.

"What? I don't understand. Everything seemed fine when I was up there visiting. What's happened?"

"I guess things weren't working out," Miss Stinson said. "We've asked your mother to keep Jane overnight and think about her decision. But if she does decide to give her up again Jane will have to go back to Languard House, at least for a while."

I couldn't bear to think of Jane having to go back to Languard House on her own. She was so young, and Justin wasn't there any more to keep her company.

"Where is she now?" I asked.

"Your mother still has her. She's to let us know in the morning what she plans to do."

"Do you know where they're staying?"

"At your father's place in Exeter, I believe. I'll let you know as soon as I hear any more."

"Thanks," I said, barely above a whisper, "Merry Christmas."

I slept fitfully that night. By morning I had worked myself into quite a tizzy, flip flopping between anger and angst. I wished Mum would call and tell me what had gone wrong, and why she was doing this.

Shortly after breakfast Miss Stinson called me again. She said she had received news of my parents, although she hadn't actually seen them yet. Mrs. Fackrell, Justin's foster mother, had called to say that they had shown up at her home unexpectedly to visit with Justin. They still had Jane with them. They had told Mrs. Fackrell that they planned to visit me on Sunday, and asked if they could bring Justin to see me too. Sunday seemed like a lifetime away to me.

Next day, Miss Stinson phoned me from Languard House.

"I wanted to let you know that your sister is here now," she said. "Your mother decided to give her up and they dropped her off at the Exeter office this morning."

"Can they do that?" I asked, "Can they just drop her off and walk away?"

Miss Stinson avoided my question.

"Jane is doing well. She seems happy here and I'm sure she'll be fine."

"So where's my mother now?"

"I'm not sure. She's with your father somewhere. I believe they're living together again."

"Did Mum seem upset?" I asked, groping for an explanation. "Did she say why she's doing this?"

"She said Mr. Brooks was in some financial difficulty. That's why she's come back to Devon."

"But why did she have to give up Jane, again? It doesn't make any sense."

"I agree, but I don't have an answer to that. Maybe when you see her on Sunday, she'll be able to tell you more."

When Mum arrived at Willowrey on Sunday afternoon I was waiting for her. Dad and Justin were with her. Dad looked very pleased and puffed up, and Mum giggled a lot and smoked endless cigarettes. I could barely conceal my anger and disgust for what they had done to little Jane. Justin, oblivious to the undercurrents of confusion and anger, was beaming from ear to ear as usual.

Dad drove us to Languard House to see Jane. Much to my relief she seemed quite content there and had to be coaxed away from a game she was playing with another little girl. Mum said she couldn't wait to get out of the place so we all piled in the car and went for a drive, even though it was cold and windy and we had no place to go. Mum carried on like everything was fine, but conversation was sparse.

"Only a few days until Christmas," Dad said, trying to cheer us up, but instead Jane burst into tears.

"What if Santa can't find me?" she wailed. "Maybe he doesn't know where I live now."

Justin looked anxiously at Dad, not wanting to believe Jane. "Do you think he knows where I live now?" he asked.

"Don't you worry your pretty little heads about it, chil'ern, Santa knows everything, and he'll find you no matter where you are," Dad said, smacking his lips together like he always did whenever he said something he thought was particularly important.

When I got back to Willowrey, I went in search of Nurse.

"Do you think Jane can come and spend Christmas Day with us? She's worried that Santa won't be able to find her."

"I'm afraid that won't be possible, dear," Nurse said, "but I know for a fact that Santa will find all the children at Languard House. He always does."

"But she's going to be on her own for Christmas. Can I at least go and visit her there?"

"The buses aren't running on Christmas Day, but you can certainly go and see her on Boxing Day, if that would make you feel any better."

"Yes, it would," I said, feeling somewhat relieved.

"Did your mother say what her plans are?"

"Not really," I said, shrugging, "I don't know why my father went and got her. She said she's going back to Birmingham after Christmas. It's like she just came down here to dump Jane and have a little holiday. If Dad hadn't gone and fetched her she'd have kept Jane, I bet. It's all his fault."

"I'm sure your mother wouldn't have come back with him if she didn't want to," Nurse said, as she sewed a missing button on a blouse. "She's quite old enough to make up her own mind about these things."

I wasn't so sure she was.

Later that day I asked Nurse if I could call my mother at my father's place to wish her merry Christmas. Long distance phone calls cost money, she reminded me as she handed me the phone. I chatted briefly with Mum and said I would see her at Aunty Barbara's wedding the weekend after Christmas. Within minutes of me hanging up, the phone rang again. Nurse answered it. From what she was saying I could tell it was my mother calling back.

"I'm afraid that won't be possible," Nurse said into the receiver, then listened some more.

"I can't speak for Languard House," she said, "but I'm sure they have their reasons. As for Gail, you'll see her in Riverton after Christmas. Sorry I can't help you."

Nurse said goodbye and hung up.

"It seems that your father is working Christmas Day, and your mother doesn't want to spend the day on her own. If you ask me she should have thought of that earlier."

Christmas didn't seem real that year. It was our first Christmas apart and I missed my family. I missed the rough and tumble stampede downstairs in the morning, racing to see if our stockings had been filled. I missed Mum's mince tarts and sausage rolls and the fancy boxes of Turkish delight and candied citrus slices which she always set out after Christmas dinner.

The day after Boxing Day I went to Riverton to have my bridesmaid's dress fitted for Aunty Barbara's wedding. Mum arrived the morning of the wedding. Dad dropped her off outside my grandparents' home, knowing better than to come in himself. Mum leaned in the car window and made a big show of giving him a goodbye kiss. I heard my grandfather scoff behind me.

"Should be ashamed of herself, after all that man's done," he grumbled.

We were all glad of the distraction of a house full of guests and the wedding festivities over the next two days. It saved us having to deal with my grandfather's disapproval of my mother or talk about what had happened to her children. When it was time to go back to Willowrey, Granddad said he would drive me. He seemed glad of an excuse to get out of the house.

"Can you drop me off in Exeter on your way?" Mum asked.

Granddad grudgingly agreed.

I was curious to see where my father was living now and hoped to be invited in, but my grandfather said he wouldn't wait so we just dropped Mum off. Granddad wouldn't even say goodbye to her, he just kept staring straight ahead, waiting for her to get her bags out of the boot and say her goodbyes to me.

I saw my father's convertible Morris Minor parked on the street. I tried to imagine him walking out of this strange house, getting into his car here in a town where I had never known him. I wondered what his life was like now, living without his children. Did he sit alone at nights in a darkened room, watching television while the reflection danced across the ceiling? I tried to imagine my mother living there with him, without us. My parents' lives had become like a migraine headache to me: the space in the middle was a dark blur and I could only see the fuzzy bits around the edges.

And then, as suddenly as she had come, Mum was gone. At least this time she phoned first. She said she was on her way back to Birmingham. Apparently Norman Brooks had sorted out his financial difficulties and she didn't need to stay with Dad anymore. I wondered if Dad would feel the sting of rejection as acutely as her children.

COUNTY OF DEVON CHILDREN'S COMMITTEE
EXCERPT OF SIX MONTHLY REVIEW OF GAIL PUDDICOMBE
File 7952/2

EDUCATION:

Attends Stoneleigh Grammar School. She seems to have settled down well and goes for any activities which are taking place. She ran in the area sports though she did not win. She is also in the school choir and plays net ball. They feel at the school she will be able to do reasonably well in four "O" level subjects when the time comes. She is well liked at school.

RELIGION:

Gail attends Church in the mornings and is receiving instruction for confirmation.

FAMILY CONTACTS:

Mr. Puddicombe [father] fell in quite readily with all this and he visits quite regularly. This was fortnightly at first, then every three weeks but he has not now been for a month.

Mrs. Puddicombe [mother] is not over keen to have Gail back now but wants her later.

Jane: There is no jealousy of Jane on Gail's part, she is more maternal in her attitude towards her.

SOCIAL PROGRESS:

There are times when the Willowrey staff feel that Gail is not a "nice" girl. They feel that she has a nasty streak and that she can be insincere and ingratiating but that this is probably because she has had to do so much fighting. She gets on quite well with the others in Willowrey.

On 11.10.63 she absconded with another girl. They disappeared after they had gone to bed and were found walking from Brixham with a 19 year-old youth. This has not really been discussed with the girls concerned but Mr. Puddicombe had seen Gail the following weekend and told her how silly he thought she had been.

Gail sleeps badly. It takes her a long time to get off to sleep and she wakes up early. She also has nightmares on occasions.

Gail is neat and clean and careful about her clothes. She is reasonably helpful. She tends to belittle both the other girls and the staff and can be very scathing, though when she has been put in her place about this she has taken it quite well.

Matron feels that she has never seen Gail relax and Miss Stinson said that the only time she had seen her relax was with her grandmother at Riverton.

Gail seems to have to be occupied all the time and has a vivid imagination. Matron felt that she has never really been at home with them but is torn apart the whole time because of her desire to be in her own home and her realization of all that this would involve.

Child Care Officer

CHAPTER SIX

As 1964 dawned Beatlemania was running rampant and I couldn't help but get swept up in it. With my Christmas money I bought myself an imitation-leather Beatles hat, like the one John Lennon wore in the movie *A Hard Day's Night*. I wore it everywhere, unless I had my school uniform on that is - then we had to wear our school beret or else risk a detention. They were very strict about things like that. Two fourth form boys were suspended for wearing their hair in the long basin cut like the Beatles and refusing to get it cut. School regulations said boys' hair had to be kept off the collar. I suggested they simply lower their collars.

One day when I got home from school Maureen's child care officer, Miss Harvey, was there waiting for her. I assumed she had come to talk to Maureen about our recent moonlight escapade. Maureen and I had slipped out after bedtime and gone in search of excitement. We were on our way back to Willowrey when the police picked us up shortly after midnight.

Miss Stinson had already raked me over the coals for my part in the escapade and even my father had gone on about with a silly thing I'd done. I tried telling them I was used to running free at night in Riverton and going to nightclubs with my mother, so didn't see what the problem was, but apparently they did. Such behaviour simply wasn't appropriate for a girl my age, they said. I'd grumbled about having to grow up backwards, and asked how I could go back to behaving like a child when I already knew so much. They told me I should try. So now I was keen to make a good impression on Miss Harvey in an attempt to mitigate my role in the whole affair. I chattered on about the latest fashions, pop music and the Beatles but she didn't even know who they were. I invited her to the playroom and showed her our collection of Beatles posters and records.

"See, here they are," I said, pointing to the wall of posters. "George is my favourite. Isn't he cute?"

"I suppose," Miss Harvey said, obviously not impressed.

"That's Cliff Richards over there," I said, pointing. "Maureen likes him. She's so square. I really liked her when I first got here but now I can't stand her. She's always in trouble."

"Oh, really," Miss Harvey said, arching her brow, "I thought the two of you were friends. In fact, I understand the two of you went off on a nighttime junket recently. That would indicate friendship, surely?"

I blushed and giggled.

"Well, yes, there was that. We just snuck out one night after bedtime to see what was happening in town. They wouldn't have known we were gone if the police hadn't picked us up and brought us home. And besides, Maureen gets on my nerves now. She's boy crazy."

I was eager to change the subject. It was bad enough having Nurse and Miss Stinson lecturing me, without having to put up with it from someone else's worker too. And besides, if they insisted on having such ridiculously early curfews they could hardly blame us for sneaking out now and again. We weren't babies after all.

"Would you like to see some pictures of my family?" I asked, steering the conversation into safer waters. "Here's a photo of my sister, Jane. Isn't she adorable? And this is my brother, Justin."

Miss Harvey studied the pictures.

"I saw Jane when I was at Languard House the other day," she said, handing the photos back to me. "She was busy playing with another little girl and seemed quite settled."

I was happy to hear this, but curious.

"You seem to know a lot about me and my family, even though you're not our worker. How come?"

"I hear about you all when Miss Stinson makes her regular reports to the Children's Committee, just like she hears about my cases. We discuss any issues which are causing concern."

"Oh, really" I said. I felt like one of the insects we examined under the microscope in biology class.

In late February my mother wrote to Miss Stinson and asked if I could spend my Easter holidays with her in Birmingham. Miss Stinson wrote back to say she would discuss the request with the Children's Committee when they met in March.

"Your mother says it would give you both a chance to see how you'd get on living with them in Birmingham," Miss Stinson said, when she came to tell me about my mother's invitation.

"I suppose it would," I agreed, picking my words carefully, "but I've been thinking about that a lot lately. I'm not really sure I want to go and live with my mother anymore. For one thing, I don't like the idea of having to change schools again. I'm just getting settled at Stoneleigh Grammar." I paused, trying to find the words to express what I was really feeling, but none seemed adequate. "Of course, I'm really looking forward to seeing Mum again ... it's just that I'm not really sure about anything else."

"Well, one step at a time," Miss Stinson said. "I thought it was what you wanted."

"It was. It is. I guess. It's just that I'm not sure I could handle being dropped off at Children's Services if things don't work out, like she did to Jane."

We sat in silence for a few moments.

"Actually I'm not sure about anything, anymore. I still have nightmares about what happened in Riverton, and I can't seem to get the bad memories out of my head. I remember that one morning my brother, Graham, asked me why I'd been making so much noise in the night, but I couldn't tell him. During the day I had to pretend it wasn't happening. It was too horrible to think about. And besides, Dad was a different person in the daytime. He was nice, and never got angry or hit us or anything like that. People wouldn't believe me if I told them what he did at night."

I felt strangely detached as I spoke, as if recounting the events of a book I had read. It didn't hurt so much that way.

"How long did it go on?" Miss Stinson asked, gingerly broaching the subject we had only skirted around before.

"I'd just turned eleven when it started. He'd come to my room at night when Mum was out with her boyfriend. But then, after his motorbike accident, when he was home all day and in bed most of the time, he pestered me more and more. I thought it would stop after the accident but it didn't. Mum said he'd crushed his pelvis when he was knocked off his motorbike and he was in the hospital for ages. I hoped he wouldn't be able to do it anymore, but he could. When they brought him home from the hospital Mum made up a bed for him in the living room because he couldn't get up the stairs. My bedroom was upstairs, so I thought I'd be safe. But then Mum went out to see her boyfriend the very first night Dad was home from the hospital. Dad told me to come to him in the living room. I was too scared to say no or run away. I didn't know what to do; there was no one there to stop him."

Try as I might, I couldn't keep back the tears. It was several minutes before I could carry on. But now that I'd opened Pandora's box I needed to get the words out, let my tears wash away the pain and start the healing process.

"And then after Mum left home for good there was no stopping him. He even made me do it at lunch time once, while the others were outside playing and no one was around to see that he was the bogey man really. And then he started talking about bringing his friends home. He said they'd probably like horsey rides too. If Mum hadn't come back with the police when she did, I don't know what I would have done. It was getting worse every day and I couldn't stop him. I stayed away from home as much as I could, but with Mum gone I had to be there to look after the other two, at least until Dad got home from work."

I wiped snot and tears across my sleeve. Miss Stinson passed me a clean white cotton hanky with the initial 'J' embroidered on it. I blew my nose loudly before offering it back to her. She suggested I hang on to it for now.

"Mum said he used to do the same things to her but I can't understand why he would do those things to me, especially when I was crying and gagging. It's disgusting. Normal married people don't do things like that. Mum said so. She told me about the things that normal married people do, and she said these were clean and decent, but I don't know. It still sounds pretty yucky to me. I can't imagine wanting anyone to do those things to me."

"How's your father's behaviour since you've been in care?"

"He hasn't done those dirty things to me, if that's what you mean," I said. "But I don't even like it when he touches me now. One time I was crying about something and he hugged me, to try and comfort me, but I panicked. It felt like I couldn't breathe. I hate the smell of him. When he let me go I couldn't help but shudder. I think maybe he noticed but I couldn't help it. I didn't want to hurt his feelings or anything, I just don't want him touching me and holding me. I'm afraid he won't let me go."

I wrapped my arms tightly around my waist and started rocking back and forth. I didn't want to talk about it anymore; it hurt too much.

"How's Jane doing now?" I asked, needing to talk of easier things.

"She's well," Miss Stinson said. "The Children's Committee has decided that she should be fostered again. She needs the stability of a home environment. I'll let you know as soon as we find a placement for her."

A couple of weeks later I got a letter from my mother, postmarked Leicester.

> Dear Gail:
>
> Well, as you can probably tell from the postmark, I am writing to you from Leicester. Norman has a fabulous gig at a swank nightclub here – much nicer than the dives he played at in Birmingham. We found a nice little furnished flat close to the shops and

buses, and I'm busy getting the place organized ready for your visit. Which brings me to my most exciting news …Norman has asked me to marry him!! We've booked the Registry Office for March 26, which is only three weeks away! I was hoping we could get married while you're here at Easter, but the Registry didn't have any openings. I'll write to Miss Stinson and let her know about the change of dates and make sure you can be here for the wedding. No one else from the family will be here unfortunately, but we'll have fun anyway. I can hardly wait!

Must dash, or I'll miss the post. Write soon.

Love Mum

The Children's Committee were not impressed with Mum's abrupt change of plans and kept me on tender hooks for two weeks waiting for their decision. Three days before I hoped to leave Nurse told me the Committee had approved the visit. She was to travel with me as far as Birmingham, at which point I would change trains for Leicester and continue on my own. Miss Stinson would come and pick me up on April 2.

Mum and Norman met me at the Leicester train station. Norman had managed to scrape together enough money to buy an old beater car and we clattered and chugged our way to Saxby Street, where they were living. They had rented a furnished bedsitting room on the third floor of a tall terraced house. There was a shared bathroom on the floor below. The room had a gas ring for cooking, a double bed pushed up against the far corner, a tatty sofa that had obviously seen better days (and probably too many passionate nights), a wobbly dining table, two straight back chairs, and a dresser. I took it all in with a glance and wondered where we were all going to sleep.

"You and I will sleep here," Mum said, seeing the worried look on my face. "Norman will stay with one of the blokes from the band while you're here. I have a job as a barmaid at the Highgate Hotel, so I'll have to work a couple of nights while you're here," she continued, as we unpacked my few belongings and put them in one of the dresser drawers vacated by Norman. "You can come with me if you like or maybe go to the pictures if there's something good on. I get off at midnight."

Norman came back to the bedsit at eleven o'clock next morning and after a breakfast of toast and jam, with copious amounts of strong tea, we went exploring Leicester. We looked around the shops, which were filled with the latest fashions, and Mum bought me a red boucle coat to wear to her wedding. She said it would probably be too cold to take my coat off anyhow, so there was no sense in wasting money on a new dress too.

March 26 dawned cold and windy. Shortly before two o'clock Mum and I took a cab to the Registry Office where we were to meet Norman. She didn't want him to see her before the wedding. She said it was bad luck. He was standing outside the Registry Office wearing a trench coat and grey pants. He had his collar turned up against the wind and was smoking a cigarette. He looked like someone from a spy novel.

Mum took off the wedding band she had been wearing for over a year and gave it to Norman. He did the same with his. We went into the Registry Office and were directed to a room at the end of the corridor. A tall, thin man with greasy black hair and an equally greasy black suit came in holding a dog-eared Bible. He looked around the room as if expecting to see a throng of people.

"Are we all here?" he asked.

Norman nodded and tried to say that we were, but his stammer left him gaping and wordless.

"Yes," my mother interjected, "this is it."

"Very well, let's begin," said the greasy man. "Dearly beloved, we are gathered here together ..."

Within minutes it was all over. When we got outside my mother handed me a packet of confetti and asked me to sprinkle it on them. For good luck, she said. I took some pictures with my Brownie camera, then Norman handed me his camera and asked me to take some with that too. A passer-by asked if we would like a picture of the three of us so we lined up against the wall and smiled, then thanked him for his trouble.

Norman suggested we go to the Grand Hotel for a drink to

celebrate the happy occasion. He ordered Babychams for Mum and me and a pint of ale for himself. The Babycham made me feel lightheaded, especially as we had hardly eaten anything all day. As we were leaving we saw a poster advertising an Oscar Peterson concert that evening. A yellow 'sold out' sign had been pasted across it.

"Oh Norman, look! Oscar Peterson is playing here tonight and I've always wanted to see him," Mum said.

Norman shook his head in a most mournful way.

"Sign says they're sold out, sweetheart," he said.

"That's too bad," Mum groaned, making a pouty face. "I'd really love to have seen him."

Norman's mournful expression re-arranged itself into a huge smile as he put his hand in his inside coat pocket.

"Then it's a good job I managed to get some tickets before they sold out!" he said triumphantly, waving the tickets above his head.

"They only had stage seats left," he said, as he lowered his arm and let my mother take the tickets, "We'll be behind him, but it's better than nothing."

"Just being in the same room is good enough for me," Mum said, clutching the tickets to her bosom. "Let's go and have some dinner before the show starts. There's a great little Indian restaurant close by."

Their wedding feast consisted of curried lamb, biryani and papadoms, and their future was toasted with more Babychams and beer. By the time we left the restaurant Mum and I were giggling like schoolgirls and lightheaded. The three of us linked arms and did a little song and dance routine along the pavement. I was glad Nurse couldn't see me. I knew she wouldn't approve of one of 'her girls' carrying on like this in public but what the heck, it isn't every day you get to go to your mother's wedding. And besides, Mum didn't seem to mind at all. In fact, she seemed to rather enjoy it.

Mum had to work the next three nights so I was left to amuse myself. The first night I went with her and spent most of the evening reading in the lobby. While I was there I saw a poster advertising a Dave Clark Five concert the following evening. They had just returned from a tour of the States, where they had become an instant sensation. Some said they were the hottest thing next to the Beatles. Their hit song *Glad All Over*, with its upbeat 'Tottenham Sound', had made the number one spot on the hit parade, and their latest release, *Bits and Pieces* was already number two. Mum said I could go if there were any tickets left and, much to my delight, there were.

Mum dropped me off at the theatre on her way to work the next night. Feeling slightly self conscious about being on my own, I joined the line-up and made my way into the theatre. Within minutes I was swept up in the hype and hysteria of hundreds of teenagers screaming and clapping in frenzied delight. The noise was so loud you could hardly hear the music, but that didn't really matter - you could see the Dave Clark Five, right there in front of you, and you could feel their music pulsing through your body, sweeping you up into a rhythmic ecstacy.

After the concert I joined the throng of fans waiting outside the stage exit hoping for a glimpse of the band. I found myself pushed towards the front of the crowd and eventually wound up against the railing adjacent to the stage door. The excitement in the air was electric as girls screamed and swooned chanting 'Dave, Dave, Dave'. Some of the fans became restless and tried scrambling over the barricades. Suddenly there were police everywhere trying to control the crowd. One of them had a megaphone and told the crowd to disperse.

Most of the fans started drifting away, but others kept pushing towards the stage door. I felt myself being swept along and heard someone say there was another way in, around the side. Half a dozen teenage girls started running in that direction. I followed. A frenzy gripped hold of me. All I could think of was seeing the Dave Clark Five in person.

We made it inside the building and found our way to the dressing rooms - but they were empty. The Dave Clark Five had obviously slipped out another exit. Some of their things were still there though, so I knew I was in the very same room that Dave Clark had been in only moments before. I felt dizzy with excitement. I picked up a silver embossed cigarette case from the table. It had *To Dave, with love*, engraved on it. I slipped it into my pocket. Beside it there was an ashtray with half a dozen cigarette butts in it. I heard footsteps and turned to see a security guard filling the doorway. I grabbed a handful of the cigarette butts and put them in my pocket along with the cigarette case. To think, his lips had touched them!

"Hey, clear out of 'ere, you bloody louts," the guard barked, as he approached us menacingly. I slipped past him and ran out the door.

The crowd outside had thinned considerably and I wasn't sure what to do next. I was pumped and looking for more excitement.

After a while, a ripple went through the small crowd that remained. Apparently the cigarette case had been missed and Dave Clark himself had put out a plea for its return. It had strong sentimental value and he wanted it back. I clutched the case in my pocket as I weighed my options. The girl beside me gave me a knowing look. She had seen me take it.

"Why don't you tell them you'll give it back to him as long as you get to deliver it personally," she suggested. "I'll come with you," she added eagerly.

"Great idea," I said excitedly, but quickly had second thoughts. "But what if they arrest me for stealing it?"

"Don't be daft," she said, laughing, "you didn't steal it, you were just looking after it for him, so no one else could steal it. Right?"

"Yeah, right, I guess so," I said, laughing too.

We made our way through the crowd towards one of the security guards.

"We know where the cigarette case is," the girl said, appointing herself as my spokesperson.

"What cigarette case?" the guard asked.

"The one Dave Clark is looking for," the girl said, her tone of voice implying that the whole world should have known what she was talking about. "We'll give it back to him, if you tell us where he is."

The security guard didn't look convinced.

"You can check. It's true, honest. Dave Clark wants it back, and we know where it is. If you tell us where he is, we'll take it to him."

"He's probably staying at the Grand Hotel, just like every other big shot performer that comes to town," the guard said. "Why don't you try there?"

We ran the short distance to the hotel. When we arrived a concierge stopped us at the door.

"But we're here to see Dave Clark," I said, breathlessly. "We have something very important of his, and he wants it back."

The concierge looked skeptical. He went inside to check with someone, then re-appeared and signaled for us to go in.

"They're in the bar, having a drink," he said, pointing to the far left corner of the lobby.

"Thanks, mister," I said over my shoulder, as my companion and I started across the lobby. Several other teens tried to follow us but the concierge put a halt to it.

"Doesn't take a whole army to drop off whatever it is, does it?" the concierge said as he moved to stop the trail of teens.

When I got to the bar I stopped dead in my tracks. There, not ten feet from me, was Dave Clark and his band having a drink just like any other blokes off the street. I recognized Dusty Springfield sitting next to Dave Clark. The girl I was with nudged me in the back.

"Go on then. Give it to him," she said excitedly.

I suddenly had cold feet. I was thinking about turning on my heels and running when Dave Clark noticed the two of us huddled in the doorway and smiled. I took a deep breath and approached him.

"I have your cigarette case, Mr. Clark, I mean Mr. Dave."

I blushed beet red and just stood there, staring at him. Dusty Springfield and a couple of the band members chuckled. I felt like a total clutz.

"You can call me Dave," he said, smiling.

"Oh, thank you," I said, recovering somewhat. "I found this and someone said you wanted it back."

I held out the cigarette case. As he reached to take it his fingers touched my hand. I thought I would faint with the thrill and excitement of it all. He turned the case over in his hands as if to verify that it was his and then put it in his pocket.

"Thanks," he said, "I wouldn't want to lose that. Good of you to bring it back, luv."

"Sorry I took it," I said, eager to make the moment last as long as possible. "You left it behind in the theatre. I thought maybe you didn't want it anymore."

I stood there, transfixed. I could see a twinkle of amusement dancing in his eyes. I was just another star struck teenager to him.

"Do you think I could have your autograph, please?" I managed to ask.

He picked up the Guinness coaster his drink had been sitting on, signed the back, and handed it to me.

"This is my friend, Dusty Springfield," Dave said.

I nodded and smiled at her.

"Hello," I said. "I've seen you lots on television."

She smiled, in a bored kind of way. I had obviously interrupted their conversation and she seemed impatient to get back to it. I saw the concierge moving towards me and realized I was about to be asked to leave. I wanted the moment to last forever but it seemed it wasn't going to.

"Can I kiss you," I blurted out.

Dave laughed.

"Sure," he said, proffering his cheek.

I leaned forward and pecked him on the cheek.

"Nice to meet you," he said, as the concierge put his hand on my shoulder and gestured towards the exit.

Dave Clark turned his attention back to Dusty and I was forgotten.

I got back to the Highgate Hotel just as Mum was finishing work.

"You look like you had a good time," she said, as she squiggled into her coat. "Did you have a good seat?"

"More than that," I said breathlessly, "I got to meet him. I actually got to meet Dave Clark and his band, and I even kissed him."

I told her the story from beginning to end on the way home.

The next night Mum was working again. I wasn't keen on staying home alone so said I would go to the pictures and meet her at the hotel after. The cinema was crowded and a black man sat next to me. As I was leaving, he fell into step with me.

"Would you like go to drink?" he asked me. His English wasn't very good.

"No, thank you," I said, wrapping my scarf around my neck. There was a cold wind blowing.

"Maybe just coffee?" he persisted. "We talk about films we like."

It wasn't even ten o'clock yet. I had two hours to kill before Mum would be finished work.

"Alright," I said. What harm could it do?

We went to a nearby Wimpey restaurant where he ordered two coffees. He told me he was from Jamaica, studying engineering at Leicester University. When I said I liked jazz, he told me he had a good collection of jazz records and invited me back to his room to listen to them. I didn't know enough to say no.

His room was in the basement of a large terrace house. It was sparsely furnished but clean. Text books were piled everywhere. On the table there was an old record player and a pile of jazz LP's. I started flipping through them.

"Can we put this on?" I asked, holding up an Oscar Peterson record. "I just went to see him the other night. He's great."

As we listened to the music he started rubbing my back. Then he leaned over and kissed me. His lips were thick and soft; his touch gentle yet strong. His hand came around to my breasts. I pushed it away.

"It's okay," he said in a husky voice, "I no hurt you."

He kissed me again, all the while rubbing my body, exploring. He ran his fingers through my hair, the blackness of his large hands contrasting sharply with the blondness of my hair. I wanted to run but couldn't move. A sense of foreboding had immobilized me and I became a spectator in an all too familiar scene. I hoped he wouldn't hurt me. His hand was moving up my legs, squeezing my thighs. Now his fingers were tracing the line of my knickers, picking and lifting the elastic to get his hand inside. A sob escaped my lips. He stopped.

"How old you are?" he asked, looking at me closely as if seeing me for the first time.

"Nearly fourteen," I said, avoiding his eyes so he wouldn't see my tears.

"Why you out on you own, so late, so young? Where you mother?"

"Working," I said.

"Not good," he said. "Not good at all. Mother should keep you safe at home at night. Young girl like you, find big trouble in big city like this."

He smoothed my skirt back down, obviously struggling with a range of emotions. His erection was still quite obvious. He took my hand and put it on his penis.

"It okay?" he asked. I shrugged. It was nothing I hadn't seen or done before. He put his hand over mine and started sliding it up and down along the shaft of his penis. His breathing quickened and he closed his eyes. He took a hanky out of his pocket and placed it over his penis to catch his cum. Some of the sticky stuff got onto my hands and a shudder of revulsion ran through me. I smelled his semen and thought of my father.

Afterwards he walked me to the bus stop where I got the bus to the Highgate Hotel to meet Mum.

"How was the show?" Mum asked, once we were in the cab on our way home.

"Okay, I guess."

"What did you do after?"

"I went for a coffee at Wimpeys, with a bloke I met at the show."

"Oh, good for you," she said, her tone of voice teasing. "Was he nice?"

"Yes," I said. "Very."

"Are you going to see him again?"

"No, I don't think so."

"What's his name?"

I suddenly realized I didn't even know his name. If he'd told me, it hadn't registered. He was just another man with a penis as far as I was concerned.

"Dunno," I shrugged.

Two days later Miss Stinson came to take me back to Willowrey. I wasn't sorry to see her. Staying with my mother was proving to be a little more exciting than I felt I could handle. Miss Stinson arrived just as we were finishing our breakfast. Mum was still in her dressing gown, the bed was unmade, and the remains of our breakfast were still on the table. Miss Stinson took it all in with a glance.

"Sorry about the mess," Mum said, as she cleared away our plates and empty tea cups. "We were just having breakfast. Have a seat."

Mum offered her the chair where I'd been sitting. Miss Stinson sat down. She looked strangely out of place in this dingy flat and I could see she was struggling not to show her disapproval. I sat on the unmade bed.

"It's not much of a home, I know, but Norman and I only really sleep here. We both work full time," Mum offered, by way of apology. "Norman has been staying with friends while Gail's here. He just comes over in the morning for his breakfast. We tend to get a late start because we both work nights."

Mum took some clothes out of her drawer.

"I'll just run downstairs and get dressed," she said, as she headed for the shared bathroom on the floor below.

Miss Stinson asked me how my visit had been. I told her about meeting Dave Clark and showed her my collection of cigarette butts which I had taken from his dressing room. I didn't mention meeting the Jamaican man. I could tell by her reaction to the Dave Clark story that she wasn't ready to hear what I'd done the following evening.

Mum came back upstairs and carried on with her apology for the state of the place.

"We aren't going to be here long," she said, straightening the bed covers around me, "Norman's got a job in Morecombe for the summer season."

This was the first I had heard about it.

"Where's Morecombe," I asked.

"It's a seaside town in Lancashire," Norman said.

"We hope to spend a few days in Devon before we start at Morecombe though," Mum added.

"Please give us plenty of notice if you want to see any of the children," Miss Stinson said. "I think my supervisor, Mr. Brill, explained to you in his letter that the Children's Committee needs time to consider requests for visits. They weren't very happy about the short notice for this trip, and then to have the dates changed at the last minute. It would make things much easier if you let us know your plans in plenty of time."

"What about future visits for Gail," Mum asked. "Mr. Brill's letter made it sound like this might be a problem."

"I don't really know what the Committee might say in the future, but I believe they'd be unwilling to allow Gail to come and visit, unless you're prepared to give fuller notice about your plans."

Mum looked taken aback by the brusqueness of Miss Stinson's tone.

"I couldn't help the last minute change of plans," she said, bristling. "I didn't know we'd be moving when I first wrote to you. But when Norman was offered a gig here in Leicester he had to come right away, or risk losing it. I let you know as soon as I knew."

"Yes, of course," Miss Stinson placated, "but I'm sure you realize by now how slowly the system works at times. The Committee has many other children to concern itself with, besides Gail."

There was an uneasy silence. Mum lit a cigarette. Norman offered to make more tea.

"You mentioned in your letter that this visit would give each of you a chance to see how it might be if Gail lived with you permanently," Miss Stinson said, after the tea was poured. "Have you given any more thought to that?"

Mum shrugged. I squiggled into the corner of the bed and leaned against the wall, wondering what her answer would be, and if they were going to ask me what I thought of the idea.

"Well, we were living in Birmingham when I wrote that but obviously the situation has changed a bit now. I'm not sure it would be that good for her, moving all the time like we seem to do. And besides, Gail sounds like she's pretty settled in that new school of hers. Maybe she can stay at Willowrey, just until she's finished school, and spend the school holidays with us."

"I think the Committee is looking for a more settled arrangement for Gail," Miss Stinson said.

There was a long silence. Norman offered biscuits to go with the tea.

"Well, like I said, Norman has this job in Morecombe for the summer so we can't possibly have her then and I don't know where we'll be after that." Mum's voice trailed away.

I sat there feeling like a stray dog at the pound whose owner was reluctant to reclaim them.

"Well, perhaps when you're more settled you'll consider asking to have Gail again, if this is possible," Miss Stinson concluded. It seems there was no more to be said on the subject.

"How are Justin and Jane doing?" Mum asked, as if suddenly remembering them too.

"Justin seems to be settling well with the Fackrells. And the Committee has decided that Jane should be fostered out again as soon as possible."

"That's nice," was all Mum said. "Tell them I said 'hello' next time you see them."

I guessed those dogs weren't going to be claimed from the pound today either.

CHAPTER SEVEN

It felt good to get back to the relative tranquility of Willowrey. Nurse and Aunty Dawn seemed genuinely pleased to see me home. I told everyone about my Dave Clark Five adventure and each time I told the story it became just a little bit more exciting.

My father came to visit a few days after my return. He had a new lady friend with him. This one was called Terry. I was glad he'd stopped seeing that juvenile drip, Carol. At least Terry looked old enough to know what she was getting into. My father announced that he and Terry planned to marry as soon as her divorce came through. I wondered if he meant it this time but doubted it somehow.

April 19th was my fourteenth birthday, Aunty Bridget, who filled in while Nurse or Aunty Dawn was on leave, made a birthday cake for me, complete with icing and candles. Mum and Dad each sent birthday cards with money tucked inside and my brother, Graham, sent a box of writing paper with matching envelopes. But best of all was a red patent leather handbag, with black and white houndstooth plaid on the front, which Nurse and the Aunties gave me. It matched the new coat Mum had bought me for her wedding perfectly and I loved it.

In with my mother's card was a letter telling me that she would be coming to Devon on May 4 for a week before moving to Morecombe for the summer.

"It's unfortunate your mother isn't coming a day sooner," Miss Stinson said, when I told her of my mother's plans. "She could have come to your confirmation service at church on the Sunday."

I shrugged. "She wouldn't want to come to that anyway," I said. "She isn't much on church or anything like that. I already invited my Dad but he said he was busy, right away, without even thinking about it."

I'd been attending classes at Church in preparation for my confirmation and was looking forward to it. My parents, who to my knowledge never actually stepped foot inside a church, couldn't understand my need for the unconditional love offered by God. They seemed to think I was a little odd in this regard.

Much to my delight, Miss Stinson said she would come to my confirmation service even though it was on her day off. I was deeply touched by her gesture.

"I have some other news," Miss Stinson said. "Justin's foster mother isn't well so he has gone back to Languard House for a while. Just until we know what's happening. Maybe I could bring him with me to your confirmation service. I'll check with the matron at Languard House."

As it turned out, Mum and Norman managed to come to Devon a day early and made it to my confirmation. They slipped into the church a few minutes after the service had started. I didn't know they were there until after it was all over. Justin came with Miss Stinson and it was great to see him again but he was even quieter than before. The move back to Languard House was obviously weighing heavily on him. He cheered up though, when Mum and Norman slipped into the pew next to him and he spent the rest of the day glued to Mum's side.

My grandparents were on their annual vacation in Nestleton that week, so they came to the service too. Even Nurse came, along with Aunty Dawn and most of the other girls. The twins wished me well but said they couldn't come because they were Catholic. I told them we were all worshipping the same God so what did it matter, but they couldn't be persuaded. Nurse and 'the Aunties' gave me a small, white leatherbound bible as a confirmation gift. I told them I would treasure it forever. My mother joked that I had more people at my confirmation than she had had at her wedding. I thought she probably needed to think about why that was, but didn't say anything.

Nurse invited everyone back to Willowrey for lunch after the service. We all piled into the living room where plates of sandwiches and goodies had been set out. For a few glorious hours I was able to forget why I was living at Willowrey and why my grandfather always stayed on the opposite side of the room from my mother. And I could overlook the fact that my mother was there with her new husband, while my own father had been too busy to come; and that my little brother had been brought here by a social worker on her day off; and that my little sister was living somewhere miles away with strangers.

When it was time for them to leave, Mum said she would come and see me again on Thursday and that they'd bring Justin with them.

"What about Jane? Can you bring her too?" I asked.

"Huh, fat chance of that," Mum said. "They've been right touchy about me visiting her, some nonsense about not wanting to upset her and giving her a chance to settle into her new home. I'll see what we can manage but don't build your hopes up. And I want to get up to Riverton too, to see Graham, so we might just go to see Jane on the way back up north."

I shrugged, trying to hide my disappointment.

"Have you seen your father lately?" Mum whispered to me as we were getting her coat.

"Yes, I saw him when I got back from Leicester. He came and took me to see Jane. He said he was busy and couldn't come today," I added, seeing the question in my mother's eyes.

"Did you tell him Norman and I are married now?"

"I mentioned it. Why? Is it supposed to be a secret?"

"No, no, of course not. I was just wondering how he took it, that's all."

"He didn't really say anything about it. He says he and Terry are going to get married as soon as her divorce comes through."

"Huh, he didn't waste any time did he? Whatever happened to that other dipstick, Carol?"

"Dunno. I never saw her again after you came down at Christmas."
I tried to keep the note of accusation out of my voice.

"Well, say 'hello' from me next time you see him."

"I don't know when he's coming again."

"I thought he came to see you every fortnight?"

"He used to, but lately he only seems to come and visit if I call
and ask him to. And then half the time he doesn't show up when he
says he will. I don't bother much anymore."

The tug of war between love and hate for my parents was endless.
I would have an angry outburst one day, wishing they were dead and
never wanting to see them again, only to cry myself to sleep because
I missed them so much, the next. I didn't know what I could do to
make them love me. And I so wanted them to love me. It was weeks
since I'd seen my father. It was almost as if he had forgotten about
me. My mother wrote fairly often from her new home in Morecambe
but it wasn't the same as having her there.

Miss Stinson came to see me at least once a month. She became
my role model and I wanted to be just like her when I grew up. I
grew to trust her and started to open up.

"I wish my father liked me more," I confided to her one day. "He
hasn't been to see me in ages. I think he still blames me for what
happened to him and our family."

"It wasn't your fault, Gail. You were the victim not the cause of
the problems," she tried to reassure me.

"Is it true that he's on probation now?" I asked.

"Yes, it is. The court gave him three years probation."

I thought about this for a while. I'd be fifteen by the time he
finished his probation. I'd still have three more years under the care
of the Children's Committee before I turned eighteen, and was free
from their supervision. I wondered who the guilty party really was.

"I think he's kinda fond of me in a way," I said, "but I don't think
he really likes me for myself. I don't think either of my parents like
me for who I am."

"The important thing, Gail, is that you like yourself for who you
are," Miss Stinson said. "But I believe your father is very fond of you
all, despite everything that has happened."

I shrugged as I struggled to make sense of it all.

"When Dad was in the hospital after his accident my mother took me to see him. I started crying when I saw him. I don't know if it was the sight of him in so much pain or whether I was just scared of him. Mum said he kept asking to see me, so she made me go even though I didn't want to. Part of me hated him, because of what he was doing to me, but it was hard to see him like that and most of me still loved him." I fell silent.

After a while Miss Stinson spoke, bringing me back to the present.

"I thought you'd like to know we've found a new foster home for Justin. It's a nice family, just outside Exeter. They have one son, just a bit younger than Justin, so they should be good company for one another."

"That's good," I said, still lost in my own thoughts.

It hurt to think about the past. In the silence that fell between us, I could hear music coming from the television in the sitting room.

"Cilla Black is singing and I want to go and hear her," I said, feeling emotionally drained and anxious to end the interview. "It's 'Top of the Pops', my favorite show, and I want to see who is number one this week. Is it okay if I go and watch it? I didn't realize we'd been talking so long."

"Yes, that's fine. I'm glad you were able to open up and talk a little, Gail. It isn't good to keep these feelings bottled up inside you. We can talk some more next month when I come to visit."

By the time Miss Stinson came for her next visit there had been a lot of changes at Willowrey. The Devon County Council had decided that Willowrey would become a working girls' hostel rather than a children's home. The twins had gone home to live with their father now that he was back on his feet; Maureen had gone to another foster home; and Pam had moved on to independent living. For a couple of weeks during the transition I was the only girl at Willowrey while they decided what should be done with me. Eventually the Children's Committee decided to make an exception in my case and allow me to stay at Willowrey, at least until I finished my 'O' levels.

I enjoyed having the undivided attention of Nurse and Aunty Dawn during that time and became resentful when the new girls started arriving. Not wanting to be totally upstaged by the 'working girls', I told Nurse I wanted to find a Saturday job so that I could make some extra money.

"I hear the beach concession is looking for part-time help," Nurse said. "You might want to try there."

The following Saturday I applied at the beach hut and was hired on the spot. I was to make sandwiches and serve the customers. The boss said it could develop into a summer job if things worked out. When I told Miss Stinson about my job she urged me not to spend my whole summer holiday working.

"Plenty of time for that when you're older," she said. "And besides, the Committee has agreed that you can spend some time with your grandparents during the summer holidays. They've also agreed that your friend Trina can come and visit you here for a few days, provided her parents agree. I've written them a letter and will let you know as soon as I hear. We still have a few weeks before the school holidays begin."

As much as I looked forward to visiting my grandparents over the summer, there was someone closer at hand who held more appeal for me these days. His name was Thomas Weston. Not Tom, or Tommy, but Thomas. He was a prefect in the Lower Sixth and had taken me to see the Rolling Stones' concert in Torquay. I was very proud of the fact that I, a mere third former, had a boyfriend in Lower Sixth. Thomas was quiet but self assured; good looking but not gorgeous. And he was just shy enough not to be pushy. I felt safe with Thomas. His parents owned a mid-size hotel on the sea front in Nestleton. Thomas was their eldest son and his father let it be known that he had great ambitions for him.

Mr. Weston wasn't impressed when he discovered his son was dating a girl from a children's home. He took small consolation in the fact that I was only allowed out on Saturday evenings and had a curfew of ten o'clock. He didn't seem to mind our daytime excursions so much. He naively believed that young people only got up to no good after dark.

When our school reports were issued at the end of the year, I was delighted to find I was now in the top third of all the students in my year. Mr. Carter, the headmaster, called me into his office shortly before last period. He told me I would be receiving the Progress Cup Award at the year end assembly being held that evening. I was so excited I ran all the way home to tell Nurse my news.

"Parents are invited to the assembly," I said, "but obviously mine can't come, so I was hoping you'd come with me."

"I'd be honoured," Nurse said.

I toyed with the idea of telephoning my father to invite him too, but was reluctant to open myself up to another disappointment from him so decided against it.

After tea I rushed upstairs to get ready. My hair was greasy and badly needed washing. Bath nights at Willowrey were Saturday and Wednesday. This was Tuesday.

"Nurse," I called over the banister, "I need to take a bath and wash my hair before we go to the assembly."

Aunty Dawn heard me and called back. "Bath night is tomorrow."

"I know, but my hair is so gross," I wailed. "Can't I have my bath tonight? I'm going to have to walk across the stage in front of everyone!"

"It's an assembly, not a fashion show," Aunty Dawn called back.

I ran downstairs in search of Nurse, hoping she would be more reasonable. I found her in her office doing paperwork.

"I have to wash my hair but Aunty Dawn won't let me," I pleaded. "I can't walk across the stage looking like this."

"You look just fine," Nurse said. "Just tie it back in a ponytail and no one will notice. You're getting the award for your brains not your beauty."

I spun on my heel and stormed back upstairs to my bedroom, slamming the door as hard as I could behind me. I heard Aunty Dawn's footsteps coming along the corridor towards my room.

"Anymore outbursts like that and you won't be going anywhere," she chided me.

I felt my temper rising like bile in my throat. I couldn't believe they could be so unbending, so totally unreasonable. I'd been so proud of getting the Progress Cup Award and now it was all going to be ruined because they wouldn't let me wash my hair. I burst into tears and threw myself onto the bed, wishing with all my heart that my mother was here. She'd let me wash my hair for sure.

After a while I calmed myself. I had worked hard for this award and I wouldn't let these witches spoil it for me. I went into the bathroom and studied the damage. Now, not only did I have greasy hair but my face was swollen and blotchy from crying. I splashed water on my face and held the cold facecloth over my eyes for a few moments. Next I sprinkled talcum powder on my hair, to absorb some of the excess oil, then brushed it out and put my hair into two bunches. It looked marginally better, but my fringe still hung in greasy clumps across my forehead.

A few days later the local newspaper carried a picture of me being presented with the Progress Cup Award - greasy bangs and all. Mum wouldn't have made me go on stage looking like that. She always washed and curled her hair and put on makeup when she was going on stage. Mum understood about these things, not like Nurse and Aunty Dawn.

There were now three new girls at Willowrey and a lot of the staff's time was taken up with getting them settled in. I began to feel left out, not knowing where I fit in with the new scheme of things. I missed my mother.

Two weeks into the summer holidays my pent up emotions finally exploded. I was tired of Nurse and Aunty Dawn controlling my every move. I had a summer job, I was doing well at school, and I had a boyfriend. I thought I deserved more freedom and resented being treated like a child. I wanted to be treated the same as the working girls, even though I was a bit younger. Nurse thought otherwise and we started locking horns on a regular basis.

"You shouldn't talk to Nurse like that," Kathleen, one of the new girls, told me as I sat pouting in the hobby room after tea one day. "If you act like a spoilt child you can't blame Nurse and Aunty Dawn for treating you like one."

Kathleen was an easygoing Irish girl and I normally got along quite well with her, but not today.

"Mind your own fucking business," I said. "It's nothing to do with you."

Kathleen gasped. "Don't swear at me or I'll tell Nurse," she threatened.

"Go ahead; see if I care. Don't think I haven't heard you say 'fuck' a few times when you didn't think Nurse was listening. Who do you think you are anyhow, Nurse's little spy? Running and telling tales on us like some wimpy goody two-shoes. You think you're so high and mighty but you're no better than anyone else here."

Kathleen's Irish temper flared.

"I'm only here because my mother got sick and had to go into the hospital. As soon as she's better, I'll be going home. Not like you. Your own mother doesn't even want you."

Her words stung me to the quick. I flew into a blind rage and lunged at her, grabbing a handful of her hair and pulling her to the ground. She screamed as I pummeled her, trying desperately to escape. But she couldn't. I was like a wild animal, kicking, biting, and scratching her. I wanted to kill. She had said what I couldn't bear to hear and I wanted to silence her forever.

I felt strong hands on my shoulders. Nurse pulled me to my feet, while Aunty Dawn helped Kathleen up. I could see red welts rising on Kathleen's cheeks where I'd scratched her.

"What on earth is going on?" Nurse said, not really expecting an answer. "I've never in all my life seen two young ladies fighting like dogs before. Who started this?"

"She did," Kathleen and I said in unison.

"Well you can both take yourselves off to bed," Nurse said, steering me towards the door before finally letting go of my arm. "Maybe a good night's sleep will put you both in a better frame of mind."

I ran up the stairs and locked myself in the bathroom. My face was a blotchy mess and my eyes still looked wild. I hardly recognized myself. I stood staring at my reflection wondering who this mad woman was. I wanted to smash the mirror into a million tiny pieces and obliterate the image of my face forever. My ugly, unloved, unwanted face. A groan started deep in my throat, a primordial sound of deep, agonizing pain. I wanted my mother. I needed to hear her say she loved me, cared for me and wanted me. I had never heard her say she loved me but I needed to hear it now.

I would go to her, I decided. I clung to the idea like a drowning man clings to a log. They couldn't keep me here against my wishes; I wasn't a prisoner here. I splashed cold water on my face and brushed my teeth, slipping the toothbrush into my pocket before going to my room.

Jackie, the newest working girl to come to Willowrey, came into my room to see if I was alright. She had witnessed the fight.

"It wasn't very nice of Kathleen to say that," she said, obviously trying to make me feel better. "Are you alright?"

"Do I look alright?" I said, dripping sarcasm, "I hate this place and I'm leaving."

"Leaving? What do you mean 'leaving'? Where are you gonna go?"

"I'm going to find my mother. She's in Morecambe, wherever that is, and I'm going to run away and find her."

A glimmer of excitement shone in Jackie's eyes. "Can I come too?"

"Sure, if you want. Do you have any money?"

"Only a couple of shillings. I don't get paid until Friday."

"Well bring what you have. I have nine shillings, so that'll help." I lowered my voice. "We can't go until after Nurse has been to tuck us in and say goodnight. Come to my room as soon as the coast is clear. We can get onto the garage roof from my window and it's easy to get down the drainpipe from there. You better go and pretend you're getting ready for bed. Remember, don't bring too much stuff 'cos we'll be hitchhiking."

Shortly after nine thirty Jackie snuck back into my room. I was dressed and waiting for her. My gondola basket sat waiting by the window. I had packed a change of clothes, my leather writing case, and Mum's most recent letter describing where they were staying. Jackie had tucked a few belongings in her guitar case and looked eager for an adventure. We climbed out the window, crossed the flat garage roof and shimmied down the drainpipe onto the dustbins lined up below. Within seconds we were scurrying across the lawn and had flung ourselves over the boxwood hedge to freedom.

As soon as we made it to the main road I stuck my thumb out for a ride. We managed to get a lift as far as Exeter with a middle-aged couple who spent the whole time tut-tutting about how dangerous it was for young girls to be out on their own at this time of night. We thanked them for their concern and assured them that we would be careful.

The next ride got us from Exeter to Gloucester in a car with three young men. They offered to take us all the way to Birmingham but I thought better of it. I didn't like the way the man beside me was leering at me. He'd put his arm across the back of the seat, ostensibly to make room for us to squeeze in, and had started rubbing my neck and shoulders. I sat rigid, not wanting to give him the slightest encouragement. The man driving asked how far we were going.

"Morecambe," Jackie said before I could answer. We were approaching Gloucester.

"Actually, we're only going as far as Gloucester tonight," I said, poking Jackie in the ribs with my elbow. "We'll carry on to Morecambe tomorrow. You can drop us here."

Jackie looked at me, confused. "But I thought .."

"We're staying here with my grandparents tonight," I lied, anxious to get away from the man with the roving arm. I glared at Jackie to be quiet.

"You can drop us off here," I said. "We can call them from that phone box over there to come and pick us up. They're expecting us."

Instinct told me it wasn't a good idea to let these men know we were runaways. We scrambled out of the car and thanked them for the ride. As their headlights faded into the distance I breathed a sigh of relief.

"Whaddya wanna say that for?" Jackie asked. "They could've taken us as far as Birmingham."

"No thanks," I told her. "I'd rather walk than sit beside that creepy guy with his dirty hands all over me."

"He wasn't that bad. And besides, what could he do with us all there?"

"You're so naïve at times, Jackie" I told her, as I stuck my thumb out again. There was another car coming.

Much to my dismay it was a police car. The officer got out of his car and walked around to where we were standing.

"Bit late for young ladies to be out on their own," he said, eying us closely. "Where are you going?"

"We're on our way back from holidays in Cornwall," I told him off the top of my head.

"I see, and where's your luggage?"

I kicked myself. I should have thought of that.

"Her brother has it in the car but there wasn't room for us and the luggage," I said, as calmly as I could manage. My mind was racing. Had Nurse discovered we were gone already? It wasn't even midnight yet, and I was pretty sure she wouldn't miss us until morning. But I couldn't be totally sure. The radio crackled to life in the police car and the officer went to answer it.

"Don't tell him where we're going," I hissed at Jackie. "Just pretend we live here and are waiting for our parents to come and pick us up."

Jackie nodded her head, a look of panic on her face.

The officer came back and told us to take care. He had to respond to an emergency call. I assured him our ride would be here any minute to pick us up and thanked him sweetly for his concern. He turned on his police lights and headed off at high speed, leaving us relieved but shaken by the side of the road.

"When you're running away you have to keep out of sight of the police," Jackie said, as we watched the tail lights fade into the distance.

"I know that, stupid," I said scathingly. "How was I to know it was a police car?"

Jackie looked like she might cry. I turned away in disgust. I had enough on my mind without having to babysit her. I stuck my thumb out again as I saw headlights approaching. Two young men stopped and asked us where we were going.

"Morecambe," I said, peering into the car to see how many of them there were.

"It's your lucky day, darlings. Hop in," the young man said, smiling. "We're going to Lancaster."

Shortly after dawn next morning we were dropped off on Morecambe seafront. We were hungry, tired, and lost.

"Where's your Mum's place?" Jackie asked, looking around expectantly.

"Not far from here, I hope, but it's too early to telephone her; she probably doesn't start work until nine o'clock. I just want to sleep right now. I can't even think straight anymore."

We spread our coats out on the seafront lawn and fell asleep in the early morning sunshine. When I woke up, I was even hungrier than before. I told Jackie we had to get some food before we starved to death. We packed up our things and set off in search of a supermarket. I hadn't spent a lot of time shopping for food before and was shocked by the price of it. What little money we had would soon be gone if we had to spend it on food so we decided to simply bypass the cash register. I tucked a Melton Mowbray pork pie and a bag of crisps into my basket and strolled out of the store. When we were outside Jackie proudly produced the can of beans she had stolen.

"That's bloody brilliant, Jackie. And how the hell are you going to open that?" I asked, too tired to really care.

"Dunno," Jackie said, on the verge of tears once more. Hunger had obviously addled her brain.

"Here, have some of this," I said, ungraciously offering her some of my pork pie, "and then let's get going. Someone has to know where the Middleton Holiday Camp is."

When we got to the camp there was a security guard on duty. He asked to see our pass.

"Actually, we're here to see my mother," I told him, trying my hardest to sound matter-of-fact and confident. "She works here."

He eyed me suspiciously. "Which department?"

I didn't have a clue where she worked. She'd never told me that much, just that Norman was playing the piano and she was working here too. I decided to side step the question.

"She's with Norman Brooks, the piano player," I told him.

His face lit up.

"Oh, you mean Peggy. I should have guessed," he said, smiling, "you look just like her."

I smiled back as sweetly as I could manage while he reached for the phone.

"She's in housekeeping. I'll give her a call and let her know you're here. She expecting you, is she?"

"Not really, it's a bit of a surprise visit."

I hoped she would like the surprise but I suddenly had cold feet. Maybe this wasn't such a good idea after all. After a few minutes Mum came scurrying down the path. She seemed more excited than shocked and eagerly led us off to the back section of the camp to where the staff quarters were.

"Well, isn't this a nice surprise. How long are you here for?" Mum asked, as if my dropping in for a visit was the most natural thing in the world.

"Dunno really," I shrugged, "I guess it depends on how long it takes before they miss us."

A pang of guilt washed over me as I thought of Nurse. I hoped she wouldn't be too upset to find us gone. Now that I was here in Morecambe, I felt rather silly. I realized my mother's life had no room in it for me, living in the cramped staff quarters at the back of a holiday camp. I wondered what I had been thinking, when I decided to come here. I had wanted so badly to see my mother but now that I was sitting here with her I didn't know what to do next.

"Well, we might as well enjoy ourselves while you're here," Mum said cheerily. "Are you hungry?"

Jackie and I nodded eagerly. "We're starving," I said.

"They'll be serving lunch in the cafeteria soon and I always meet Norman there. He had a band practice this morning but should be done by now. Come on, I'll give you a tour on the way."

Jacquie glanced at me, expressions of relief and confusion playing across her face. Mum was carrying on as if our arrival was cause for a party, not concern. It didn't seem to occur to her that we had broken all the rules by coming here.

It was the peak of the holiday season and the camp was packed with families and young children, grandparents and newlyweds.

As we passed the main hall, Mum saw Norman and waved at him excitedly. He smiled and waved back, but then his hand stopped moving in mid-air as he recognized me. He started walking towards us.

"What in heaven's name are you doing here?" he asked, not unkindly.

I shrugged.

"I felt like seeing my mum," I told him.

"And they let you come all the way up here on your own?"

I looked at Jackie. "I'm not on my own," I told him, "Jackie came with me."

"That's not what I mean and you know it," he said, slightly annoyed now.

I shuffled my feet. "I didn't bother to tell them I was leaving," I said.

Norman looked at my mother.

"They can't stay here, you know that don't you?" he asked her in that tone of voice adults usually reserve for young children.

"They don't have to go back right away though, do they?" Mum pleaded. "They can at least spend the day here, can't they?"

Norman looked uneasy. "I don't want any trouble. Next thing you know the police will be all over the place looking for them."

"They wouldn't even know we were gone until this morning," I said, trying to appease him. "I don't think they'd call the police right away."

I tried to imagine what might be going on in Willowrey at that moment. Another wave of guilt washed over me as I thought of the worry I was causing them. If in fact they cared.

"Whatever you think best," Norman said to my mother, "but they can't spend the night here, so you'll have to do something before that."

Mum looked like a teenager who had been given an extension on her curfew.

"Let's go and eat first," she said brightly, "and then I'll show you girls around. Maybe we can even catch the bus over to Blackpool later and you can see the pier."

We spent the afternoon playing tourist and acting like we didn't have a care in the world. For a few hours I was able to pretend that I belonged to one of those happy families staying at the camp. We swam in the pool, played bingo in the amusement hall, and had a round of mini golf before heading back to the cafeteria for dinner. Norman, who had been sleeping before going to work in the evening, joined us there. He was obviously not impressed with my mother's handling of the situation and asked her what she planned to do next.

"We still haven't seen Blackpool pier," I said, misunderstanding his question. He shot me a withering look and turned his attention back to my mother.

"I guess they've got to go back," she said, reluctantly. "I'll take them over to Heysham Police Station after dinner."

It seemed the party was over. We finished our meal in silence.

As Mum was explaining the situation to the police officer at Heysham, Jackie and I sat in silence. I thought of Jane and how she must have felt when Mum handed her back over to the authorities. There was a flurry of phone calls back and forth to Devon as they tried to decide what to do with us and eventually it was agreed that Jackie and I should take the overnight train back to Devon on our own.

The police took us to the station and put us on the train. Mum stood on the platform beside the police officer waving us goodbye.

"Thanks for coming! Come again soon!" she called out, as the train pulled away from the station.

We arrived in Newton Abbot very early the next morning. Miss Suckling, Jackie's care worker, was there to meet us off the train. We made the journey to Willowrey in complete silence. When we pulled up outside the house Miss Suckling told me to go in and find Nurse, while she had a word with Jackie. My feet felt like lead as I walked the few steps to the front door. As I stood there trying to find the courage to ring the bell, the door opened.

"You better come in," Nurse said. "We were worried sick about you."

I sheepishly mumbled an apology and was only able to glance at Nurse before looking back down at the ground. She looked tired and strained and it occurred to me that she had been genuinely worried about us. She told me to go and tidy up before breakfast. I scurried off to my room, too embarrassed to say another word. I was home.

CHAPTER EIGHT

The day after my return from Morecambe, Miss Stinson came to see me. She wanted to know why I had run away. But I couldn't really remember why. I had just done it. It had been a spur of the moment thing, a teenage reaction to an emotional crisis which was overwhelming one moment, forgotten the next. She asked me what I thought I had accomplished by my escapade. I thought about this for a several moments before replying.

"I have seen my mother."

"And was this important to you?"

I shrugged. "I guess I thought it was at the time."

"And do you think it was important to her?"

A longer pause before I answered.

"I think she thought it was a party."

"And a party is what you were looking for?"

"No, not really. I was just looking for my mother."

The look on Miss Stinson's face told me what I already knew. I hadn't found a mother, I had found a playmate. I wasn't sure I would ever find my mother. I was no longer sure she really existed. My mother was now a kaleidoscope of people. She was Nurse and Aunty Dawn when I needed someone to care for me. She was Miss Stinson when I needed someone to talk things over with. She was the faceless Children's Committee when I needed permission to do things.

My mother didn't have a lap I could curl up on; she had committee reports which were circulated and reviewed. My mother didn't kiss my scraped knee better; she requested medical reports which were forwarded and filed. My mother didn't cherish my uniqueness, she demanded that I conform and live by rules established for the countless other children who had passed this way before me. I was file number 7952/2 of the Devon County Council.

"How are things going here at Willowrey?" Miss Stinson asked.

"Not bad, if you don't mind living in an institution," I grumbled. "It's the summer holidays and I'm still only allowed out one night a week. It's so pathetic. None of my friends invite me to parties anymore 'cos they know I won't be able to go. And even if the party is on my night out, I still have to be back by ten. Half the parties don't even get into the swing of it till nine."

Miss Stinson looked sympathetic and made a note in her book. I continued, encouraged by her apparent empathy.

"And all my friends are wearing make up now but I'm not allowed to. I look like a baby next to them. It isn't fair. Maureen was allowed to wear make up when she was my age. I am fourteen, you know. It isn't as though I'm still a child. Ever since the new girls came Nurse and Aunty Dawn hardly have any time for me anymore. They're the 'big girls' and I'm treated like the baby."

I expected some form of rebuttal from Miss Stinson, but there wasn't one.

"And another thing," I blurted out, fuelled on by her lack of argument, "I don't even know if I'm allowed to be on Thomas's scooter 'cos Nurse says she has to check with the Committee first. Why can't I do anything without a thousand people giving their opinion on whether I can or can't. At least Thomas understands me," I said indignantly, implying that absolutely no one else in the whole wide world did.

I was actually amazed by Thomas. When he first invited me out I had been apprehensive. What if he was like all the other men I had known in my life? But he wasn't. He was gentle and kind and seemed more interested in land formations and rocks than he was in kissing and carrying on. We would spend hours sitting on beaches or hilltops while Thomas explained the geology of the area and how the earth's crust was formed and shaped. We would explore the back roads of Devon, riding everywhere on his Honda 50 cc scooter, until Nurse put a halt to that. She said I didn't have permission to ride the scooter.

"I'm sure Nurse is only concerned for your safety," Miss Stinson said. "She cares for you a great deal and only wants what's best for you."

I shrugged, reluctant to admit that this might be true. All I could see was that Nurse's caring for me was a huge impediment to my social life.

"Perhaps we need to consider some alternatives," Miss Stinson suggested. "We thought you'd be better able to settle here at Willowrey than elsewhere, but maybe that's no longer the case. Maybe you would be better off in a foster home where it's more of a true family environment."

I thought about this for a moment before discarding it as a viable option. I didn't really want to leave. I was developing a strong circle of friends at school and, if truth be known, I was very comfortable at Willowrey. If only there weren't so many rules. And then there was Thomas and my summer job and the church choir and youth club on Fridays. No, I didn't think I wanted to give all that up and start over again.

"What about your grandparents? Now that Graham has joined the Merchant Navy they might have room for you there."

"No, I don't think that would work. I think my grandparents are getting too old. Trina's parents even said I could go and live with them, if I ever needed a home, but I don't think that would work either. I don't think I could bear to live in Riverton again. And obviously my father's a dead loss," I said, not feeling a need to elaborate. Which only left my mother, and even I had to admit she wasn't much of an option at this time.

"I suppose I should just stay at Willowrey, at least until I finish my 'O' levels," I said. "Or do I have to leave now?"

I was suddenly struck with a terrifying thought. What if Nurse had told the Committee she didn't want me at Willowrey any longer? Even I could tell I'd pushed her to her limits over the last couple of months. She made no secret of the fact that she was nearing retirement and I guessed she must be getting pretty tired of my antics. Maybe I'd gone too far by running away.

Miss Stinson reached out and touched my hand.

"I'm sure Willowrey will be your home as long as you need it," she said. "Just try to get along with people. You'll find life is so much easier that way."

I settled back into life at Willowrey, and had to admit that things were good. It was summertime, I had a job, some extra money in my pocket, and a boyfriend. There was a feeling of magic in the air, of invincibility. We were young and the sky was the limit. There was nothing we couldn't do. If we could dream it, we could do it. The world was bursting with energy and we were the generation of tomorrow. The airwaves were full of music urging us on, confirming our belief that we were invincible. The Who's hit song, *My Generation*, told the older generation to '…just f-f-f-fade away'; and the Rolling Stones urged those in authority to *Get Off of My Cloud*. Our generation was determined to make love not war. As soon as we got a chance, that is.

Two weeks after my jaunt to Morecambe, my mother wrote and invited me for a holiday before going back to school. When Miss Stinson came for her monthly visit she informed me that the request had been denied by the Children's Committee.

"However, they have given permission for you to ride on Thomas' scooter, provided you wear a crash helmet," Miss Stinson informed me, anxious to take the sting out of the denied visit.

"I always do," I said. "And so does Thomas, so that's no problem."

Miss Stinson cleared her throat before continuing.

"Did your mother mention to you that she is planning to ask for Jane back again after the summer?"

I hadn't known this and was taken aback by the news. I sat staring at the floor as a familiar gnawing started in my gut. That feeling of worthlessness, of being unwanted and unloved by the one person who's love I needed more than anyone else's. I was so confused. Even though I didn't really want to live with her, I needed her to want me. It seems I was good for the occasional holiday but it was Jane she really wanted.

"Do you think the courts will let her have Jane again, after what happened last time?" I asked, once my emotions were under control.

"It's hard to say how they'll react, but I know the courts always try to keep children with their families if at all possible," she said.

Her words cut through me like a knife. Then why wasn't I being kept with my mother? Why didn't she ask to have me to live with her? Why was it always Jane that mother asked for? What about Justin? He was young too. Didn't the courts think he should be with his family? Mum obviously didn't think so, or she would have asked for him too. But she didn't. She only wanted Jane, it seems. I told myself I didn't need her. I wouldn't let myself need her.

Sometimes on our day off I would take the bus to Nestleton with one or two of the other girls to go shopping. We'd tour the shops, admiring trinkets we couldn't afford to buy, and testing make-up we weren't supposed to wear. But there was never enough money to buy all those lovely things we saw.

"No problem," Jackie said, when I grumbled about not having enough money, "just watch this."

She sidled up to the counter in Woolworth's where I'd been admiring an ornament of three brass monkeys. The plaque said 'See No Evil, Speak No Evil, Hear No Evil'. Jackie picked it up, studied it, and then motioned as if to put it down as she reached out with her other hand to pick up something else. Only she didn't put the three monkeys down. Instead she tucked them into the palm of her hand and casually slipped her hand into her pocket, all the while pretending to study the object in her other hand.

I was amazed at the ease with which she'd done it and followed her out of the store in a state of excitement. As soon as we were around the corner we burst out laughing, triumphant in our crime.

"Wow, that was tooooo easy," I said.

Jackie gave me the ornament.

"Go on, you try it," she urged, heading back towards the store.

"There's nothing to it and besides if you get caught just say you were about to pay for it. What can they do? They aren't going to throw you in jail for nicking a trinket worth two quid."

Suddenly the store was my oyster. I could have anything I wanted. Just pick it up, put it in your pocket, and walk out the store, cool as a cucumber. Jackie, Kathy and I strolled up and down the aisles, surveying the bounty before us. It was like Christmas Day and I was my own Santa.

As we walked out of the store I half expected an arm to reach out and grab me, or alarm bells to ring and lights to flash, but there was nothing. We ran all the way to the beach, where we collapsed on the hot sand, laughing and carrying on until our nervous energy had dissipated. We admired our booty and congratulated ourselves on a job well done.

Our appetites had been whetted and before long we were heading back towards the shops in search of more. I found a handbag I wanted and slipped it on my shoulder as I discreetly tore the price tag off. I needed a bag to put all my new-found goodies in.

When we got back to Willowrey I stashed most of the things in my drawer, except for the brass monkeys. Those I gave to Nurse as a gift. She seemed touched by my gesture and a pang of guilt stabbed at my heart as I saw the joy on her face.

It was arranged that Trina, my friend from Riverton, would stay for a week at Willowrey. She had never been away from her parents before and was obviously apprehensive about staying in a children's home. It meant a lot to me that she cared enough about our friendship to overcome her own fears. She had doubtless imagined all sorts of draconian horrors taking place behind the closed doors of Willowrey. She seemed vastly relieved to discover we lived our lives pretty much as other people did. We had breakfast at eight, helped with some chores and then hung around the house, like teenagers the world over, listening to records or playing games or just sitting on the lawn watching the world go by.

Afternoons were free for playing. We could go to the beach or romp through the woods along the shore or take the bus into town and look around. As long as we were home by five thirty in time for tea. After tea we could watch television or hang out in the hobby room, listening to records, doing hobbies or playing games. Bed time was at nine, lights out at nine thirty. Pretty normal stuff, all things considered.

On the days that I was working at the beach concession Trina came with me. The owner was pleased to have another pair of hands to help and even offered to pay her for her time there. On my day off we took the bus into Nestleton to look around the shops and explore the town. I took Trina to Woolworths and showed her how easy it was to shoplift. I urged her to give it a try, but she wouldn't. She said it was wrong and I should know better.

She was right, of course. I did know better, but it was so easy and the thrill of getting away with it was so exhilarating I couldn't help myself. Except afterwards it wasn't so much fun and I was beginning to realize that the things I stole gave me no pleasure. It was especially hard on Sundays as I sat in the church pew saying my prayers and singing the psalms. I sat in dread of a thunderbolt striking me dead, right there in the middle of the choir pew, and then the whole world would know I was a common thief.

After our week together at Willowrey, Trina and I returned to Riverton so that I could spend a week with her family. But after a few days I became restless. I missed Thomas. And although Trina and I had been best friends since we were five, I realized we were starting to grow apart. She had led such a sheltered life that we simply couldn't relate on many issues. I felt like a wild creature compared to her. Her goodness only amplified my badness. But mostly I was annoyed with myself for bragging to her about my shoplifting, only to have Trina tell me what I already knew - that it was wrong.

Nonetheless, the day after I got back to Willowrey Jackie, Kathy and I went 'shopping' again. A new girl, Rosina, tagged along. We took the bus into Nestleton and strolled around the shops eyeing the goodies. But the thrill was gone. As I wandered from shop to shop I realized that none of these trinkets would bring me any happiness. In fact, they did the opposite. They reminded me what a wicked person I was for stealing them - and that made me miserable.

"I don't see anything I really want," I told the other girls after a while. "I think I'll just go and see if Thomas is home."

"I thought we were coming here to get some stuff," Jackie grumbled "not go and see your boyfriend."

"Suit yourself," I said, setting off towards Thomas' hotel.

The other girls fell into step beside me.

"I used to have a boyfriend," Jackie said, struggling to keep up, "and we slept together and I had a baby."

I groaned in disgust.

"I know that Jackie, you told me already."

"Are you still a virgin?" she asked.

I stopped dead in my tracks, spun on my heels, and put my face very close to hers. She had hit a nerve.

"No, I'm not. What's it to you?"

Jackie looked triumphant. "You better watch out, or you'll be having a baby too."

"Not bloody likely," I snarled, "I'm not as stupid as you."

Kathy looked aghast.

"Have you slept with Thomas?" she asked.

"Course not!" I snapped, "What kind of girl do you think I am?"

Kathy looked confused, but decided to drop it.

When we got to the hotel, Thomas wasn't home so the three of us just hung around the pier for a while before catching the bus back to Willowrey. Jackie looked very smug and we hadn't been in the door two minutes before she was making stage-whisper comments that implied I had slept with Thomas. I was horrified.

"Shut up, you stupid bitch," I cried, as I shook my clenched fist near her face.

"That's no way for ladies to talk," Nurse called from the kitchen, ever mindful of what was going on in the house.

I stormed into the kitchen, complaining bitterly about Jackie's accusation.

"Is it true?" Nurse asked.

"Of course not," I replied indignantly.

"Then you'll just have to ignore her," Nurse said.

"But what will people think if she goes around saying things like that?"

My eyes filled with tears again at the injustice of it all.

"Sticks and stones may break your bones," Nurse said, in a sing-song voice.

"But it's not true," I cried.

"Then you have nothing to worry about, do you," Nurse said, turning her attention back to the pie she was making.

I stomped upstairs and lay on my bed, feeling rotten to the core. A girl's reputation was one of the most important things she had in 1964 and, once lost, it could never be regained.

Jackie's comments gnawed at me for the rest of the day, leaving me short tempered and jumpy. As I was getting ready for bed, Aunty Dawn chastised me for being so snippy. I snapped back at her and before I knew it we were having a full scale row.

"Fine way for a young lady to carry on," Aunty Dawn said, pursing her lips. "I don't know what we're going to do with you. Sometimes I think you're just a lost cause."

Her words stabbed me like a knife. She was right, I was a lost cause. I was less than worthless. Who would ever want me after what I had been through? I wanted to rip my insides out, rid myself of all my wrong doings. I only wanted to be loved and accepted for who and what I was. But what was I? I was a common thief and, worse yet, I wasn't even a virgin. It didn't matter that I went to church every Sunday, sometimes twice. It didn't matter that I studied hard, and did well at school. It didn't matter that I had tried to keep my brother and sister safe. None of it mattered. I was worthless. Before I knew it my pent up emotions were spewing out of me like bile.

"I hate you and I hate this stinking place," I screamed at Aunty Dawn.

In a blind rage I picked up a vase and threw it at her. It shattered on the floor around her. I looked in horror at the glass shards scattered at her feet, then fled from the room, leaving Aunty Dawn speechless. I ran down the stairs two at a time and collided with Nurse, who was just coming out of the sitting room.

"What in heaven's name is going on up there?" she asked, startled.

I took one look at her and broke down in tears, sobbing hysterically.

"You'd better come and sit down, and tell me what this is all about," Nurse said in her gentle, unflappable way as she led me into her office. She sat down and pulled me onto her lap, like a small child. Between sobs I told her the whole story.

"I've been stealing things," I wailed, "and now God will hate me too." I cried as if my heart would break.

As the words tumbled out of my mouth I began to understand why Catholics go to confession. I felt the tension and strain of the last few weeks lifting as I unburdened my conscience in a torrent of words. When I finished telling my tale of woe Nurse looked saddened, but said I had done the right thing by telling her.

"This is a very serious matter," she said, still holding me on her lap, "and we'll have to discuss it further of course, but for now I think you need a good night's sleep."

After breakfast next morning, Nurse called me into her office. She asked me to go to my room, gather up all the things I had stolen, and bring them to her. When I laid my stash out in front of her it made a considerable collection. The three brass monkeys I had given Nurse as a gift were sitting on her desk. I added them to the pile.

"I've rung Miss Stinson," Nurse said. "She'll be here later to talk to you about this."

I hung my head in shame, unable to look Nurse in the eye.

Miss Stinson arrived mid afternoon and asked me to join her in the office. The pile of stolen goods sat on the coffee table between us.

"I see you've been very busy," Miss Stinson said, her tone of voice uncharacteristically distant. "What do you have to say for yourself?"

I stared at the floor, unable to speak.

"I'm sure you realize this is a very serious situation, Gail. What made you do it?"

"It was just stuff I wanted and once we saw how easy it was, it was hard to stop."

"We? So you didn't do all this on your own then," Miss Stinson said, making a sweeping motion over the pile with her hand.

"Not all of it, but most of it," I sheepishly admitted. It was bad enough to be a thief; I didn't want to be a snitch too.

"Stealing is a criminal offense, you realize. We'll have to notify the authorities. It will be up to them to decide what action is to be taken. I'm really disappointed that you would do such a thing, especially as I know you know its wrong."

I sat there, withdrawn and scared, unable to speak. Miss Stinson decided to change tack.

"Nurse tells me you were upset yesterday over some comment Jackie made about you and Thomas."

My cheeks burned red.

"She asked me if I was a virgin and when I said I wasn't she assumed I'd slept with Thomas, so now she's telling everyone I have, but it's a lie, I haven't. I hate sex." I could hear the venom in my voice.

"Sex isn't all bad, in the proper time and place," Miss Stinson said.

"Well I hate it and I'm fed up with people telling me that it can be a happy experience. It's dirty and disgusting and I never want to do it." I shuddered involuntarily. Miss Stinson decided to drop the subject.

"I just want to go and live with my mother," I said through clenched teeth, fighting back tears. "It's not fair."

"I know," Miss Stinson said, her tone softening. "We all know that's what you want. But none of us are trying to replace your bond with your mother. We're just trying to make the time as happy as possible until you can rejoin her. Everyone's trying their hardest to help you grow up into a responsible and happy person."

There was nothing I could say in response.

"We'll talk some more later," Miss Stinson said after a few moments.

I could hear the voices of the other girls as they came in from work. It would be tea time soon.

"You can wait in the sitting room with the other girls for now. Miss Sucklin will be here soon to talk to Jackie about her role in all this."

After a while Nurse, Miss Stinson and Miss Sucklin joined us in the sitting room.

"You've been called together for a very serious purpose," Miss

Sucklin began. "We have reason to believe that you have each been engaged in shoplifting activities."

She paused and looked from girl to girl, letting her words sink in. Rosina squirmed in her seat; Jackie thrust her chin out defiantly; Kathy and I sat motionless, staring intently at the worn carpet.

"I want each of you to go to your rooms in turn with Nurse and bring down all the things you've stolen."

Rosina, who had a childlike innocence despite being seventeen, seemed confused by the turn of events. Nurse asked her to go first. After a few moments they returned with Rosina's small collection of stolen trinkets. They were placed in a pile on the table as Nurse escorted first Kathy, then Jackie back upstairs to get their stuff. Then I went with Nurse and collected my stash from her office. When it was all together Miss Stinson and Miss Harvey made a list of the items, noting where they had been stolen from and who had actually stolen them. None of us made any attempt to deny our activities.

The police were called.

Two policemen arrived as we were clearing away the tea dishes. I had to fight back the urge to run. One by one we were taken into Nurse's office to give our statements. I went first. I half expected to be handcuffed and marched out the front door, never to return. I'd heard stories of reform schools and remand homes where the 'bad' children were sent. I had no wish to find out, first hand, what they were really like.

When I finished giving my statement they told me the matter rested in their hands now and warned that I could well face court charges. Then they told me I could go. I was so relieved I practically ran from the room, thanking them profusely for letting me go, apologizing for causing so much trouble and promising never, ever to do anything like it again, the words tumbling out of me as I fled from the room.

I went to bed that evening with a clearer conscience than I had felt for many weeks. I said my prayers and begged for God's forgiveness. I hoped the police would be equally as forgiving.

CHAPTER NINE

By the time September rolled around I was glad to return to school and start Fourth Form. It had been an emotionally exhausting summer. And besides, school meant I was able to see Thomas every day.

Since being awarded the Progress Cup I had started to enjoy a certain status among the other students. Now, instead of being the new girl struggling to catch up, I was seen as one of the bright academic lights. I also had the good fortune to look a lot like Twiggy, the top fashion model whose picture adorned every fashion magazine. I was welcomed into the 'in' crowd at school.

When the weather turned wet and cold, my friends and I would congregate around the radiator in the back corridor during lunch and breaks. Other students would be shooed outside by the on-duty prefects, but we weren't. They turned a blind eye to our little group mainly because my boyfriend was in Upper Sixth. I'd gained a certain prestige and respect, at school - but at home in Willowrey it was different.

Miss Stinson's monthly visits were invariably met with a barrage of complaints, mostly about my lack of freedom and how tired I was of being treated like a fourteen-year-old child.

"But a fourteen-year-old child is exactly what you are," Miss

Stinson said, in her usual calm manner, "so how else would you expect to be treated?"

She had a point.

Boys had become a big topic of conversation among my friends at school. But when the girls twittered about whether or not they should keep their virginity until they were married, I'd hang back in silence. It wasn't an option for me. When they giggled about boys and wondered what it would be like to kiss one or 'go all the way', I kept silent. They seemed so childish and naïve. I wanted to tell them what it was really like, how ugly it was and how disgusting a penis tasted, but of course I couldn't. So instead I said nothing and my silence was interpreted as innocence.

But inside my head a maelstrom of emotions crashed around, colliding with each other and often erupting into angry outbursts. I had been robbed of my innocence, my childhood, by the very people who should have protected me. I was jealous of my friends with their mums and dads who cared for them and kept them safe. I'd listen to them grumbling about their parents and how they couldn't do this, or couldn't do that. I'd try to join in with my list of complaints about my lack of freedom at Willowrey, but really I wanted to scream at my friends for taking their parents for granted. They should be thankful they had parents they could live with. I had to make do with the occasional Sunday afternoon chaperoned visit from my father, or an infrequent holiday with my mother.

At school I did my best to keep a lid on my emotions, but at home in Willowrey I railed against their rules at every opportunity. The more difficult I became, the sterner they were. The sterner they became, the more rebellious I was. Nurse had her hands full as she struggled to corral the wild side of my nature into some semblance of a polite young woman. I often wondered why she bothered. Couldn't she see I was hopeless? But she never faltered in her steadfast caring. Nor would she bend an inch.

Shortly after school started I learned that my sister's new foster home hadn't worked out. She was being returned to Languard House, yet again. Once more I asked Miss Stinson if she could come and live with us at Willowrey. She promised to discuss the possibility at the next Children's Committee meeting.

"But you said that last time, and nothing happened," I said.

"You know it isn't up to me, Gail, but I'll do my best."

"But what if Mum gets her, like you said she wanted, and then dumps her off at Children's Services again like she did before?" I queried. "We can't keep moving Jane around like baggage. It isn't fair on her. No wonder she's getting to be such a brat. If she came here she could be settled. Like me."

A look crossed Miss Stinson's face which said a thousand words, but she made no reply. No doubt Nurse had filled her in on how troublesome I had been of late.

Almost a month after my shoplifting confession I arrived home from school to find a police car parked outside. I went in, prepared for the worst. Nurse called me into the sitting room where she and two police officers were waiting. I was told to take a seat. One of the officers was shuffling through some papers. He cleared his throat before looking directly at me.

"Well, young lady, we've talked to the store owners you stole from and you'll be happy to know they've decided not to press charges - this time."

I stared back at him, not trusting my ears, and waited for him to continue.

"However, you need to know that this was a very serious offence. There could be dire consequences if you ever do anything like this again. You can't expect to be so lucky, next time."

I nodded imperceptibly, afraid to move.

"What do you have to say for yourself?" he asked.

I didn't know what to say. What do you say to someone who has just handed you back your life? I'd been so sure I was going to be charged as a common thief that it was taking a few minutes for his words to sink in. I'd been bracing myself for the shame and humiliation of people knowing what I had done. Now he was saying it was all behind me. Case closed. Carry on as if you are normal. The relief was so great I felt I was floating. I hadn't realized until that moment how much it was wearing on me, how much energy I was putting into stuffing my shame deep down inside me, or how the worry had been fuelling my angry outbursts and tearful tantrums of late.

"Thank you," was all I could mumble.

"Let this be a lesson to you," Nurse chimed in. "You're very fortunate, young lady, to have gotten off so lightly. You can be sure it won't be the same next time."

"There won't be a next time," I told her.

A few days later Mum arrived in Devon by herself. They had finished their summer jobs at Morecambe and Norman had gone to Manchester to start a new gig. Mum was going to join him there after visiting her family, which still very much included my father it seems. They both came to visit me at Willowrey next day.

Dad, who had stood me up on more than one occasion and could be considered an infrequent visitor at best, tried to impress my mother with assurances that he visited me every fortnight. I looked at him through narrowed eyes, not wanting to call him a liar but refusing to play along. I watched as he beamed at my mother, obviously still quite besotted with her. And she played him like a fiddle.

Mum stayed with Dad for ten days before heading to Manchester to join her husband. I wasn't particularly upset when she left. My life was here in Devon and her cameo appearances were becoming less and less important to me. I was more interested in Thomas.

Thomas was the one person I felt I could talk to. We saw each other every chance we got and slowly, ever so slowly, I started to let down my guard. He wanted to know all about me. None of my friends knew why I was living at Willowrey. It was a secret I kept very close to my heart for fear that the truth would bring shame and rejection on me. But Thomas was different. He understood me in a way that no one else did.

"My Dad did things to me," I told him one day, as we sat on the beach watching the sail boats go by. "Bad things."

I waited for his response. I was quite prepared for him to hate me after what I had to tell him, but if we were to have an honest relationship I needed him to know the truth. I didn't want to keep up the pretense any longer. Not with Thomas.

"What kind of things?" Thomas asked, his voice small with trepidation.

"You know, grown up things like people do when they're married."

Thomas stared at me open mouthed while he digested this information.

"You mean …" His voice trailed off.

"Yes," I said.

We sat in silence for a few moments.

"Did he hurt you?" Thomas asked after a while.

"Kinda." I shrugged. "He did weird things mostly like make me give him horsey rides up the stairs."

Thomas stared at me, confused.

"He liked to jerk off on my back," I said, wanting my words to shock him.

I watched Thomas closely, trying to gauge his reaction. If there was the slightest hint of rejection, I would reject him first. Thomas sat in silence.

"So you might as well go and find yourself another girlfriend," I said, suddenly regretting telling him.

I was a fool to think he'd understand and now I hated him for knowing. I was soiled goods and now I couldn't pretend differently to Thomas anymore.

"I don't want another girlfriend," Thomas said, reaching out and putting his arm around me, "I want you."

"But what about, you know?"

"None of that was your fault," he said, pulling me closer, "You're here now, with me, and I'm going to keep you safe. He won't hurt you anymore."

I buried my head in Thomas's chest and let the tears flow. A huge weight had been lifted from my shoulders. I no longer had to carry my dreadful secret around alone. Thomas would help me carry the burden of truth from now on.

As autumn settled in around us and nature put on a dazzling show of yellows, oranges and reds, my life entered a period of calm. My father, who had made such a big show in front of my mother of promising to come and visit me the fortnight after she was there, never showed. I stayed home waiting for him, but as the late afternoon sun slipped below the horizon I accepted the fact that he wasn't coming. I was angry and upset, but it wasn't the same as before. I just resented the fact that he jerked me around like that.

Thomas and I visited back and forth in each other's homes quite frequently. Nurse obviously liked him and said he was a good influence over me. The same could not be said for Thomas's father. Mr. Weston was definitely not in favour of our relationship. He had high hopes for his eldest son and couldn't understand why Thomas was wasting his time with 'that waif from the Children's Home', as he insisted on referring to me. He chided Thomas repeatedly for spending time with me. He said his time would be better spent studying for his "A" levels. Mr. Weston seemed to live in mortal fear that I would get 'knocked up' and trap his precious Thomas Weston into marrying me. If only he'd known how little interest I had in such things. And if he'd bothered asking, he would have realized that I had high hopes for my future too.

At tea one day Nurse dropped a bombshell.

"I went to see the Weston's this afternoon," she said, as if it were the most natural thing in the world for her to do on a Tuesday afternoon.

"You did what?" I asked, hardly believing my ears.

"I went to visit with Thomas's parents," she repeated.

"Why?" I asked, with a look of horror on my face.

"I thought it was probably time I met them," she said.

I groaned.

"You've been spending a lot of time at Thomas' place, so I thought it only right that I should go and introduce myself."

I didn't know whether to be embarrassed or annoyed.

"Mr. Carter rang me to say he was concerned about the amount of time you and Thomas were spending together at school, so I thought his parents should be aware of this also."

Mr. Carter was the headmaster and on several occasions recently he had shooed me away from the sixth form corridor during lunch breaks. Only the prefects were supposed to be inside during lunch and he wasn't prepared to make an exception for me, even if the prefects were.

"Oh my God," I gasped, "can't I do anything without everyone spying on me and checking up on me all the time."

"We only have your best interest at heart dear," Nurse said, a note of irritation in her voice. "Mr. Weston was out when I first got there but I had a nice visit with Thomas's mother. She seems very fond of you."

Nurse carried on eating, while I digested this piece of information.

I was pleased to know Mrs. Weston liked me. She had just had another baby, much to Thomas' consternation and embarrassment. Thomas was eighteen and his brother, Mike, was fifteen. After a twelve year hiatus their mother had produced a baby a year for the last three years. I suspected that much of his father's concern about Thomas' relationship with me was based on his own alarming fertility rate. Thomas would joke that his father only had to look at his mother and she got pregnant.

Whatever the reason, Mr. Weston did not approve of Thomas dating me. The thought that Nurse had gone to see them mortified me. Thank God Mr. Weston hadn't been home.

Nurse continued. "They're hoping Thomas gets accepted at Portsmouth University next year, and they don't want anything interfering with his studies."

I was obviously the 'anything' they were referring to.

"If he wasn't dating me he'd probably be dating someone else," I said defensively, "Everyone in Upper Sixth has a girlfriend."

"His father came home just as I was leaving, so I had a brief chat with him before I left."

Oh my God, no. I cringed inside, imagining what the conversation must have been like.

"He seemed very concerned about the fact that you live in a children's home," Nurse said, looking up at me.

Was that a hint of defiance I saw in her clear blue eyes? I knew how she felt about 'her girls' and it suddenly occurred to me that she had gone to the Weston's to defend me, not check up on me. She'd heard me grumbling about the way Mr. Weston treated me and how judgmental he was. Perhaps Nurse had let the Weston's know that while I may not live with my parents I was, nonetheless, cared for too. I smiled back at Nurse, as if truly seeing her for the first time.

"So what did you tell him?" I asked, suddenly very proud of her for daring to challenge Mr. Weston's prejudices in ways that I would never be able.

"I simply told him the truth, which is that you're here through no fault of your own. I also told him we had very high hopes for your future, too."

She gave a little nod of her head, as if to say 'so there'. She turned her attention back to her dinner. She had said all she was going to on the subject.

When I saw Thomas at school next day I told him about Nurse's visit. He already knew. Apparently his father had been very impressed by Nurse and had grudgingly admitted that perhaps I wasn't such a bad influence on Thomas after all.

When Miss Stinson came to see me in the middle of October she commented on how relaxed and contented I seemed.

"Well, things are going pretty well at the moment," I said, settling into the armchair in Nurse's office. I tucked my feet up under me and wrapped my arms around my knees. "I've joined the Sea Rangers with two of my friends from school, Wendy and Amy. We get to go rowing and are learning all about semaphore and how to tie knots and lots of neat things like that."

"I didn't know you had an interest in that sort of thing," Miss Stinson said.

"Oh yes, very much so," I said enthusiastically, "and we get to go to regattas all over Devon."

It was true, I was enjoying Sea Rangers, but in reality it had more to do with being allowed out one more night a week than any burning desire to learn how to tie reef knots.

"Well, I must say how happy I am that things are going so well for you at the moment. Let's hope it stays this way," Miss Stinson said, a faint note of skepticism in her voice.

I heard the theme tune of "Top of the Pops" coming from the sitting room.

"Oh, I have to go," I said excitedly. "Top of the Pops is just starting and I want to know who is number one this week. It's too bad you always come on Thursdays, when my favourite show is on."

Miss Stinson started gathering up her papers.

"Is there nothing else you wish to tell me?"

She hardly seemed able to cope with my lack of complaints or problems.

I couldn't think of anything to grumble about at that moment, but didn't want to disappoint her. I turned and looked at her very solemnly.

"Well actually, Miss Stinson, there is one thing I should mention. I'm pregnant."

"Oh, really?" she said, straight faced. "I'm very sorry to hear that Gail. How many months pregnant do you think you are?"

"Three," I said, equally straight faced.

"And who do you think the father is?" she asked.

"I don't know. I was drunk at the time." I lowered my eyes, not wanting her to see the laughter dancing there.

"It's a good job I know you're teasing me," Miss Stinson said.

I thought so too.

I didn't hear from my mother for several weeks after her visit to Devon. When she did finally get around to dropping me a line, it was to tell me that she and Norman had bought a house in Manchester. I finally realized she was never coming home to Devon. When Miss Stinson came to see me early in November she was glad to know I'd heard from my mother. She asked me for her address so that she could write to her.

"We need to let her know what arrangements have been made for Jane," she said, jotting down Mum's address. "The Children's Committee has decided she should go to St. Leonard's Childrens Home in Riverton."

"Oh, I think Mum's hoping Jane can go and live with them again," I said.

I wondered how Mum would take the news.

"Her letter implied that they'd bought the house especially so she could have Jane and me live with her. Actually, I don't know if I really want to live with Mum anymore, at least not till I'm finished school. But Mum says she wants Jane to live with her so she won't grow up with the same inferiority complex I have. Mum says I have a chip on my shoulder, always feeling sorry for myself."

I looked down at my hands. There was blood oozing out of my thumb cuticle. I had been absent mindedly picking at it while I spoke.

"It's funny really, my friends at school think I'm so stuck up but my mother thinks I have an inferiority complex. I wonder which is right."

"Probably a bit of both," Miss Stinson said. "You've had more than your share of things to deal with for a girl your age and you tend to hide your feelings behind a screen of jibes and jokes. Sometimes it's hard to know what you're really thinking or feeling."

"Sometimes I don't even know what I'm thinking or feeling. I hear these words coming out of my mouth and I wonder who said them. Anyhow, maybe I won't have to go and live with Mum when I'm finished school. Maybe I'll just get married as soon as I'm old enough. What do you think of early marriages?"

Miss Stinson shifted positions in her seat as she tried to catch up with this abrupt change of topic.

"I want to get married and have children and live in my very own house," I continued enthusiastically, "and I'll make sure my children have a very happy time of it indeed."

"Well, no doubt what you want for your own children is influenced by your own childhood," Miss Stinson said, catching up. "I suppose young marriages can be very happy, sometimes. But I think you have to be sure you enjoy your freedom long enough before settling down to the ties of marriage and children. Perhaps your mother regrets marrying so young."

"Perhaps," I agreed.

Miss Stinson turned her attention back to her notes, then looked back at me.

"I was wondering how your pregnancy is coming along," she asked, straight faced.

"Oh," I said, trying to look suitably upset, "I had a miscarriage."

"Probably for the best," she said.

"Yes, probably," I said, quite seriously. "Actually, I was wondering what you think of sex outside of marriage. It's the big topic of conversation at school these days."

She considered my question for a moment before responding.

"I believe, from my own feelings and what I know of other people's experiences that a loving sexual relationship can only truly happen within a marriage. And of course, on the practical side, there's also the danger of pregnancy. No contraceptives are one hundred percent certain."

I thought about this for a few moments.

"It's funny, the way they refer to sex as 'making love'," I said. "It's supposed to be an act of love but I'm not so sure it is. Some men can be horrid about sex. My mother says that's why she left my father. I don't know how Terry can stand to live with him, knowing what he likes to call 'sex'. And now I hear her daughter, Marcella, is living with them too and she's only fifteen. It just doesn't seem right to me."

"I didn't realize Marcella was living with your father and Terry," Miss Stinson said. "But I knew the daughter hated being so far from her mother."

"I hate being this far from my mother too," I said, "but I'm getting used to it."

Towards the end of November my mother wrote and invited me for Christmas. Before approving the visit the Children's Committee sent Miss Stinson to Manchester to assess the situation.

"Well, how was it?" I asked Miss Stinson when she came to see me after her visit.

I was almost afraid to hear the answer.

"Your mother and Norman both seemed well," she said. "They've bought a two bedroom terraced house in a neighbourhood not unlike Coronation Street. They have the only house on the street with an indoor bathroom, apparently, although the toilet is a privy outside the back door."

I sank back in my chair, not much liking the sound of it.

"Your mother is most anxious for you and Jane to visit at

Christmas. I pointed out to her that it was up to the Committee to decide, but she seems to have set her heart on it."

"But I've already told Trina I'd come and spend Christmas with her. Isn't it a bit late to be planning a trip to Manchester? Christmas is only two weeks away."

As much as I wanted to see my mother I was reluctant to cancel my other plans. Besides, I had a sinking feeling that it wasn't really me she wanted to see. She just didn't want to be alone at Christmas.

"Your mother and Norman both said they hope to have you girls live with them. They plan to apply to the Courts as soon as they're settled."

This didn't come as a total surprise to me. Mum had said in her letter that she was busy trying to fix up the house so that Jane and I could come and live with her.

"The Committee has decided that you and Jane should go for a visit with them first though, before making any decisions. If things don't work out for a Christmas visit we should aim for one at Easter."

"I guess," was all I could think to say. These things weren't up to me anyhow.

"Your mother seemed quite disappointed when I couldn't give her a more definite answer. I suggested that perhaps she could come to Devon for a weekend around Christmas, if she's so anxious to see you both. But she's more interested in having you come to see her in Manchester. She's keen to show off her new home."

"Always the performer, looking to put on a show," I said sardonically.

When I told Thomas I might have to go to Manchester for Christmas he seemed crestfallen.

"That's too bad. My parents always have a big gathering for New Year's Eve," he explained, "and I've asked them if you could join us this year. I was going to talk to you and Nurse about it tonight."

"Really," I squealed with delight, "I know what your dad thinks of me, I can't believe he'd say yes."

"Well he did. He's been much more reasonable since Nurse went to visit them. My mother said she'd put the invitation in writing, just to make it official. You can stay the whole weekend if it's agreeable with Nurse."

Two days later Nurse called me into her office. She had the letter from Thomas's parents in her hand and said she saw no reason why I shouldn't go. She was obviously pleased about the invitation. Her efforts hadn't been in vain.

"Of course, I expect you to behave yourself while you're there and mind your manners," Nurse said.

"Yes, m'lady," I said, catching the hem of my skirt and dropping into a low curtsy, "I shall be on me best behaviour, mam, and no one will know I'm just a lowly serving girl from the orphanage."

Nurse chuckled. "No need to overdo it. I'll telephone Mrs. Weston in the morning and let her know you can come."

"I've also heard from the Children's Committee," she said. "They feel a visit to Manchester is a little premature at this time. Miss Stinson's supervisor, Mr. Brill, is going to write to your mother and explain the situation to her. Hopefully something can be arranged for Easter."

"That's too bad," I said, feeling a need to respond but not really caring. I was far too excited about being invited to stay with Thomas' family.

"Perhaps you could write to your mother and let her know how disappointed you are," Nurse suggested.

"Yes, yes, of course. I'll write to her this evening. The sooner I let her know the better so she can make other plans. I know she hates being alone at Christmas."

My father had become a non-entity in my life since my mother's visit in October. Although he managed to visit Justin and Jane on a fairly regular basis, he never seemed to make it down my way. When I phoned to let him know I'd be going to Riverton for Christmas he said he'd come and see me on Sunday before I left. But Sunday came and went and he didn't show. He phoned two days later to say a band job had come up unexpectedly so he hadn't been able to make it. He wished me a Merry Christmas.

Christmas at Trina's was hectic and happy. I took great comfort from the fact that there was still a place where I could go and it seemed like nothing had changed. Trina thought my life was exciting, while hers was dull. I thought my life was terrifying, while hers was safe. But at the same time I no longer believed I could fit into a world like Trina's. Not now, not after what I'd seen and done.

We promised to be friends forever. We were the yin and the yang. We talked of finishing school and getting a flat together. I said I wanted to travel the world. Trina said she wanted to stay close to Riverton. I said I wanted to be rich. Trina said she wanted to be happy. I told her I had a boyfriend. She said she wasn't ready for one yet. She asked if I'd 'done it'. I told her I hadn't, but maybe I would soon. She said she was going to keep her virginity until she was married. I told her she was being old fashioned. If you really loved someone you should 'do it' first, to make sure you liked it. I told her it would be terrible to marry someone only to find that you didn't enjoy 'doing it' with them. Some men did it differently than others, I told her, and you needed to make sure you married one who did it right. I didn't tell her how I knew these things and she didn't ask.

On Christmas Eve Trina and I walked across town to St. Leonard's Children's Home, to see Jane. I took her a colouring book and some crayons and a doll's outfit Trina's mum had knitted for her. St. Leonard's was relatively new and seemed sterile and institutional with none of the homey comforts of Willowrey.

Jane seemed happy to see me, in an offhand sort of way. She had changed from that cute little four-year-old who had left Riverton two short years before. There was a wary look in her eyes now, as if she didn't trust anyone or really believe anything they said. She was learning to survive on her own and probably saw me as just another person who had let her down. I didn't stay long. I didn't know what I could say to reach her. She seemed so distant. I promised to come and see her again next time I was in Riverton.

"Yeah, sure," she said, as I kissed her goodbye. At six and a half she'd already learned not to form attachments or develop expectations.

New Year's Eve Thomas picked me up from Willowrey and took me home to his place. I was given the room next to his parents. I imagined Thomas's father standing guard outside my door all night, protecting me from Thomas or Thomas from me? Thomas' room was another two floors up and the stairs were notoriously creaky. Thomas showed me to my room and put my small suitcase on a stool beside the dresser.

"Wow, is this ever nice," I said as I sat on the plump bed, reveling in the luxury of hotel accommodation. Thomas took a few steps towards me then stopped abruptly, a look of alarm on his face. I followed his gaze. His father was standing in the doorway, scowling.

"I'll talk to you downstairs," he said to Thomas. "Now!"

Mr. Weston spun on his heel and marched down the stairs, followed by a devastated Thomas.

"Come downstairs as soon as you're ready," Thomas said over his shoulder.

"But Dad, I was just showing her to her room." I heard him saying, as they hurried away.

When I finally plucked up the courage to venture downstairs Mrs. Weston looked pleased to see me. She was busy in the kitchen overseeing dinner preparations, the youngest baby draped over her shoulder. I offered to hold the baby, glad of something to focus my attention on. The house was rapidly filling with friends and family and Thomas was kept busy helping his father set up for cocktails in the hotel lounge.

Mr. Weston seemed to have calmed down but I took a wide berth around him nevertheless, preferring the warmth of Mrs. Weston's company. While Mr. Weston was polite and pleasant towards me, it was obviously a bit of a struggle. I wouldn't have stood a chance with him if it wasn't for Nurse. He just couldn't see beyond the fact that I lived in a children's home. I simply wasn't a person of substance in his mind and nothing I said or did was going to change that. Better just to keep out of his way.

It was almost a relief to get back to Willowrey, away from the scrutiny of Mr. Weston and his persistent warnings of grave consequences should Thomas so much as put a hand on me. He obviously had no trouble putting his hands on Mrs. Weston though. On New Year's Eve she proudly announced that she was pregnant with their fourth 'second generation' child. She looked so happy, I wondered what it would be like to be pregnant with Thomas' child.

Chapter Ten

January 14, 1965

Dear Mum:

I hope you are well and enjoying your new home. I can't wait to see it.

I saw Miss Stinson the other day and she says she's going to Manchester to see you again soon, to talk about Jane and me coming to visit sometime. They say we might be able to come and live with you now you're settled in your own home.

The thing is, I'll be sitting my 'O' levels next year, so you see it might not be a very good time for me to think about moving right now. It's taken me ages to get settled here at Willowrey and Stoneleigh Grammar and I don't much like the thought of having to get to know new teachers and a new school all over again before the exams. After this term there's only one more year and then I'll be done, unless I decide to sit my 'A' levels of course, and even if I do, I could maybe move to Manchester in time for that. I just don't feel like it's a good idea to move right now. I'm sure Jane is really looking forward to it though, but she doesn't have school to worry about like I do.

I'm still seeing Thomas and even got to stay at his parent's hotel for three nights over the New Year. Thomas has even taken me to see Dad a few times too because he never seems to have time to come and visit me anymore, not that I care really.

It seems like ages since I saw you – you wouldn't believe how tall I am now, and my hair is getting really long. Nurse won't let me wear make up, but sometimes I wear mascara. Maybe you can show me how you put on eyeliner when I come to Manchester.

I saw Jane at St. Leonard's while I was in Riverton. She sure is growing fast! I haven't seen Justin in ages – I hope he's doing alright. I never hear from him so I guess he's okay. I'll write to him soon, and send him a card for his birthday. Hard to imagine he's going to be 10 in February!

Well, I'd better go now as I have lots of homework to do. Thomas is coming over this evening so I want to be finished before he gets here.

All my love,
Gail.

It took my mother several weeks to reply. By the time she did, Miss Stinson had already been to see her.

19 Sun Street,
Manchester
February 16, 1965

Dear Gail,

Thank you for your letter telling me all your news. Miss Stinson was here the other day and seemed quite impressed with our home and the furnishings we've managed to gather together. I told her I had heard from you and that you didn't seem that keen on coming to live with us at the moment. Obviously I'm very disappointed. I understand that your studies are important to you, but I have to wonder what role Thomas is playing in all this. Would you feel the same way if you didn't have a boyfriend in Devon? There are lots of nice young men in Manchester you know! I'm sure you could have your pick of the crop, if you lived here.

Anyhow, it looks like you and Jane will be allowed to visit at Easter and I'm sure we'll have great fun while you're here. I haven't heard from Justin in a while either, but maybe he'd like to come and live here if you aren't coming.

See you soon,

Love Mum

xxxx

Miss Stinson drove Jane and me to the station and settled us on the train to Manchester. She asked the conductor to keep an eye on us. Jane was wide-eyed with excitement and sat so close to me the whole time that she might just as well have sat on my lap, and saved the price of a ticket.

Mum met us at Piccadilly Station and we took a taxi to her new home on Sun Street. Miss Stinson was right - it did look just like Coronation Street, only shabbier.

"Welcome to my humble home," Mum said with a flourish, as she unlocked the front door and threw it open.

We stepped into a sparsely furnished front room. It felt cold and damp.

"We haven't been using this room much," Mum said, "it's warmer in the dining room, so we keep the telly in there. Come and have a look."

The dining room had a table with four chairs, a sofa, and armchair. A television, which had been acquired on hire purchase Mum said, sat proudly on an upturned carton in the corner, rabbit ears askew. An extremely small kitchen led off from the dining room, with a door leading to the outside. I opened the door and peaked out. There was an outhouse and a small back yard, which had been completely bricked over.

"Bring your bags upstairs," Mum said. "You'll be sleeping in Jane's room, on the left at the top of the stairs."

"What makes it 'Jane's room'," I asked, sibling rivalry instantly raising its ugly head.

"Well you don't seem to want to live here and Jane does, so it makes sense to call it Jane's room, doesn't it? Don't go getting touchy, the minute you're in the door."

I started up the stairs behind Mum. Jane went ahead. There was only one bed in the room, which we would have to share. Fortunately it was a double bed.

We stayed in Manchester for almost two weeks, rehearsing how it would be to live like a normal family. But it didn't seem real, probably because it wasn't. A fifteen year old doesn't have a whole lot in common with a seven year old, even if it is your little sister who you love and haven't seen for ages. I felt bored. Jane demanded, and got, Mum's undivided attention, leaving me feeling left out. I wrote to Thomas every day.

None too soon Miss Stinson was knocking at the door, ready to escort us back to Devon. She asked how the visit had gone and how Mum and Norman were feeling about future plans. Mum offhandedly said it would probably be best for me to stay at Willowrey, at least until I finished my 'O' levels. While I agreed with her wholeheartedly, I was stung by the casual, offhand way she said it. I felt like I'd failed an audition of how to be a lovable daughter.

"But we're really looking forward to having Jane live with us," Mum told Miss Stinson, brightening considerably. "She's had a lovely time here, isn't that right, Jane. She was such a pleasure to have around."

She was a pain in the ass, Mother!

"She's such a little sweetheart, don't you think, and she's such a help around the house."

In case you didn't notice, Mother, she didn't lift a bloody finger the whole time we were here.

I sat there, listening to my mother prattle on about Jane's virtues like I didn't even exist. But Mum knew I was there alright, taking it all in. She knew how to push my buttons.

When I got home to Willowrey, Thomas was waiting for me. We went outside and sat on the lawn, enjoying the late spring sunshine.

"Are you going to go and live in Manchester?" he asked.

"No, it doesn't sound like it, thank goodness. I don't think I'd like living in Manchester. It isn't at all like Devon and I can hardly understand what people are saying, they have such thick accents."

"Oh aar me dear, us sure knows 'ow to talk proper down eer in Debon, doan us?"

I laughed at his phoney Devonshire accent and put my arms around him, kissing him lightly on the cheek.

"Did you miss me?" I asked.

"Of course I did. You were always on my mind."

"I missed you too," I said. "I wish you didn't have to go away in September. I don't know what I'm going to do without you. Do you have to go?"

"If I want to have a future I do. You know that. But it's not forever and besides I'll be home for the hols at Christmas and Easter and all summer. I'll be back before you know it."

Thomas put his arm around me and I felt his sweet breath on my cheek. There was an unfamiliar stirring in my groin, urging me closer to him. I wondered what it would be like to make love to him, gently and willingly.

I heard Nurse calling me in for tea, putting an end to my reverie. The moment was lost.

That night as I got ready for bed I studied my naked body in the mirror. My arms and legs were long and skinny; my breasts small. My fine blond hair draped over my shoulders, falling across my breasts and covering the pale pink nipples. My body had changed in the two years since my father had used it. I was much taller now, with gentle curves where my ribs once poked through. It was no longer the body of a child. I was becoming a woman, with a woman's desires and passions. But I was repulsed by the thought of sex. It was ugly, dirty. It was what grown ups did at night, in the dark, when no one was listening. It hurt. It felt bad. I couldn't imagine what sex had to do with love. And yet I felt this stirring deep in my groin which spoke of a different kind of sex, where I was a willing participant and it was a beautiful.

Next day, as Thomas and I strolled along the beach, I plucked up the courage to broach the subject with him.

"Thomas, have you ever wondered why they refer to sex as 'making love'?"

"Well, I guess it's because that's what people in love do."

I shrugged. "It doesn't seem like a very nice thing to do to someone, especially if you love them."

Thomas laughed. "Well, I guess we don't know enough about it to know for sure, but from everything I've read, it seems like the perfect thing to do with someone you love. As long as it's what you both want, that is."

We walked in silence for a few moments.

"Do you want to do it?" I asked after a while.

Thomas stopped and turned to face me. He put his hands on my shoulders and looked directly into my eyes.

"I can't imagine anything I'd like to do more. I dream about making love with you, long into the night." He stopped, embarrassed by his honesty. "Maybe one day when you're ready, you'll come to realize that sex can be a beautiful thing between two people. What your father did was wrong. It shouldn't be like that and it wouldn't be like that, not between us."

We walked on in silence, holding hands, each lost in our own thoughts.

The summer term flew by in a flurry of studying and homework. Thomas and I hardly had time to see each other. If he wasn't studying for his "A" levels he was helping out at his parents' hotel, serving behind the bar. But on weekends we'd head off on his moped every chance we got, exploring the back roads of Devon.

One time we saw my father's convertible Morris Minor parked outside a pub. We went inside to surprise him. Dad bought us each a shandy and ordered another pint of beer for himself. We took our drinks outside and sat in the pub garden, enjoying the sunshine.

"Terry and I are splitting up," Dad said, between great gulps of beer.

I thought I detected a slight slur in his speech, and wondered if he was going to cry. I hoped not.

"It's probably for the best, if that's what you want," I said, not knowing what else to say.

Dad just shrugged and ordered himself another pint. Thomas and I declined his offer of another drink. Dad took some long swigs of beer, draining half the pint mug before putting it down on the table with a thud.

"Ahh, you can't beat a good pint of Whitbread's on a sunny afternoon," he said, smacking his lips together and wiping beer foam off his lips with the back of his hand. "And there's nothing like a bit of sunshine, to make a fellow want to sow some wild oats, eh Thomas?" Dad gave Thomas a knowing wink.

I cringed with embarrassment. I wondered how many beers Dad had had before we found him.

"We have to get going, Dad," I said, flustered. "Thomas has to work this afternoon."

A white lie could be forgiven, surely, under such circumstances. Dad promised to come and visit the following Sunday. I said that would be nice, but doubted he actually would.

The heat of the summer sun only served to intensify the yearning in my groin, much to my confusion and dismay. I felt my body was betraying me, urging me towards something I had sworn I would never, ever, willingly do. I wanted to be a nice girl and nice girls didn't do things like that. Bad girls did. I became short tempered and irritable as I grappled with my confusion and raging hormones. My body wanted to be caressed and loved but my mind was repulsed by the idea.

I poured my pent up energy into Sea Ranger activities, participating in regattas up and down the Devonshire coast. I also signed up for the Duke of Edinburgh Ten Tors Hike across Dartmoor. It was totally exhausting and not much fun, but at least I didn't have time to think about sex.

As the summer season got into full swing, my lack of freedom seemed even more oppressive. I continued to rail against the restrictions placed on my life at Willowrey. Refusing to be restrained, I would sometimes sneak out my bedroom window after lights out on Saturday nights. Kathy was a willing companion and we became regular night-time escapees from the confines of Willowrey, only making it back to our beds in time for a few hours sleep before Nurse woke us next morning.

Nestleton was a popular seaside resort and during the summer of '65 hundreds of Mods and Rockers congregated there. Their motorbikes and scooters would be lined up along the seafront in packs, lights reflecting off their polished chrome piping. It was a party I didn't want to miss.

As Kathy and I strolled along the street I couldn't help but notice the admiring looks young men gave me. I pretended not to hear their wolf whistles as I fluttered past, taunting them in a way I couldn't begin to understand. You can look, but don't touch! I believed I was in control.

When I told Thomas I wasn't ready for sex he had respected my wishes. I assumed it would be that way with all boys. So, when a couple of them offered us a ride home one night Kathy and I eagerly accepted. They seemed like nice boys. They were from Liverpool and told us they knew the Beatles personally. We believed them.

I got into the front beside Jock, the driver. Kathy climbed into the back seat, giggling as Mack put his arm around her. We hadn't gone far when Jock parked the car in a secluded spot. He suggested Mack take Kathy for a walk, some place private. Kathy giggled nervously and looked at me for reassurance.

"You alright here?" she asked, as Mack tugged on her arm.

"Yeah," I said, "I'll be fine here, but don't be too long."

Jock put his arm around me.

"How old are you, sweetheart?" he asked, between tongue thrusting kisses.

"Seventeen," I lied.

"Hmm, thought so," he said, sliding his hand up under my blouse. I squirmed, embarrassed by my small, albeit fashionable, breast size.

"Come on now, sweetheart, don't be shy. How 'bout we slide into the back seat where it's more comfortable."

I felt light headed from all that kissing and was surprised to hear myself agreeing. Within minutes we were writhing and clawing at each other in the back seat, oblivious to our surroundings. I felt the hooks of my bra spring open, as Jock deftly undid them with his left hand. A little voice in my head kept telling me to stop, get out of the car, run! But it was drowned out by a louder, more persistent voice which said Yes! Yes! Touch me, kiss me, tell me you love me!

I felt his hand sliding up my legs, his fingers struggling to probe my vagina. I groaned and thrust my hips towards him, all the while knowing I should stop before it was too late. But I was no longer in control of my body. My body was in control of me.

I wondered if this was 'making love', but how could it be? I didn't feel any love for this stranger, just an animal lust. Jock slipped my knickers off and I felt the cool leather upholstery against my hot flesh. I heard the rattling of his belt buckle as he struggled to undo his fly, releasing his swollen penis from his skin tight jeans.

I saw a flash of light. There was a rapping on the window.

"Oh shit," Jock gasped, fighting to get his penis back inside his pants. A flashlight beam shone across us.

"Police! Open up! What's going on here?"

A bleary eyed Nurse opened the door. The police had called ahead to say they were bringing us home. She stood rigid as Kathy and I slithered into the house, followed by two police officers. She listened straight-faced as the police officer explained where they'd found us - me in particular. I could tell from Nurse's expression that this was beyond a childhood prank. This was serious.

I wanted to tell her that nothing had happened, that we were only kissing, but I didn't dare speak. I hoped Thomas wouldn't find out about this. It would break his heart.

I awoke next morning with a start, the memories of the night before flooding over me. I pulled the covers over my head, ashamed to face the light of day. I didn't understand what I had done or why I had done it. I remembered the cold, distant look in Nurse's eyes and wondered how I could ever face her again.

My bedroom door opened abruptly. Aunty Dawn stood over my bed. She pulled the bedcovers back.

"Time to get up," she said, a look of pure disdain on her face.

"I'm not hungry," I said, trying to pull the covers back over me. "I don't want any breakfast today."

"Get up anyway," she said, then spun on her heel and left the room.

Breakfast was eaten in silence. As soon as I was able, I excused myself from the table. I said I was going to get ready for church. I heard Aunty Dawn scoff. Anger burbled up through my shame. They had no right to treat me like this. I hadn't done anything wrong, or so I told myself. I was just kissing some fellow in the backseat of his car. Big hairy deal. I could have stopped him, and would have, if the police hadn't come along. We were just having some fun. Except it hadn't been much fun. And now Nurse and Aunty Dawn seemed to think I was some sort of low life form. I had crossed some invisible threshold and shattered any good opinion they ever had of me. I had been judged and found to be lacking, and there was nothing I could do about it now. Well to hell with them. They could keep their opinions to themselves. I told myself I didn't care what they thought of me anymore. But I did. I cared more than they would ever know.

I hated them for treating me this way, but mostly I hated myself for giving them reason. I wanted to break down in tears, run to Nurse and tell her how sorry I was to have let her down, but my shame was too great and her disappointment too palpable to overcome. Instead I held my head high and pretended I didn't care, because to care would hurt too much.

When I got home from church Thomas was already there. I could tell from the expression on his face that Nurse had filled him in on the previous night's activities. He looked like he'd been crying. He suggested we go for a walk before lunch.

"Why d'you do it?" he asked, as soon as we were out of earshot of Willowrey.

I shrugged, unable to speak. I was bracing myself for the 'of course you realize we can't go out together anymore' part of his speech. Heck, I didn't even want to go out with me anymore, so I couldn't blame him. I obviously wasn't worthy of his love and affection. He was a good boy, from a good home. I was a bad girl, from a bad home. They were the cards we'd been dealt.

"What were you thinking to do something like that? Anything could have happened."

"Well nothing did," I said defensively.

"That's not what I heard."

"Well you heard wrong. We were only kissing and I would have stopped him before he went any further."

"Maybe that's what you think but once a man gets that far, it's pretty hard to stop him going further. He could have raped you and there'd be nothing you could have done about it. You only weigh seven stone, soaking wet. How do you think you could stop a grown man from doing what he wanted to do, once things have gone that far?"

I remembered how I'd been unable to stop my father from doing what he wanted to do. I shuddered, secretly relieved that the police had intervened. In the cold light of day the prospect of having sex with a stranger no longer seemed so thrilling. I didn't understand why my body had betrayed me so, with its eagerness to be touched and caressed. And now everyone hated me for it and I didn't know what I could do to right the wrong I had committed. I was consumed with self hate and loathing.

"I don't know what the big deal is anyway," I retorted. "It's not as if I was a virgin or anything."

Thomas looked at me with tears in his eyes.

"Just because you're not a virgin doesn't mean you have to behave like that."

"Well I did, and there's nothing I can do to change it, so if you don't want to go out with me anymore, I don't blame you."

Thomas looked shocked.

"I love you, Gail, and I still want to go out with you. But I need you to promise that you'll never, ever, do anything like this ever again."

When I got home from school next day, Miss Stinson's car was in the driveway. She had obviously been summoned by Nurse.

"I hear you've been up to no good," she said, as soon as we were alone together in Nurse's office. "Do you want to tell me about it?" Her tone wasn't angry or judgmental, just curious, in a tired sort of way, like she wasn't really surprised.

I let down my guard a little. It was exhausting keeping up the façade of not caring what Nurse and the others thought.

"Kathy and I decided to go to Nestleton to see what was going on there and these two blokes offered us a ride home, but on the way we parked for a while and now everyone's treating me like the biggest slut this side of Bristol."

Tears sprang to my eyes and trickled down my cheeks. I wiped them away with the back of my hand.

"I don't believe anyone thinks you're a slut, Gail, but you must surely realize how upset and disappointed other people are at your behaviour."

"But what's it to them? We were only kissing. I wouldn't have let it go any further."

"You may think that but in reality you were in a situation you had little or no control over. Anything could have happened. You could have been raped and left for dead on the side of the road."

"Maybe that would have saved everyone a lot of trouble," I retorted.

Miss Stinson ignored my comment.

"If you remember, Gail, your curfew was extended last year because you felt you weren't allowed out as much as your friends. And now you've abused that by sneaking out your bedroom window in the dead of night. Do you think your friends are allowed out until after midnight?"

I shrugged, reluctant to admit that they probably weren't.

"But everybody hates me now. It's so unfair!" I broke down in tears.

Miss Stinson waited for me to regain my composure.

"I don't believe anyone hates you, Gail, but at the same time we're all struggling to understand why you behaved this way."

I wished I could tell them why, but I didn't understand it myself.

"Nurse and Aunty Dawn have hardly spoken to me since it happened. What about Kathy? She did it too."

"No one's excusing Kathy's part in all this but you're only fifteen. She's seventeen. In your case it would have been a criminal offence for that young man to have sex with a minor."

"We didn't have sex," I yelled in frustration, "we were only necking!"

"In all likelihood it was just a matter of time. The police told

Nurse that if they hadn't intervened it was obvious that intercourse would have taken place."

I slumped back in my seat, deflated. But I got a grim satisfaction from them calling it 'intercourse'. It sounded so clinical it couldn't possibly be mistaken for making love.

"We'll talk about it some more later. I'm sure the Children's Committee will take a very dim view of this turn of events and will undoubtedly want to take steps to ensure it doesn't happen again. I'll be back to see you next month, after they've met. In the meantime, try to behave yourself."

In the days and weeks that followed, I felt like a pariah at Willowrey. Aunty Dawn's lips became permanently puckered and she looked at me as if I was a stranger. Nurse's pale blue eyes looked cold and distant, the usual twinkle gone. I so much needed them to tell me it was alright, that they still cared for me and wanted to keep me safe. But they said nothing. And nor did I. I couldn't find the words to tell them how badly I felt, how deep my shame went, or how cruel my self hatred was. So I masked it all in a veil of arrogant nonchalance. A line was drawn in the sand, our trenches too deep and too far apart to negotiate from. I hurled snide remarks and angry retorts across the wasteland of our existence. They retaliated with enforced rules and denied favours.

Only Thomas seemed to understand and be able to find it in his heart to forgive me. I clung to him like the rock he was. Aunty Dawn told me I didn't deserve him. Nurse told me I should thank my lucky stars that I had found someone as good as Thomas. Men like him didn't come along very often.

But our days together were numbered as Thomas would be leaving for university in September. I promised to wait for him. He promised to be true to me. We talked about love and passion and how it would be when we were older. We dreamed of nights spent making love and living happily ever after. Thomas told me he read about a man who had died in the act of making love, at the very moment of orgasm. He said it seemed like the perfect way to die. I wasn't so sure. Sex had never brought me anything but trouble.

"But it needn't be like that," Thomas protested, "in the right time and place it's beautiful."

I thought about this for a few moments.

"Perhaps if we made love I would understand how beautiful it can be."

Thomas laughed nervously, sensing there was more to my words than idle chatter. We walked on in silence, each lost in our own thoughts. After a while he spoke.

"My parents are going to be away this weekend so perhaps, you know, it might be possible to, kinda, you know," his voice trailed away. He pushed his hands deep into his jacket pockets and kicked a pebble across the pavement. I felt a stirring in my belly.

"You mean?"

"Well, only if you really want to."

I nodded, slowly. "Yes, I think I do."

Thomas reached out and took my hand. "I'll have to get some rubbers. The last thing we need is for you to get pregnant."

On Saturday Thomas picked me up shortly after lunch. I told Aunty Dawn I would be having my tea at Thomas' place so wouldn't be home. I didn't mention that his parents weren't going to be there. She reminded me of my ten o'clock curfew.

"How could I forget that?" I said as I ran out to meet Thomas, slamming the door behind me.

We spent the afternoon exploring Dartmoor before heading back to Thomas' place. I sat and watched television while Thomas tended the bar in his father's absence. Shortly after seven Thomas joined me. We told the babysitter we were going out for a walk. But we only walked as far as the rear entrance of the hotel, before slipping back inside and scurrying up the rear stairwell to the guest rooms. Thomas had a list of vacant rooms and the master key.

The first door he opened had two twin beds. That wouldn't do at all. We tiptoed down the hall, to the next vacant room. But it was being redecorated and the bed was covered with a plastic tarp. Thomas signaled for me to follow him up the stairs to the third floor. There, nestled under the eaves, was a vacant room with a double bed. We slipped inside, locking the door behind us. Thomas flicked the light on and we stood there, too shy to actually look at each other.

We'd been dating for over a year but suddenly felt like strangers. I went and looked out the window. Thomas sat on the bed and patted the space beside him.

"Why don't you come and sit down," he said gently.

"I was just looking at all the people down there. They look so small from up here."

Thomas came and stood beside me, putting his arm around my waist.

"I don't get to go up this high very often," I explained, "it's neat to be able to look down and watch everything. It's like being a bird."

We watched in silence for a few minutes.

"We don't have to do this if you don't want to," Thomas said, "it was kinda your idea and I really don't want to force myself on you."

"No it's alright, really. It's just that it seems so strange, being alone in a bedroom with you like this. It's so, how can I say it, premeditated. I don't know what to do or where to begin."

Thomas pulled me close and kissed me slowly, gently, making me lightheaded with anticipation.

"How 'bout we start here," he said, taking my hand and leading me towards the bed.

We lay on the bed and kissed some more, slowly at first, exploring each other's bodies and reveling in the joy of being alone together. Our breathing quickened as we groped and squirmed and wrapped ourselves around each other. Pieces of clothing began falling to the floor like autumn leaves and soon we were naked under the bedclothes. Thomas pulled away slightly, propping himself up on one elbow. I opened my eyes.

"Are you totally sure about this?" he asked, his voice heavy with lust.

"Yes, I am," I said, burying my face in his chest. His nakedness was beautiful. He kissed the top of my head, then reached for the package he'd put on the bedside table. I pretended not to look as he fumbled with the box of condoms, struggling to get the cellophane wrapper off. He pulled out a chain of foil wrapped condoms and tore one off. He opened the foil, exposing the slippery rubber contents. His hands were shaking as he tried to pull the condom over his erect penis. The room was growing dark and it was hard to see. He put the condom on inside out, making it impossible to unroll along the erect shaft of his penis. He pulled it off, embarrassed, and put it on the right way, before sliding back under the covers.

In the growing darkness of that little room tucked up under the eaves, Thomas and I made love. It was beautiful but there were no fireworks, no drum rolls, no screaming orgasms, like I'd expected. I was too tense and Thomas too inexperienced.

"These things take time," Thomas reassured me later, as I sat on the edge of the bed getting dressed.

"I guess, but I don't see what all the fuss is about, do you?" I asked.

I had somehow thought it would be different. And it was different, in a way. This time I'd been an eager participant, not a frightened child. But I'd been looking for more, some hidden mystique, some holy grail that would help me make sense of this madness we call life. I wanted to understand how sex could drive a woman to abandon her children for the man she loved, or how it could drive a man to drag his daughter out of bed in the dead of night to have sex with her. But I understood it less now than I had before.

Thomas and I slipped out of the hotel and went for a walk along the beach. I needed to get my thoughts together before going home. Thomas was grinning like a Cheshire cat. I told him everyone would know what we'd been doing if he was going to walk around looking like that.

Aunty Dawn was waiting up for me when I got home. For once I was a few minutes early. I thanked her for waiting up.

"Just doing my job," she said, tight lipped.

"I know," I said, "but thanks anyway."

I was tired of fighting. Perhaps those beatniks were right, the world would be a better place if we made love, not war.

CHAPTER ELEVEN

The chill at Willowrey continued unabated despite my insipid attempts at reconciliation. I just wanted to forget the whole ugly incident of the young man in the car but Nurse and Aunty Dawn remained distant, waiting for an apology. But how could I apologize? How could I undo what I had done? Sure, I could say I was sorry, but it would seem so trite. Of course I was sorry. Of course I wish it hadn't happened the way it had, but all the apologies in the world wouldn't change that. So what was the point in apologizing?

Nurse told me I hadn't heard the end of this incident, that the Children's Committee would be discussing the issue at their next meeting. I told her it was a pity these people had nothing better to talk about than my non-existent sex life. She told me to watch my manners and sent me to my room for the evening. I used the time to write to my mother and tell her how unbearable life was becoming in Willowrey. I overlooked mentioning why.

When I arrived home on the last day of school, a tradesman's van was pulling out of the driveway and nearly ran me over.

"Jerk," I yelled, as I jumped to avoid him. The driver scowled at me and rolled his eyes as if to say 'what can you expect from a place like this?' I gave him the finger and went in the house. I plopped my overstuffed satchel in the hallway, then went to the kitchen to check out what was for tea. I was starving and ready to eat a horse. Aunty

Dawn and Aunty Bridget were in the kitchen chatting and preparing the meal. They stopped talking abruptly when they saw me.

"Where's Nurse," I asked.

"She's off until Monday," Aunty Dawn said.

"Oh right, I forgot this was her weekend off," I said, rummaging in the fruit basket for something to eat. "Just think, I'm off till September. No more school, no more homework, no more exams, just six glorious weeks of summer hols. This is going to be my best summer ever."

Aunty Dawn shot Aunty Bridget a knowing look, but didn't say anything. I wondered what they were up to but was too excited about my summer plans to pay them much attention. I took an apple and went upstairs to change out of my school uniform.

It took a second or two to register that something wasn't quite right. The furniture was still the same, my things were where I'd left them, but something wasn't right. It was hot in the room. I pulled back the curtains to open the window and stopped dead in my tracks. I couldn't believe what I was seeing. There were bars on my window. They'd put bars on my window! My bedroom had become a prison cell. I had become a prisoner. I rushed at the bars and grabbed them with both hands and shook them as hard as I could. They wouldn't budge. I yanked harder and harder, grunting like a caged animal. It felt like my arms would pop out of their sockets but still I wrenched on the bars. A stream of obscenities gushed from my lips, punctuated by blood curdling screams.

I ran to the top of the stairs, hysterical, my breath coming in sharp gasps.

"You put bars on my window!" I screamed down at Aunty Dawn. "You fucking cow! I hate you! You can't do this to me. You can't make me stay here."

I ran back to my room, slamming the door so hard a picture fell off the wall and smashed on the linoleum floor. The sound of tinkling glass heightened my hysteria. I turned and swiped all the bottles and jars off my dresser, staring like a madman at the splintered shards of glass. I lunged at the bars again, hanging on like a monkey as I kicked at them with my feet. I felt hands pulling me off. I was hyperventilating and felt dizzy as my body went limp. The hysteria had exhausted all my strength. Aunty Dawn and Aunty Bridget put me on my bed where I curled up in a ball and sobbed.

"What did you expect?" Aunty Dawn asked, her voice cold, "We have to keep you safe."

When Miss Stinson came to see me a few days later, I told her I refused to stay at Willowrey a minute longer.

"I hate this place," I told her, "and you can't make me stay here."

"Where do you think you could go?" Miss Stinson asked. I wasn't sure if she was toying with me, or if leaving really was an option.

"I dunno, but any place is better than this hell hole. It's worse than being in prison. At least in prison you're there because you committed some crime. I haven't broken any laws."

"No one says you have, Gail, although you were very close in that young man's car. The fact is we need to keep you safe. We can't have you wandering around town at all hours of the night like you seem to like to do. It isn't the first time you've snuck out at night. It's only a matter of time before something really terrible happens to you out there. It's our responsibility to make sure it doesn't. We'll do whatever it takes to protect you, from yourself as much as anyone else it seems."

I just sat there feeling sorry for myself and wishing with all my heart that I could live with my mum and dad in a regular house, like a regular family. Miss Stinson seemed to read my thoughts.

"You just have to deal with the reality of your situation, Gail, and make the best of it. It's just the luck of the draw which parents we get and unfortunately yours weren't able to do very well by you. But you're here now and you have every opportunity to make the most of your life. Willowrey has provided you with a good home where you can focus your energies on your schooling. You must remember how difficult it was for you in Riverton and how poorly you were doing in school as a result of your home life. At least here you don't have those issues to worry about. A lot of people are putting a lot of time and energy into trying to make life good for you. You're being given every opportunity we can offer, to give you a good start in life."

I grudgingly admitted to myself that Miss Stinson was right. I was better off here. Or at least I had been, before they turned my room into a prison cell.

"But it's so unfair," I protested. "Now that I've blotted my copy book, I've been branded as a slut by Nurse and Aunty Dawn. I can see it in their eyes when they look at me. I guess once you break a vase you can always see the crack, no matter how carefully you glue it back together again. I'll always have that crack as far as they're concerned."

"Can I see the bars on your window?" Miss Stinson asked.

"I suppose so. My cell is the one at the end of the hall," I said, standing to lead the way.

"Well, they certainly are ugly," Miss Stinson agreed when she saw them, "but perhaps there's something you can do to cover them up in some way."

I scoffed. "Like what? Paint pretty flowers on them?"

"Maybe hang a trailing plant in the window, or put some net curtains up. The unfortunate reality is that you have to learn to live with them, so you may as well make the best of it."

If only I could do that. I just had to get through this summer and one more school year and then my 'O' levels would be done.

That summer I managed to get myself a job at the Woolworth's store in Nestleton - the very same store I'd so freely shoplifted from the year before. I was a sales girl and got paid a guinea a day. I used most of the money to buy fabric. The fashion scene was exploding and I wanted to be part of it. I became a devotee of 'mod' fashions, mimicking Mary Quant and Twiggy every chance I got. Although the Children's Committee provided me with clothing it was just the basics, nothing more. I made the rest.

Life at Willowrey continued to be a battle field throughout that summer. The bars on my bedroom window were a constant reminder of where I was. Every time I looked at them salt was rubbed in a wound, a wound that went so deep I could barely discern its origin. Any pretext of a normal home life had been shattered by those bars. Willowrey was an institution and I was an inmate. If they were reacting like this about a necking session in a car, how would they react if they knew what Thomas and I had done? But I didn't care what they thought anymore. I obviously couldn't live up to their standards. Riverton was too ingrained in me.

Nurse said I was getting out of control, but I didn't care. I was locked in a battle of wills and to surrender would mean the death of my spirit, the very essence of me. Nurse was the face of the Children's Committee's and she bore the brunt of my anger. I vented my rage on her without mercy, refusing to acknowledge my role in the whole affair. I hurled insults and rude remarks at her every chance I got, taunting her to distraction.

During a heated exchange one day I called her an old witch, before running up the stairs as fast as I could. I heard her chasing after me. I stopped on the top landing and spun around to face her, prepared to do battle. Nurse stopped on the center landing and we stood there staring at each other, wondering who was going to make the first move. Much to my surprise Nurse chuckled.

"Maybe I am an old witch," she said, shaking her head, "but I'm too old of a witch to be chasing after the likes of you."

And she turned and went back down the stairs.

I could hear the clattering of dishes and bantering back and forth in the kitchen, as the other girls cleaned up after tea. I wished I knew how to be included. I was getting battle weary but didn't know how to call a truce.

"Perhaps if you weren't so rude to them, they would be nicer to you," Thomas said when I complained to him.

"But how can I be nice to them when I know they hate me!" I retorted indignantly.

"Nurse doesn't hate you. She just hates the way you're carrying on these days. You behave like a caged animal half the time you're there."

"Shit, they put bars on my bedroom window. Of course I act like a caged animal. Wouldn't you?"

"Perhaps if you weren't so defiant, so head strong, it wouldn't be like this. Nurse is only human you know. Even a mother would have trouble putting up with your outbursts."

I laughed.

"What's so funny?" Thomas asked.

"My mother is the queen of temper tantrums. I grew up in a

house where dishes were thrown around on a regular basis. I learnt from an early age to keep clear of 'poor Peggy' when she was having a tantrum. I wouldn't dare talk back to her like that. She'd kill me."

"Perhaps that's the problem," Thomas offered. "Nurse is too nice to you. You wouldn't talk to her the way you do if you thought she was going to hit you around the way your own mother did, would you?"

"She doesn't care enough about me to even touch me anymore. She'd never slap me."

"Then perhaps you should count your blessings," Thomas suggested.

I began to fret about Thomas' departure for university in September, which was fast approaching. How would I manage without him? He was my confidant, my friend and, occasionally, my lover. But most of all he believed in me. He saw something in me that I couldn't see in myself and I secretly marveled at his undying patience and understanding. At school, my sharp tongue and sarcastic retorts often got me into trouble and I was glad of the protection that dating a sixth former gave me. I learned to bend the rules to breaking point and would have gone further if Thomas hadn't been there, pulling me back from the edge of the abyss of my not caring. I feared I might fall in once he was gone.

Thomas came to see me the night before he left for university. He gave me a white teddybear to keep me company while he was away. We kissed and hugged and promised to write every day. Thomas said he would come home on weekends as often as possible. I said that would be nice, but secretly doubted it would last for long. I had said goodbye to too many people already and knew from experience that in time they simply fade away. The visits become less frequent and the letters become shorter until they are just a vague memory. That night I fell asleep hugging the teddy bear Thomas had given me. At least teddy bears never went away, unless you wanted them to.

I started fifth form like a marathon runner entering the home stretch. Thomas, true to his word, came home for several weekends in a row before begging off one weekend to swot for a mid term exam. My school friend, Amy, invited me to a party at her place that same weekend.

When I got to Amy's there were several people there already. Her parents had gone out and wouldn't be home until late. We sat around the living room with the lights down low and the music up high. There was a tall blond man standing in the doorway talking to Shelagh, another friend of mine from school. He was smoking a Disque Bleu cigarette and the thick sweet smoke curled up towards the ceiling.

"Who's that?" I asked Wendy, nodding in the direction of the doorway.

"He's a friend of Shelagh's brother. I think his name is Anthony Vanderhof. He just moved here from London."

"I thought he looked a little different from the regular Devonshire country bumpkins," I said.

As the evening wore on more and more people arrived, until there was hardly room to stand in the living room. The party was really starting to hop when I realized I would have to run for the bus if I was going to make it home in time for my curfew. I went in search of Amy, to say goodbye. I found her talking to Anthony in the kitchen.

"Thanks for inviting me," I said, interrupting them, "but I have to go or I'll miss my bus."

"Do you really have to go so soon," Amy asked, "things are just beginning to get going?"

"I know," I groaned, "but it can't be helped. I'm already in enough trouble at home, without getting into any more."

"I'll walk you to the bus stop," Anthony offered, "Its dark out." He turned to Amy, "I'll be back in a bit."

"Thank you," I said, somewhat surprised at the offer, "but we'll have to hurry."

We grabbed our jackets and headed for the door. Anthony wound a long navy blue and yellow striped scarf around his neck, casually flipping the long tail over his left shoulder. He seemed very sophisticated and I was flattered that he would leave the party to walk me to the bus.

"Wendy says you just moved here from London," I said, as we walked to the bus stop. "I'd love to live there. What's it like?"

"Big, noisy, and dirty."

"But isn't it fun, being in the thick of the music scene there and all those great shops. Devon is so behind the times."

"Well my dad's firm relocated here so I didn't have much choice, but I really like Devon. In fact, I'm getting to like it more and more," he said, smiling at me.

"Oh shit, there's my bus," I cried and started running the last few yards to the stop.

"Thanks for walking with me," I called over my shoulder. "Have fun at the party."

When I got to school on Monday, Shelagh was all atwitter.

"Anthony asked for your phone number," she told me, as we sorted our books for the first class, "but I didn't give it to him in case you didn't want me to."

"Anthony?" I asked, "You mean that fellow I met at Amy's?"

"Yes, silly, of course I mean him. How many other Anthony's do you know?"

"Gosh," I said, suddenly flustered, "I can't imagine he's interested in me. He seems so, you know, groovy and cool. I feel like a country bumpkin beside him."

"Well I'm not saying he wants to marry you, he just wanted your phone number. Maybe go to the pictures or something like that."

"I dunno," I told her, feeling sudden pangs of guilt about Thomas, "I already have a boyfriend. I don't think Thomas would like it very much if I went out with someone else while he's away."

"Well I don't suppose Thomas is sitting home alone every night while he's at university, do you?"

I hadn't really thought about it but I had to admit it was unlikely. The bell rang, signaling the start of classes.

"I've got geography first period," I called out to her, "I'll see you at break."

As I sat in the classroom pouring over maps of Asia, I began to wonder what Thomas did do with his spare time. He couldn't be studying twenty four hours a day, surely? I wasn't jealous, just curious. I thought I ought to be jealous, if what I read in magazines was true, but I wasn't. At break I gave my phone number to Shelagh. Two days later Anthony called.

"There's a young man on the telephone, asking to speak to you, Gail" Nurse said when she found me in the dining room studying. "He says his name is Anthony."

"Hello," Anthony said when I picked up the phone. "I was wondering if we could continue our conversation of the other night. D'you wanna go for a walk this evening?"

I could think of nothing I'd enjoy more at that particularly moment, but told him I couldn't go. I didn't bother explaining that I lived in a children's home and wasn't allowed out on Wednesdays, or that I already had a boyfriend even though he lived miles away, or that I was studying really hard so I'd pass my 'O' levels and maybe have a life one day. He said he'd call back another time.

The following weekend Thomas begged off coming to Devon again. He said he was strapped for cash and didn't have the train fare. It seemed so familiar – the waiting for someone to visit; the last minute excuses about why they couldn't make it; and the inevitable disappointment. It was too much like waiting for my parents to visit. That same weekend Anthony rang again. This time he invited me to the pictures. I said I'd love to go.

He picked me up on his Lambretta scooter and we headed towards Torquay. Anthony was very tall, with long straight hair that flopped persistently into his eyes as he looked down from his six foot height to talk to me. His lips were full, almost pouty, and he wore dark, horn-rimmed glasses. He told me he had gone to school with two members of the Kinks rock group. I thought he was the coolest person I had ever met. He offered me a Disque Bleu cigarette which I accepted, anxious to show that I was just as sophisticated as those London girls.

After the film we walked along the streets of Torquay looking in shop windows. Anthony put his arm around my shoulder. He felt me shivering and offered his scarf to keep me warm. I wound it around my neck, wallowing in the intoxicating scent of Disque Bleu cigarettes mingled with Brut aftershave. I inhaled the essence of Anthony. I was in love.

When Thomas came home the following weekend I told him I'd met someone else. I said I didn't want to see him anymore. I didn't think he'd care that much, now that he had a life of his own at university. But I was mistaken, and the depth of his pain took me aback. No one had ever cared about losing me before; it was always the other way around. I couldn't understand his anguish. He phoned me several times and even dropped by Willowrey once, to solicit Nurse's help in making me see reason, but I was resolute and stood my ground. I didn't want a part time relationship with yet another person who lived far away. Next time Anthony telephoned the house Nurse made a point of telling him that I was only fifteen and tried to warn him off.

"But I'm only seventeen," Anthony told her, somewhat confused. "Gail said her last boyfriend was nineteen so I don't understand what the problem is."

"Just so you know," was all Nurse said.

I wrote to my mother telling her all about my new boyfriend and grumbling as usual about the unfairness of life at Willowrey. Mum wrote back suggesting I run away to her place in Manchester. She said she wouldn't tell anyone I was there, at least not for a few days. I shook my head in disbelief as I read these words, wondering who the adult was in this relationship. Mum went on to say she was coming to Devon soon to make arrangements for Jane to come and live with her again. I tried not to care.

Anthony and I spent every moment we could together. If we couldn't afford to go out we'd go back to Anthony's home and listen to Jacques Loussier playing Bach on the record player in his room. His mother always brought tea and biscuits up to his room shortly after eight o'clock, anxious for an excuse to come and check up on us. One evening we were so engrossed in kissing that we didn't hear her footsteps coming up the stairs. When she opened the door she found us on the bed. She was not amused.

"I'd like a word with you downstairs," she said to Anthony, as she placed the tray on his dresser and cast me a disparaging look.

She told Anthony we weren't to lie on the bed together. When he said we were only kissing she said that didn't matter. Kissing could lead to all sorts of other things. There were chairs in his room for sitting on and we were expected to use them.

I was embarrassed at being caught kissing Anthony, but mostly I was devastated by that look in his mother's eyes. It was the same look Nurse had given me when I was found in the car with the man from Liverpool. That look that said more than words alone could say. It conveyed disapproval. It made me feel dirty and cheap. It told me I had been judged and found to be lacking in some moral fiber I knew nothing about. It was as if I had broken some unspoken rule that everyone else was aware of but I had somehow failed to learn. That page was missing from my text book on life. I had been absent from that class on social acceptability. I had no sense of self to shield me from the disapproving looks of protective parents. I couldn't separate who I was from what I did. If I did something bad then obviously I was a bad person. And I didn't like feeling like a bad person. Next time Anthony invited me to his home, I suggested we go for a walk instead.

Tensions at Willowrey had escalated to breaking point. Miss Stinson was summoned to come and talk to me, yet again, in the hopes that she could get me to realize just how unpleasant things were for everyone concerned.

"You have to know that everyone's patience is just about at an end with you, Gail," Miss Stinson said as soon as we were alone.

"What else is new?" I asked. "I hope you haven't come all this way just to tell me that."

"Christmas is only a month away. I think it's a good idea for everyone concerned if you make plans to visit your mother for the holidays. You need a break to help end this standoff between you and the other people here."

My heart sank. Was I really that bad? Was I being thrown out?

After Miss Stinson's visit, I began to worry about where my future lay. My days at Willowrey seemed to be numbered and as much as I couldn't wait to get out of there, I had no real plans for my future. Mum seemed to be expecting me to go and live with her when I finished school but I secretly dreaded it. I didn't think she could keep me safe like Nurse and Miss Stinson and the Children's Committee did. As much as I hated their intervention, deep down I realized I needed their protection - from myself as much as anyone. I had a wild streak in me fuelled by hurt and anger and a searing anguish which threatened to consume me.

I felt very alone and frightened for my future.

CHAPTER TWELVE

The house on Sun Street looked somewhat more inviting when I arrived a few days before Christmas. Mum had put up some pictures in the dining room and installed an electric fireplace which flickered like a real fire, casting a cozy glow. On the mantle there was a jam jar full of shilling coins, ready to feed the electric meter which had a ferocious appetite when the electric fire was on.

We saw very little of Norman. He worked most nights until the early hours of the morning and then slept till one or two in the afternoon. But when he was there he always had a joke to tell. Except Mum didn't laugh at his jokes much anymore; she'd heard them too many times already it seems.

"I hope you at least have Christmas Day off," Mum snapped one afternoon, as Norman was getting ready to go to work for the tenth night in a row. "It's no fun sitting home alone night after night while you're out playing."

"Don't you start in again," Norman retorted. "You know I have to grab these extra jobs while I can. There won't be much work around in January."

Norman went upstairs to change into his band clothes. Mum followed him. I could hear them arguing upstairs, their voices rising above the noise of the television. I turned up the volume and pulled

Jane close. Some things never change, I realized. I wondered how long it would be before Mum started throwing things around.

"I miss my real Daddy," Jane said.

"I expect you do, sweetheart," I said, smoothing her hair. "I miss him too sometimes."

I was meant to stay in Manchester until after New Year's but once the excitement of Christmas was over I became restless. Things obviously weren't perfect in paradise and I was anxious to get back to my own banana tree. Mum and Norman had frequent spats and Mum seemed torn between Norman and Jane. I felt I was just in the way.

I telephoned Anthony on Boxing Day and told him I was missing him. He suggested I come home early and spend the New Years' Eve weekend at his place. He was sure his parents wouldn't mind. I wasn't so sure about Nurse but decided to risk it. Miss Stinson had told me that everyone at Willowrey needed a break from me over Christmas as I was so hard to handle. I hoped I'd been away long enough for them to get over me. It was a chance I was prepared to take.

I left Manchester on December 30, amid hugs and kisses and accusations. Mum was miffed that I wouldn't be there for New Years Eve. She grumbled all the way to the station about how difficult and expensive it was going to be to find a babysitter at this late date. She'd already made plans to go to the club with Norman, thinking I would be there to look after Jane.

Before leaving Manchester I had telephoned Willowrey to let them know I would be arriving in Nestleton that afternoon. They weren't overly happy about that piece of news. I had also called Anthony and arranged for him to pick me up at the station. I was no sooner in the door of Willowrey when Nurse started chastising me about changing my plans at the last minute.

"Anthony invited me to his place for the weekend," I said. "I wasn't having much fun in Manchester, listening to my mother and Norman fighting all the time, so I thought I'd go to Anthony's instead. Miss Stinson said you needed a break from me and didn't much seem to mind where I went, as long as I went somewhere. So now I'm going to Anthony's."

"I don't think so, young lady," Nurse said. "I can't let you just waltz off to Anthony's for the weekend. We don't know anything about his family and precious little about him."

"That's not true," I protested. "You've seen Anthony loads of times. You've even met Mr. Vanderhof too, when he and Anthony come to pick me up in the car."

"Saying 'hello' to someone hardly constitutes getting to know them," Nurse retorted.

"But they're expecting me. I've come home especially. You can't do this to me."

"If you ask me, I'd say you were doing it to yourself. Arrangements were made for you to stay with your mother for New Years. Now just because you've changed your mind doesn't mean the rest of the world has to jump."

"But I was miserable in Manchester," I wailed, "I didn't want to go there in the first place only I was told I had to. I don't get you people."

I stormed upstairs to my room, slamming the door behind me. Welcome home, Gail! I lay on my bed staring at the bars on my window, feeling totally hard done by and sorry for myself. I couldn't wait to finish school and get out of here. I'd get a job earning gobs of money and live in my very own flat and never, ever, have to ask anyone's permission to do anything ever again. Only another six months until I sat my "O" levels, and then just two more years until I turned eighteen. Then I would be completely free of these people. No more Nurse, or Miss Stinson or the Children's Committee telling me what I could and couldn't do.

Nurse wrote a letter to Anthony's parents explaining that I wouldn't be able to spend the weekend at their place. She said such a visit might be possible in the future once she or Miss Stinson had had an opportunity to meet them. I hoped the Vanderhofs wouldn't be offended by the tone of Nurse's letter. Anthony's father was a senior executive in the new electronics factory close by and I was sure he wouldn't take kindly to being treated as riff raff.

Three days later Miss Stinson came to Willowrey to see me. She too was frustrated with me for thinking I could make and change plans at the drop of a hat.

"You seem to have no consideration for the amount of work involved for other people when you make these plans."

"I don't see why everybody has to make such a fuss about everything," I grumbled. "The Vanderhofs are respectable people, they aren't criminals or anything. The way you're all carrying on about having to make sure they're okay it's a wonder they even want me there anymore. It's so embarrassing."

"Be that as it may, you know how the system works so you might as well accept it. I've already made arrangements to visit the Vanderhofs later this afternoon, so if you're invited again we can consider allowing you to go."

I didn't know whether to be annoyed or comforted by the care and attention being lavished on me. Mostly I just saw it as an intrusion on my freedom.

"I'll come back at tea time and let you know how the visit went."

When Miss Stinson returned she said she had had a very good visit with Anthony's parents.

"They have a very nice home and seem like intelligent, home loving people," Miss Stinson told Nurse over tea.

I could have told them that.

"Mrs. Vanderhof said Gail is quite shy around them, although she seems to have relaxed a little lately. They seemed to think you were sixteen, not fifteen," Miss Stinson added, looking directly at me.

I shrugged but said nothing. I couldn't help what people thought, could I?

"I explained to them that you are a ward of the court and told them about Willowrey and what type of place it is," Miss Stinson continued.

I groaned and dropped my teaspoon noisily onto my plate. I had tried so hard to appear 'normal' to Anthony's family and now Miss Stinson had gone and blabbed the whole story to them.

"I really liked Mrs. Vanderhof," Miss Stinson continued, ignoring my groans of embarrassment, "and I'd be happy for Gail to spend a week-end with them, should she be invited again. Mrs. Vanderhof said next time she would send a written invitation directly to you, Nurse."

After tea Miss Stinson and I went to the games room, where we could be alone and talk. I was feeling quite relaxed now the ordeal of Miss Stinson visiting Anthony's parents was over, especially as it seemed to have gone so well. I tucked my feet up under me and settled down for a good chat.

"And how are things going with you and Anthony?" Miss Stinson asked.

"Just fab," I gushed, blushing slightly. "He's so much more sophisticated than the boys at school. He has a Lambretta scooter and he's a real Mod. I'm a Mod too now. All my friends think I look just like Twiggy. They say I should go into modeling when I finish school," I added whimsically.

"I don't know about that," Miss Stinson said, "but you should probably give some thought to what you're going to do when you finish your 'O' levels."

"I've actually been thinking of going to the Technical College in Torquay. They have business courses there and I could learn to be a secretary. They have a regular or an advanced course. It depends on how many 'O' levels I get. I need five to get into the advanced course, which is what I'm hoping for. That way I can study for my "A" levels at the same time."

"Have you given any thought to university? With your marks you shouldn't have any problem getting in."

"No, not really. I don't think that's an option for me. I have to learn to look after myself and the sooner the better. The secretarial course at Torquay will only take me a year to finish then I should be able to find a job and pay my own way. There are loads of secretary jobs advertised and besides, secretaries can work anywhere in the world and I want to travel a lot when I'm older."

As much as I was chomping at the bit to get out of Willowrey, I was secretly terrified. What would happen to me out there in the big wide world? Where would I live? Who would look after me once I turned eighteen? My parents? Not likely! I had to face up to the fact that I would have to take care of myself, and the sooner I did that the better. I didn't believe university offered any practical solutions for my future.

It was arranged that I would visit my grandparents during the half term break as it would be my last chance before sitting the 'O' level exams. When I bragged to my grandfather that I had a new boyfriend he didn't seem pleased. Anthony's status as a Disque-Bleu-smoking-Mod-Londoner-who-went-to-school-with-two-of-the-Kinks did nothing to increase his stature in my grandfather's eyes. Besides, he told, I should be spending my time studying, not running around chasing boys.

Life at Willowrey continued to have its ups and downs. It's not as if I didn't try to reconcile with Nurse and the others, it's just that my attempts were inconsistent, self-centered and shallow. At school I frequently commiserated with my friends about problems I was having in Willowrey and made no secret of the fact that I wanted to find somewhere else to live if I went to college.

Things reached a crisis point between Nurse and me one Saturday morning. I asked her if I could watch television after lunch as I needed a break from all my studying. When she said no, my temper exploded. Before I realized what I was doing I had jumped up from my seat, fist clenched and raised towards her face, as if to strike her. Nurse stood quickly and drew herself up to her full height, ready to defend herself. I stopped dead in my tracks and forced my hand back down.

"Don't worry, I won't hit you," I said, shocked at my own behaviour. It was one thing to wrestle the other girls to the ground, which I did with alarming frequency, but quite another to strike Nurse. I ran out of the house and all the way to the beach, across the common and along the rocky trail to Elberry Cove. I sat on the rocks, panting and sweating, too exhausted to cry. Although it was a clear sunny day the wind was cold and I soon regretted coming out without a coat. I nestled in between the rocks seeking shelter from the wind as I sat staring out over the ocean.

I felt so isolated, so alone. Why did I do the things I did? The other girls didn't fly off the handle at the drop of a hat, or say vitriolic things to each other. So why did I? My friends at school didn't wallow in self pity. So why did I? Why couldn't I be like everyone else and accept life for what it was? Why did I have to rail against everything Nurse said?

She wasn't such a bad old stick, I grudgingly admitted to myself. Perhaps if she were my real mother things would be different. Perhaps then I wouldn't have to share her with every other homeless girl who walked through the door of Willowrey. If she was my real mother she wouldn't be counting the days and weeks until I left. Would she?

When Miss Stinson next came to see me she wasted no time in expressing her concern about my ongoing rebellious behaviour. Much to her surprise, I didn't offer my usual truculent response. I knew things weren't going well for me or anyone else at Willowrey, and it was wearing me down as much as the rest of them. It wasn't easy living in a war zone.

"I try to keep out of the way as much as possible," I told Miss Stinson, "it's just that I resent people's attitudes towards me and all the petty rules in this place. You can't even put coal on the fire, or turn on the television, without asking first. It's not like we're children here. This is supposed to be a 'working girls hostel' and even though I'm still in school I'm almost the same age as the others. I'll be sixteen in a few weeks."

"It's a difficult age I have to admit," Miss Stinson said. "The transition from childhood to adulthood is often a rocky road."

Miss Stinson was in her late twenties and was one of the few adults I knew who looked like she might still remember how it was to be a teenager. It meant a lot to me that she seemed to understand me so well, and to care.

"And it's not just me," I said. "Loads of my friends are in the doldrums at the moment, what with parents and finals and wondering what to do when school is finished. We all found the recent mock exams a real strain and instead of being able to relax after exams, like we usually do, we have to just keep working even harder than before, to prepare for the real thing. And on top of that I have to worry about getting into college and where I'll live if I do go. I could take the bus from here I suppose, but I was thinking it would probably be better if I went into lodgings or a foster home some place nearer the college. They don't want me here anymore anyhow."

"You could stop fighting with everyone so much," Miss Stinson said, as if it was the simplest thing in the word to do. "Then maybe you'd feel more settled here. The way things are at the moment, Gail, I'd find it very difficult indeed to ask a foster mother or landlady to care for you. We're all very concerned, Nurse in particular, about your violent behaviour recently. I know you're under a lot of pressure but you really must try to curb these outbursts. Is there anything in particular which is upsetting you, besides your upcoming exams?"

I didn't know where to begin. It was everything. It was nothing. It was life. I clutched at a tangible straw.

"Well to start with, why does everyone have to know that this is a children's home? Whenever I get letters they're always addressed to me at 'Willowrey Children's Home' and I hate it. People think I'm orphan Annie, so then they feel sorry for me but I don't want their sympathy, I just want to be normal, like everybody else."

Miss Stinson looked at me pensively. "I believe you have a good point there, Gail. I'll pass your comments on."

She made a note in her file before looking back up at me, a frown creasing her brow.

"I was very concerned to learn that you almost attacked Nurse recently," she said, "although I must say I'm relieved to know you didn't actually strike her. What stopped you?"

"Oh I couldn't hit Nurse," I said in all sincerity, "no matter how angry I was. It just wouldn't be right."

"You must surely realize, Gail, that the difficulties you're having here at Willowrey are in large part your own doing. While you can be polite and pleasant when you want, you have an extremely ungracious manner at times. I believe your offhand way of speaking to people is often sharper than you realize. It tends to set people against you. Perhaps you could try to modify what you say, and the tone of voice you say it in. It might make your life a lot easier."

I nodded pensively as I let her words sink in.

"I suppose you have a point," I said. "Actually, my friend Wendy said something to me the other day which really surprised me. I don't remember what we were talking about, exactly, but she suddenly said 'why are you always so sarcastic' and I was totally flabbergasted by that. I had no idea I was coming across that way. I thought I was just being funny, you know, the class smart ass and all that. But they think I'm being sarcastic. I felt badly, them thinking of me that way, so I've been trying to think before I speak but half the time the words are coming out of my mouth before I can stop them."

"Well, at least you're becoming more aware of it. That's a start, I suppose. The line between humour and sarcasm is a thin one. Nobody likes to get their feelings hurt though, so you really should learn to think before you speak."

I nodded. If only life could be that easy.

"By the way," I said, thinking carefully before I spoke, "Wendy has invited me to stay at her place Saturday night. I told Nurse about it but she still hasn't said whether I can go or not. I told Wendy you were coming here this evening, so we were thinking that maybe you could go and see her parents while you're here. They're expecting you."

I felt very pleased with myself. I was finally learning to play by their rules. I realized that before I could go and spend the night anywhere, Miss Stinson had to check it out first. My pleasure was short lived.

"Unfortunately I won't be able to go and see them this evening. Perhaps if I had known in advance I could have arranged my schedule differently but as it is, I'm busy."

"But they're expecting you," I pleaded.

"Well, maybe next time you're invited, if I know in good time, I'll be able to arrange a visit. Once again you've tried to rush us into accepting something that we need time to consider. You have to learn to think about things more carefully so you'll stop being thwarted, as you seem to feel you are, by those in authority over you. We have a job to do and we're doing our best to do it well, despite what you may think."

"But I only get to see you once a month," I replied indignantly, "so how am I expected to know that far in advance that Wendy or Amy or whoever might want me to come and spend the weekend with them. Perhaps I should just give you a list of all my friends, right now, so you can go and inspect all their homes, just in case one day one of them might invite me to stay."

"I think you know you're being unreasonable, Gail, so I won't even bother responding to that. You've been in care for over three years now and you're well aware of how the system works by now. As your Child Care Officer, I'm required to make regular reports concerning you and your activities to the Children's Committee. The same goes for Nurse. She keeps the Committee informed of your day to day behaviour and any problems or issues which arise. Any decisions concerning your future or well being are made by the committee as a whole, much the same way parents would decide things about their own children."

"So, who's on this Children's Committee exactly?" I asked, wanting to know who this faceless, nameless group of individuals were who were running my so-called life.

Miss Stinson listed off several names and titles, some of which were familiar, most of which weren't.

"I don't even know most of these people," I said. "How can they know what's best for me, if they don't even know me. I'm just a file number to them, I bet." I had to laugh. "They probably only hear about me when I've done something terrible, like run away, or stolen things, or threatened to hit Nurse. They must think I'm a right piece of work."

"That's not true, Gail. They get regular reports on your behaviour, good or bad, and actually everyone on the committee is pleased to know you're doing so well in school and go to Sea Rangers regularly. There are concerns of course, but hopefully we can resolve some of those before you're too much older."

"What kind of concerns?"

"Your uncontrollable temper is one that comes immediately to mind, and the fact that you seem bound and determined to take on the whole world in some battle or another. I know you've had a hard go of it, Gail, but life could be so much easier for you if you just stopped fighting with everyone in authority."

"Me and the rest of my generation," I said.

CHAPTER THIRTEEN

Early in March I submitted my application for the Advanced Secretarial Course at the South Devon Technical College. I was provisionally accepted, pending the results of my 'O' levels. I threw myself into my studies with renewed determination. There was a light at the end of the tunnel and I was bound and determined to pass the five 'O' levels I needed to get me into college.

I hardly saw my father at all during this time but Miss Stinson told me he was no longer on probation. I wondered if that explained his conspicuous absence. Perhaps his chaperoned visits to me had been part of the probation requirements. Now that he was free there was no longer any obligation to come and visit. Whatever the reason, he became a shadowy figure in my life, along with Justin, Jane, Graham and Mum. Even my grandparents stopped visiting as often as they did before. Everyone was getting on with their lives, so I got on with mine.

In April I turned sixteen. Amy and Wendy organized a birthday bash for me on the beach at Willowrey Sands. It was arranged, and duly approved, that I would spend the night at Amy's.

I felt a special bond with Amy, mainly because she had been adopted as a baby. I believed she could understand the roller coaster of my emotions more than my other friends. I developed a whimsical fantasy that saw me living with Amy's parents and being treated like their daughter too. I eventually shared these dreams with Amy, couched in the fact that I needed a place to board if I went to college. Perhaps I could board at her place, I suggested. She thought it was a super idea and promised to talk to her parents about it.

Next time I saw Miss Stinson I mentioned the idea to her too. She agreed it was a possibility, although of course there would be many questions and hoops to go through before the Children's Committee would ever agree to such a thing. This no longer came as a surprise to me.

"I expect they'll jump at the idea," I told Miss Stinson. "Nurse says I'm the most difficult child she's ever had to cope with, like I'm some kind of monster or something."

"Well, you do seem to go out of your way to antagonize people, Gail. Nurse isn't getting any younger and she's beginning to look forward to her retirement, I'm sure. But I know she really cares for you and is anxious to see you safely on your way before she retires. A big part of growing up is learning to control your own behaviour and emotions."

I thought about this for a moment or two.

"It's just that Nurse and Aunty Dawn have no idea what life is like today," I said. "Things are changing. The world is a different place now, and people's attitudes are changing. My generation wants to make love, not war. We want to be free to express ourselves, not cramped into a little box and told to conform. We don't want to live by some stupid rules which were invented before any of us were born."

"So how do you think it should be?" Miss Stinson asked, seeming to be genuinely interested.

"Well, I don't understand this fixation with losing your virginity on your wedding night, to start with. I would never even think of marrying a man I hadn't slept with. Say if you didn't click in that department, if you know what I mean. I'd want to know before I married someone that they didn't have any kinky little habits, like my father. I know he's a nice fellow and all, and everybody thinks he's such a great musician and the life and soul of the party, but you can't marry someone based on that. You need to really know them first and the only way you can do that is by sleeping with them."

"And what if you sleep with your boyfriend and discover that you don't 'click in that department'? What do you do then?"

I shrugged. "Find another one, I guess."

"And what happens if you get pregnant during these, how shall we say, test drives?"

"There are ways to prevent that these days. There's a new thing out called the Pill which lets you have sex without any risk of getting pregnant. Everybody's talking about it. Maybe now there won't be so many unwanted children around that have to be taken into care like we were."

"True, but then we'd be out of a job and I like my job," Miss Stinson said, not buying into my attempt at self-pity. "On the subject of being taken into care, I've been wondering lately what your recollections are of the day you were brought into care?"

Her question caught me off guard.

I was silent for a few moments, thinking back to that February day when my mother had come with the police and picked me up at school. I had seen it as an ending at the time, but now I realized it was just the beginning.

"Well, I wish the police had explained the situation to me a bit more clearly. It would have been better if they'd said we were leaving for good, rather than just pretending we were going somewhere else for a night or two. We never ever got to go back to our home on Lime Road again. Sometimes I lie in bed and imagine everything in the house, just the way I remember it. I walk all around the house in my imagination, looking at the pictures and furniture and touching things. I think about it so hard I imagine I'm a ghost haunting the place. It's like part of me is still back there on Lime Road, waiting for the rest of me to come home. I think it must have been really hard for Justin in particular, but Jane was too young to understand what was happening."

"I've been wondering about that myself recently," Miss Stinson said, "particularly with respect to Justin, as he seems troubled too. I've been wondering how I or someone else could talk to him about this."

"Perhaps I would be the best person to do that because any story my mother or father tell him will be biased," I offered.

"That might be very helpful for both of you. I know he has many questions about why the family left Riverton. I've talked to him about this, but it might help him to understand better if the two of you were able to talk things through."

"Maybe during the summer holidays I'll get a chance to go up and visit him. How was his trip to Manchester over the Easter holidays?"

"He had a good time I gather, but he's been quite unsettled since he got back. I believe he's confused about why Jane gets to live with your mother and he doesn't."

"Aren't we all," I quipped.

"We did talk about you going to live with your mother, once your 'O' levels were over. Have you thought any more about that?"

"Not really. On the one hand, I suppose I should. But on the other hand, I'm really hoping to get into college in Torquay. Maybe when I've finished college I can think about living with Mum some more. And besides, wouldn't it be better for Justin; he's younger and needs her more than me? I'm pretty used to being on my own now, and by the time I'm done college I'll be old enough to work and have my own flat."

"How serious do you think your girlfriend is about you going to live there while you're at college?"

"Well we talk about it lots, but until I know whether I've made it into college there really isn't much point in getting too excited about it. It's kinda strange really, to think about leaving this place. Even though I seem to be in trouble here all the time, I'll find it hard to leave." I hesitated a moment, then added with uncharacteristic honesty, "I'm very attached to Nurse, you know, in spite of everything."

"I'm sure you are, Gail, but Nurse probably has a hard time believing that some days," Miss Stinson said with a wry smile.

"There is something else I need to talk to you about today," she added. "I'm getting married in September, so will no longer be working for the Devon County Council. This means a new child care officer will be assigned to you."

I stared at her, not wanting to believe my ears. Miss Stinson was one of the few people who really seemed to listen to me, to understand me. I had never felt judged or found to be lacking by her. I could relate to her, and now she was leaving too.

"I'm sorry to hear that, but congratulations, I guess." I managed to mumble after a few moments. I would just have to chalk it up as another loss. I too was learning not to make lasting attachments.

Knowing that I would probably be leaving Willowrey soon, I no longer felt such a compelling need to rebel. Instead I focused my energy on getting the exam results I needed to guarantee my place at college. I called a truce with Nurse and Aunty Dawn. I wasn't so kind to the other girls however, and they continued to take a wide berth around me. I taunted them without mercy, and flaunted the fact that I would be leaving within a few months. They couldn't be faulted for not liking me. I jeered at their music, their clothes, and their lives. As I watched them trudging to the bus stop each morning to go to their poorly paid, dead end jobs I vowed I would never be like them. I would pass my exams, go to college, and get a good job.

We argued about everything: which was the best pop group, who had the cutest boyfriend, who had the best record collection. You name it and we found a way to argue about it. Sometimes Kathy would side with me, sometimes not. Other times Rosina would be on my side, other times not. We squabbled about who left the magazines all over the floor, who didn't flush the toilet, and whose turn it was to do the dishes. For the most part it was harmless teenage squabbling. Until the day I went too far and put my foot through a door.

Kathy had taken refuge in her room during a particularly heated debate between us. I kicked at her door, trying to force it open. But instead, my foot went straight through. As Kathy gingerly opened the door, I did a fast step-hop to keep up with my trapped foot. I looked so ridiculous that we both burst out laughing.

"Oh my God, look what you've done," Kathy said, as she surveyed the damage. "Nurse is gonna kill you."

"Never mind that," I grunted, "give me a hand to get my foot out of here."

We heard Nurse's footsteps coming up the stairs.

"What in heaven's name is going on here?" she asked.

Kathy stifled a giggle. I wrenched my foot free and picked a large sliver out of the side of my shoe.

"Well?" Nurse said, looking from one to the other of us.

"I slipped," I said, struggling not to burst out laughing.

"Slipped?" Nurse said, incredulous. "What exactly were you doing, walking up the wall?"

Kathy and I stood there, intently studying the floor. We couldn't speak or look up for fear we'd burst out laughing, our fight of moments ago forgotten.

"You'd better go and get the broom and clean this mess up," Nurse said, realizing she would get no sense from either of us. "I'll be reporting this to the Committee, you can be sure of that," she said, before spinning on her heel and going back downstairs.

"Poo on the Committee," I muttered under my breath. "What are they going to do, throw me out? I'm leaving soon anyway."

But the Committee didn't throw me out. Instead they sent me a letter.

Dear Gail,

Nurse yesterday had to report to the Committee the damage you had done to one of the doors in Willowrey. She gave them an estimated cost of the repair to this door as 25/-.

The Committee was concerned that this should have happened, and asked me to write to you to say that they think you should pay for the cost of the repair. The Committee members know that you have a Saturday job, and that you therefore can manage to pay this money without too much difficulty.

Will you discuss with Nurse how you will pay this bill?

I know from Nurse and Miss Stinson that you are hoping for good results from your 'O' level exams. I too hope that you will be successful and that you will gain the place that you want at the Torquay Technical College.

With good wishes to you for your plans for the future,

Yours sincerely,

Children's Officer

The only consolation was the fact that the letter wasn't addressed to me at 'Willowrey Children's Home'. It had simply said 'Willowrey, Willowrey Sands Road'. At least some of what I said was getting through.

In July I sat eight 'O' level exams. I had studied and swotted for months and by the time I entered the examination hall I was as ready as I was ever going to be. I could only hope it was good enough.

As soon as school was over, I started working full time again at Woolworths for the summer. When I came home on the Friday with my first full week's pay clutched in my hand, Nurse called me into her office.

"As you know, most of the girls here are working girls," Nurse began.

I nodded, wondering where this conversation was going.

"And as such they contribute to their room and board each week."

A sinking feeling started in my gut.

"While you're in school, you get one pound a week spending money, but now you're working I believe that money should go straight into your savings account."

Sure, I could handle that. I relaxed a little.

"No problem," I said, "I was planning on saving as much as I could over the summer anyhow so that I'll have plenty of money when I start college. I was even planning on saving half my paycheque."

"Well, there's more to it than that," Nurse continued. "The Committee feels that as you are working full time you should be expected to pay room and board, just like the other girls."

"I beg your pardon?" I said, not sure I was hearing correctly. "You want me to pay to live here? But it's only a summer job and I've never had to pay room and board before when I had summer jobs. Why is it different this time?"

"Because that's what the Committee has decided. Now that you're preparing to go out into the world, it's time to start learning how the real world works."

I looked down at the crumpled pay packet in my hand and thought of all the wonderful things I had planned to buy with it.

Fabric for new clothes, records, makeup; the list went on. These things would have to wait.

"The working girls are on budgets and you should be too. We believe you can afford to pay two pounds ten shillings a week room and board, which leaves another three pounds for you. Any you don't spend can be put in your savings account for when you need it."

Three pounds a week was more than I was used to having, but still a whole lot less than I was expecting to have. I reluctantly handed the packet over to Nurse. She extracted the two pounds ten shillings for room and board, handed me three pounds as spending money, and slipped the rest inside the cover of my bank book which had been sitting on her desk. Welcome to the real world, Gail!

After handing my pay packets over to Nurse for several weeks, I decided it was time for a holiday. With the innate understanding of a teenager, I realized that if I wasn't working I wouldn't have to pay room and board, so what was the point of working this hard. And besides, Miss Stinson was encouraging me to take a break before it was time to go back to school, wherever that might be.

I made plans to go to Andover and spend a week with my Aunty Barbara. It would help to keep my mind off waiting for the exam results. I told Nurse I would call her from Andover at the end of the week, to see if the results were in.

I started counting off the days on Monday. Five days to go. Well, not exactly five. More like four and a half really, when you consider that the mailman comes just before noon every day, so you can hardly count Friday as a whole day.

Monday morning went by painfully slow. By mid-afternoon I was convinced the hands on the clock were moving backwards, not forwards. By late afternoon, I realized I needed to break the waiting into more manageable units, or I'd be a raving basket case by week's end. So, instead of counting days, I decided to count the day in two sections: daylight hours and nighttime hours. At least then I'd get to count down faster and I'd have a sense of moving towards 'the moment of knowing'. Oh my goodness will this week never end!

When I woke up Tuesday morning, the sun was already up. Great! I crossed two units off my count down sheet. Two down, seven to go. Maybe if I helped my aunt by looking after the boys, the time would pass faster. Maybe my psychic karma would be enhanced by such a random act of kindness, and I would be assured enough exam passes to get me into college in September! Oh my goodness. My belly lurched. There, I'd done it! I'd gone and mentioned the unmentionable - college. As long as I could keep my mind busy and didn't think about how much I really, really wanted to go to college, I could keep a lid on the swarms of butterflies which had taken up residence in my belly. But that 'c' word was guaranteed to set them off every time.

Wednesday evening found me consumed with self-doubt and trepidation. What if I didn't get enough passes? What would I do then? If only I'd studied harder and paid more attention in class. Did I put the correct formula for hydrogen dioxide? Is there such a thing as hydrogen dioxide, or is it monoxide. Oh dear. Maybe I can rewrite that exam. Maybe I can tell them I was suffering from a momentary lapse of memory, brought on by the disgusting fumes that had been emanating from the biology lab next door. My head started to pound just thinking about it. I took two aspirin and went to bed early.

Thursday morning, I took the boys for a walk to the library. I wanted to check on the correct formula for hydrogen whatever-it-is. The answer was inconclusive, mainly because I didn't have a clear question.

By Friday morning I could hardly breathe. I was having trouble stringing words together to form complete sentences and there was a note of hysteria in my voice. Breathe, breathe, I reminded myself. As I walked to the phone box on the corner of the street I felt my knees might buckle. I wondered if people felt like this when they walked up the steps of the gallows, when they knew it was the last thing they would ever do. I put my coins in the phone and dialed the number for Willowrey.

Aunty Dawn answered. She said the results were in. Her voice sounded to me like gravel rolling off a washboard. I asked her to read me the results but she said she had to find her glasses first. I groaned and shifted my weight nervously from foot to foot. My hand was sweating so much I had trouble keeping a grip on the receiver. I started making outrageous deals with God, if only, please God, I can have enough passes to get into college. I'll never swear again.

I'll write to my mother every week. I'll be nice to Nurse and all the Aunties. Please God!

Fortunately Aunty Dawn came back on the phone before I could promise God a life of servitude and giving all my, yet to be earned, money to the poor.

"Did I do alright?"

Aunty Dawn paused. I could hear her mumbling under her breath, as she skimmed over the results.

"Let me read them to you, dear, starting at the top. Chemistry, fail; English language, pass; English literature, pass; French language, pass; Geography, pass; Mathematics …." A lorry drove past, drowning out her voice.

"What was that?" I asked frantically, "I couldn't hear you, there's a lot of traffic here."

"Where was I? Oh yes, Mathematics, pass."

I let out a whoop. "That's it! That's five, I made it!" Tears were streaming down my cheeks. "I can't believe it, I did it."

"Not so fast, young lady," Aunty Dawn interrupted. "I haven't finished yet, there's more. Now where was I? Oh yes, here we are: Mathematics, pass; Needlework, pass; Physics, fail. That's it. Six passes in all. Congratulations, Gail. You worked hard for that and you deserve it."

I started jumping up and down inside the phone box, attracting the bewildered attention of some passers by. I waved happily at these strangers, grinning from ear to ear. Why had I ever doubted myself? The swarm of butterflies in my gut took flight, each one taking a little piece of my self-doubt with them until I was suffused with confidence and joy. I'd made it! I was going to college. I couldn't believe it, little old me, the girl from the Children's Home, was going to college.

When I got back to Devon there was a message waiting for me to call Amy. I didn't even bother taking my bags up to my room before asking Nurse if I could use the phone.

"Did you get enough passes to get in to Art School?" I asked, as soon as Amy came on the line.

"Yup," she said, "but only just. Still, as long as I'm in, that's all that counts. And Wendy got enough passes for her course at Torquay Tech too. How about you?"

"Yeah, I made it too. I got enough passes to get into the Advanced course, just like I wanted."

I paused, unsure of how to pose the big question which was on my mind.

"Are your parents still keen on me coming to live with you?" I asked. "It's just that there'll be a ton of hoops to jump through, so we'd have to start thinking about it soon, if it's going to happen." I held my breath, hoping against hope that they hadn't changed their mind.

"Oh yes, we were talking about it just last night. Mum says you can have the spare room upstairs. She'll move her sewing stuff into the dining room, 'cos we hardly ever use that room anyway. Are you still keen to come then?"

"Absolutely! I expect a woman called Miss Stinson will want to come and meet your parents and talk to them first though."

"I'll let Mum know to expect her call. What are you doing tomorrow? Maybe we can get together and spend some time on the beach."

"Great idea. I'll take the bus over right after lunch. See you then. Bye."

I hung up and went in search of Nurse. I found her in the sitting room doing some sewing.

"I was wondering when you might be expecting Miss Stinson to come again?" I asked her.

"Why dear, is there a problem?"

"Not exactly, it's just that Amy got into college too, and her parents have said that I could go and board with them, now that I've finished school and all. It's just that their place is closer to the college," I added weakly, anxious not to hurt Nurse's feelings.

I thought I saw a look of relief wash over her face, but maybe she was just tired that day.

"We can call her and arrange for her to visit," Nurse said. "She'll be anxious to know how you did in your exams anyhow. There's a lot to do before September. Which reminds me; I had a telephone call from Mr. Carter yesterday. He wants to come here and meet with us both to discuss some things. He was very pleased with your results and wants to make sure you continue with your education."

"He wants to come here?" I asked, not sure I'd heard correctly.

"Yes dear. Apparently he only lives up the road, so said he'd drop by on his way home for lunch tomorrow."

"Whatever," I shrugged, "But I've just arranged to meet Amy and the gang tomorrow afternoon, so I hope he doesn't stay too long."

Just before noon the next day Mr. Carter rang the doorbell. He looked oddly out of place away from the school grounds. I'd never thought of him as having a life outside of school. Nurse showed him into the sitting room and offered him tea, which he declined.

"I just wanted to come over and personally congratulate Gail on her excellent exam results," he said, as he beamed at me.

I was touched by his interest in my well being.

"Thank you," I mumbled. "But it's too bad I didn't get Physics and Chemistry too. I really wanted to show those boys that girls can do science as well as them."

"Well I believe in focusing on your successes, not your failures, and you had plenty of successes, which is why I've come here today. I was wondering what your plans are for the future?"

"I've been accepted at the Torquay technical college, for the Advanced Secretarial course. I start in September."

"Have you given any thought to doing your 'A' levels? With results like this it's a shame not to continue your studies."

"I am going to continue, but I'll do it at the college. I've signed up for two 'A' levels there, as well as the secretarial training."

"I was thinking more along the lines of university. If you came back and did the sixth form at Stoneleigh, you could go on to university and get a degree."

"And what would I do with a degree?" I asked.

"Well, once you have your degree you can get some training of some kind to prepare you for a job."

"So what's the point in getting a degree, if I still have to go and get training for a job afterwards? And what would I live on while I was at university?"

Nurse interjected. "The County will continue to support you until you are eighteen, if you're still in school."

I did the mental math. "But that'll only get me through to Upper Sixth. I'd still have four years of university left after I turned eighteen." It seemed like an eternity to me.

"There are student loans available, and you could get a small job to give you extra spending money while you're studying," Nurse said.

I looked from Nurse to Mr. Carter, weighing my options.

"I think I'll stick with the college," I said after a very brief moment of consideration, "At least that way I'll be able to get a job when I'm done, and it's only a one year program. I can't imagine finishing university and owing all that money. It would take years and years to pay it back. I think I'm better off learning how to be a secretary."

Mr. Carter seemed to visibly deflate. I wondered if this was how he spent his summers, trying to convince giddy fifth formers to come back to the fold after we'd all run whooping and hollering out the school doors.

I promised Mr. Carter I would let him know if I changed my mind, but I knew I wouldn't.

Two days later, Miss Stinson came to meet with Nurse and me to discuss my future plans. It was agreed that if the Desmond's proved suitable, I would go and lodge with them while attending college.

"There are those on the Committee who feel you may be destructive in the less controlled environment of lodgings," Miss Stinson said, eyeing me closely. I bristled but backed down quickly, remembering that I still owed 25/- for the door I had kicked in. Maybe they had a point but didn't they realize that that was just teenagers goofing around. I smiled weakly.

It seems that my departure from Willowrey had been a hot topic of conversation at their committee meetings and I wondered who was the most excited about my departure, me or the staff and other girls.

"Have you told your mother about your plans?"

"Yes, kinda. I told her I wanted to go to college in Torquay. She thinks I should go to one in Manchester."

"Is this something you're thinking about?" Miss Stinson asked.

"No, not really, it was Mum's idea. I told her I didn't want to do that, but I haven't heard from her since."

A few days later, Mum and Jane arrived unexpectedly for a summer holiday. It was an unpleasant visit and I wondered why they had come. Mum was angry at me for not moving to Manchester, now that I'd finished school. She grumbled about how difficult it was, trying to look after Jane and work full time. I accused her of just wanting me as a babysitter. She accused me of being a selfish snob, putting on airs and graces just because I'd managed to pass a few silly exams. I told her I was just doing my best to get an education so that I could get a good job one day.

I told Mum I would be lodging with the Desmond's if the Committee approved it, and invited her to meet them. She declined, saying she didn't have time.

Then, halfway through the week, Mum suddenly announced she was leaving. She said she'd decided to spend the rest of her holidays in Andover with her sister. I went to see them off at the station, a smile plastered on my face and a knot in the pit of my stomach. I was sorry to see Jane go.

Miss Stinson visited with the Desmond's, as promised. She met with me a few days later.

"They seem like a very nice family," she told me, obviously impressed with them. "And they have a lovely home."

I felt myself relaxing.

"I spoke to Mrs. Desmond about your situation. I didn't realize she'd known you so long, but she tells me you and Amy have been friends for a couple of years. Anyhow, she didn't want to know about any problems which may arise from you living there and is confident that she and her husband will be able to handle any issues which come up. She says she knows you quite well."

"Oh yes," I effused, "I often go to Amy's to hang out on weekends and Mr. Desmond has given me a ride home a couple of times."

"I also discussed payment for your room and board, and we have agreed on four pounds, ten shillings a week, which is the going rate for college lodgings. You'll continue to get an allowance for your clothing and spending money of course, although you'll have to budget carefully, if it is to last. Any extraordinary expenses will, of course, be covered by the County, provided they are approved beforehand."

"Did Mrs. Desmond say how soon I could move in?"

"I still have to check out the references they gave me, and go to the Committee for final approval, but the Desmond's are willing to have you any time after the end of this month. Probably the first week of September is what we're looking at."

A huge grin spread across my face. Freedom was so close I could almost taste it. Nurse just sat there, her expression distant and unfathomable.

A week later, Nurse called me into her office.

"The Committee met yesterday and approved your transfer to lodgings at the Desmond's," she announced without any preamble.

"That's great," was all I could think to say.

Except suddenly I wasn't at all sure I wanted to go. I had lived with Nurse for three and a half years and despite our endless power struggles and battles, I felt closer to her than to any other person I knew. I hated her, yet loved her; rebelled against her rules, yet felt safe within them; and railed against the confines of Willowrey, yet felt protected within them. I wanted Nurse to say I could stay if I wanted, or I could come back any time I liked. But she didn't. Instead she reminded me that I would have to get some boxes from the local grocer, to pack all my belongings in. I told her I'd manage.

The next two weeks went by in a blur. Nurse took me shopping to get some new clothes and shoes, and made up a care package of toothpaste, soaps, sanitary napkins and the like, to get me through the first month or so. I lined each of my purchases up on the spare bed in my room, in eager anticipation of my departure.

One afternoon Nurse took me aside and had a little chat with me. She made it abundantly clear that I would be responsible for my own well-being from now on. I couldn't expect Amy's mother to put up with the nonsense she had had to endure. I laughed, thinking she was joking.

"I wasn't as bad as all that was I?"

"Yes, dear, you were. I've put up with more from you than from any other child I've cared for. And I've been caring for children for over forty years, all told."

"Well at least you won't forget me," I said, refusing to let her comments dampen my mood. We were too close to the finishing line to have another row.

"I certainly won't be doing that," she said.

It was arranged that I would move to the Desmond's on September 5th. I slept fitfully the night before and woke early. I packed the last of my things into the boxes piled in the corner of my room. I was the first down to breakfast and went to the kitchen in search of Nurse and Aunty Dawn. I wanted to cling to them, tell them I'd miss them and that I didn't really want to go. But instead I stirred the oatmeal, making a mock face of disgust.

"Well, I certainly won't miss this stuff," I said. But what I really wanted to say was that I would miss them. I'd miss the sounds and smells of Willowrey, the way it smelled of floor polish on the days when Mrs. Young came to clean, or the smell of apple pies baking on Sundays. I wanted to tell them I'd miss the sounds of the other girls calling to each other when something good was on television, and the sound of Aunty Dawn humming under her breath as she worked, or Nurse's footsteps coming down the hall to kiss me goodnight. Most of all I would miss that.

Miss Stinson wasn't expected until late that afternoon. I spent the day restlessly shifting from one activity to another, unable to settle on any one thing for more than a few minutes. Piece by piece, I carried my belongings down to the front hall, piling them in the corner ready for loading into the car. Nurse teased me about how much stuff I'd accumulated.

"You've come a long way from that frightened little twelve-year-old who walked through these doors," Nurse said, looking at me in that penetrating way she had. It was as if she could see into my soul when she looked at me like that. "I hope we've managed to teach you something while you've been here, and that you'll remember us."

"How could I forget you," I said, laughing at the idea, "after everything we've been through."

Nurse nodded, a sad smile touching her lips.

"Well hopefully it wasn't all bad," she said with a note of regret in her voice. She caught me off guard. Nurse was not given to displays of emotion.

Like a drowning man, my life at Willowrey flashed before my eyes. It had been so good at first, what had gone wrong? Why were all my belongings packed in boxes and stacked by the door? I hoped I wasn't making a terrible mistake.

"I really appreciate everything you and Aunty Dawn have done for me," I said. "And I'm sorry I made things so difficult for you both, it's just that ..."

My voice trailed away. How could I explain why I had found it so difficult to live by their rules and treat them with the respect they deserved, when I had no respect for myself? I choked back my tears. I'd been dreaming of this day for so long, why was I now on the brink of tears?

At 4 p.m. Miss Stinson arrived to drive me to the Desmond's. Nurse handed me my bank book and medical card and reminded me to register with a doctor in Nestleton as soon as possible. Our goodbyes were awkward, belying the torrent of emotions attached. Nurse and Aunty Dawn stood in the driveway and waved goodbye. I promised to come back and see them soon.

As we drove, Miss Stinson reviewed the arrangements she had made for me at the Desmond's.

"If there are any problems, they can be discussed with your new child care worker," she said.

I realized with a sinking heart, that this was probably the last time I would see Miss Stinson too.

"Will she come to see me every month, like you do?"

"No, I don't think so. Now that you are in lodgings, your relationship with your child care officer will be slightly different."

As much as I liked Miss Stinson, I had been dreading the prospect of regular visits from a new worker. I wanted to be just like a regular person, and regular people don't have child care workers barging into their lives every month, wanting to know what you've been doing and have you written to your family lately?

"What about my father? Will his visits still have to be chaperoned?"

"That depends a lot on how you feel about it."

I shrugged, unsure of my feelings in this regard.

"We'll see," I said, not wanting to spoil the excitement of the day worrying about things like that.

When we got to Amy's, she and her mother were waiting for us. While Miss Stinson talked with Mrs. Desmond, Amy and I unloaded my things from the car and took them up to my room. It was at the front of the house, beside Amy's. The bed was plump and overflowing with pillows and a frilly comforter. The floors were covered with plush carpeting and there was wallpaper on the walls. It was a far cry from the institutionalized look of my room at Willowrey, with its linoleum flooring, bare walls, and thin cotton bedspread. There was even a small writing table and chair by the window where I could do my homework. I thought I had died and gone to heaven.

When it came time to say goodbye to Miss Stinson, she gave me a hug and said she hoped things would go well for me in the future.

I smiled and thanked her.

"I can't think that anything could possibly go wrong now," I told her, honestly believing it to be true.

CHAPTER FOURTEEN

I only had a few days to settle into the Desmond's before starting college. My future held nothing but promise and I was keen to put my past behind me. I was free! I didn't live in an institution anymore and there were no bars on my window. Now I lived in a normal house with normal people and I was part of a real family again. And, best of all, I was going to college. I could hardly wait.

No more school uniforms, with berets balanced precariously on our heads. Now we could pile our hair up high, slather make-up on our faces, and paint black lines around our eyes. White knee-high socks were discarded in favour of pantyhose; below-the-knee pleated skirts were replaced with mini-skirts not much wider than a belt. And our billowy white blouses and school ties were cast aside in favour of sweaters that clung to our budding bodies.

I took the bus to the South Devon Technical College early Monday morning. By the time I found my classroom there were several girls there already. They were chatting in small groups, surreptitiously glancing around and checking each other out. I sat next to a girl who introduced herself as Di. She said she was a Torquay Grammar girl, and asked where I was from. Before I could answer we were interrupted by a loud rapping sound. I looked up to see a very rotund, vertically challenged woman standing at the teacher's desk.

"Ladies, take your seats please."

There was momentary pandemonium as those still standing scrambled to their seats.

"My name is Mrs. Woodstock and my job is to teach you how to be the best secretaries in the world. English secretaries are well respected the world over, so you have a reputation to uphold."

She peered at each of us in turn, as if assessing our potential. She didn't seem overly impressed.

"We obviously have a long and challenging journey ahead of us. Now let's begin."

My life as a college student had begun.

I felt intoxicated with the seemingly endless possibilities of my new life and reveled in the joy of living with a real family. Mrs. Desmond showed me how to work the washing machine and where to hang my clothes outside on the line to dry.

"We only use the dryer if it's rainy," she said. "It uses too much electricity and besides, things smell so much nicer after a good airing in the fresh air, don't you agree dear?"

I nodded in agreement although in reality I'd never actually had much to do with laundry and washing lines and the likes. Nurse and her staff had taken care of all that sort of thing at Willowrey.

"Now that you're in college it's time to learn how to take care of these things yourselves. Amy has had it far too easy all these years, being an only child and all, but now there's two of you I won't have time to take care of everything. I explained to your social worker that I help out in Mr. Desmond's shop most days, so I won't have a lot of time to go running around looking after you."

"Oh I don't think I'll need much looking after, Mrs. Desmond," I said, smiling sweetly, "I'm pretty good at looking after myself."

The weekend after we started college Amy's parents took us to Cornwall. We stayed in a bed and breakfast and spent the day strolling along the harbour, eating cockles and ice cream and looking in all the shops. I felt like royalty. So this is what life is like, living with a normal family. We just had to look at something and Mr. Desmond would put his hand in his pocket and buy it for us. It didn't take me long to realize that what Amy wanted, Amy got. But even so, she could be demanding and cruel to her parents. They in turn vacillated between cajoling and demanding that she mind her manners.

I watched all this with a fair degree of curiosity. What must it be like, to be so sure of your parents' love that you could torment them the way she did and yet know they'd still love you in the morning? I took many of my cues from Amy's behaviour, but soon realized I was on much thinner ice than her.

As much as I reveled in my freedom, the Children's Committee wasn't finished with me yet. Every couple of months a child care worker would come armed with a list of questions about how my life was going and what was I doing. Miss Dunnett was assigned to my file temporarily. When she came to see me towards the end of September I showed her into the drawing room, proud of the comfort and warmth of my new home. I was nervous and felt I had to put on a show for this stranger who would report back to the Children's Committee about me. I talked too much and too fast.

"How are you settling in here?" Miss Dunnett asked between my babblings.

"Oh boy, it's fab!" I gushed. "The Desmond's are so neat, they let Amy and I have friends over whenever we want and Mr. Desmond will even come and pick us up after parties, so we don't have to take the bus or anything like that. And we can stay out until midnight on weekends, even later if there's a special party or something to go to. But during the week we're supposed to be in by ten, but half the time we don't make it if we've been to the pictures in Torquay, but they don't seem to mind too much."

I prattled on nervously, wishing I didn't have to go through this charade.

"That's good to hear, Gail, but don't abuse your curfew. I understand this was a problem for you quite often at Willowrey."

"Oh it's different here. They don't seem to mind at all, really. And Amy is always just as late, if not later."

"So you and Amy are still getting along?"

"Yes, just great, although we don't get to spend much time

together. She goes to the Art College in Newton Abbott and is making friends there, and I'm making friends at my college. But when we're together we have fun, sewing and listening to music and stuff. I think she'd like to have a boyfriend like me, 'cos she says she doesn't like just hanging around with me and Anthony."

"You're still seeing Anthony then?"

"Oh yes, I couldn't imagine life without Anthony. We're Mods, you know. It's so cool. We ride around on his Lambretta scooter and go to Macario's in Torquay for coffee on Saturday afternoons. All the Mods go there. They line their scooters up along the pavement to show them off. It looks really neat to see them like that: all the Mods' scooters on one side of the harbour; and all the Rockers' motorbikes lined up on the other. There were loads of them here all summer, and sometimes fights would break out, but Anthony and I kept away from that stuff. And just about every weekend we go to the Hot Spot disco to dance and see who's hanging out. We met some of Anthony's friends from London there the other night. They were so cool, they were doing this new dance called the Zizzle. I love dancing; I'd go every night if I could."

"Well it certainly sounds as though you're keeping busy. Hopefully all this dancing isn't interfering with your studies."

"Not at all, in fact I'm doing quite well now although I found it really hard at first. I just couldn't make any sense of what Mrs. Woodstock was on about."

"Mrs. Woodstock?"

"She's our shorthand and typing teacher. I think she sailed into the classroom on the same ark as Nurse. She just sits behind her desk, peering over her glasses at us and rambling on about how you absolutely *must* use this finger for this key and that finger for that key, as if it really matters as long as you get the word typed. And as for shorthand, I nearly died. She keeps going on about the difference between puh and buh and pah and bah, and how one stroke goes above the line, the other through the line and stuff like that. I hated it at first because I didn't get it but I think I'm getting the hang of it now. We had a test last week and I was almost top of the class."

"Well done. I'm glad to hear you're doing so well."

"Oh boy, I nearly forgot the best bit of all. The whole class is going to London next week for the Business Exhibition in Earls Court. We get to stay in a hotel and go to the London Palladium on Saturday night. I can't wait."

Miss Dunnett looked surprised, and I realized that perhaps I should have discussed these plans with her in advance.

"I see," she said, making some hasty notes in her file. "And how much will this cost you?'

There was something about the way she put the emphasis on 'you' that told me not to look to the Children's Committee for any financial help.

"The whole trip will only cost four pounds ten shillings, and my mother sent me three pounds towards it so I only have to pay a bit."

"Well it seems you've kept your mother well informed of your activities. I understand she was in Devon a few weeks back. How was that visit?"

I shrugged, remembering the sour note we had parted on.

"It was okay, I guess, but I think she's mad at me for not going to live with her in Manchester now that I've finished school. She doesn't understand that Devon is my home and I want to stay here. It isn't my fault she decided to go and live at the other end of the country. And besides, Mum spoils Jane so much I don't think I could stand watching her get all the attention all the time."

Miss Dunnett's lips twitched into the semblance of a smile.

"No, I can't imagine you could somehow."

She started gathering up her papers. "I'll come and see you again in a month or so, to see how things are going. You can contact me at the office if any problems come up in the meantime."

"Actually, I've been wondering whether I really need to have regular visits now that I'm in college and settled here and things are going so well. As long as the Committee keeps sending the money for my room and board and all that, I don't see that there's much else I need."

"I think the Children's Committee still has an obligation to make sure everything is alright with you, above and beyond paying your bills," Miss Dunnett said. "At least until you turn eighteen."

I thought better of pursuing the subject. My thoughts were

interrupted by the sound of the Desmond's car in the driveway. Mr. and Mrs. Desmond came in loaded down with groceries. I awkwardly introduced them to Miss Dunnett, feeling embarrassed by her prescence. It tarnished the image I was eager to create.

As Miss Dunnett was leaving I suddenly remembered some book receipts which I needed reimbursement for. I ran upstairs to get them. As I came back downstairs, I overheard Miss Dunnett talking to Mrs. Desmond.

"Please don't hesitate to call me should you have any questions or concerns. It's always better to deal with the small things before they get blown out of proportion and give rise to misunderstandings, don't you agree?"

"Absolutely," Mrs. Desmond said, apparently anxious to end the conversation. "Well, you must excuse me; I have dinner to get started. It was nice meeting you."

Just when I was getting used to Miss Dunnett's visits, my file was reassigned to Miss Harrison. She said she was Miss Stinson's permanent replacement. But it didn't really matter who came to see me, the questions were always the same: how are you doing at school; have you seen you father; have you heard from your mother; are you still seeing Anthony; how are you and Amy getting along; any problems with the Desmond's? I wasn't sure I had the emotional energy to develop a relationship with yet another worker. I would answer all their questions with assurances that no, there weren't any problems and that everything was fine, thank you very much. As indeed I believed they were.

And then they'd have a word with Mrs. Desmond, who only ever seemed to have questions about the amount of money she was paid, needing a bit more to cover this, and a bit more to cover that. But she always assured whoever asked that everything was fine with me. My wild outbursts, which were so frequent during my Willowrey days, seemed far behind me. I believed I had become the model child.

My father and I kept in touch. Whenever I saw his car parked outside a pub or heard his trombone playing, I'd go in and have a drink with him. He didn't have a band anymore but he picked up gigs wherever he could or else just played for beer money. He always seemed pleased to see me.

One day he phoned and asked me to meet him at the Black Swan pub where he'd been playing a lot lately. He said he wanted me to meet his new lady friend, whom he planned to marry. I was relieved to see that at least this one looked about the same age as him. Her name was Judy and Dad said they had rented a cottage in South Brent, not far from Nestleton.

For Christmas that year I went to London with Anthony and his parents to see his brother's new baby. My mother was annoyed when I told her about my plans. She said she wanted Justin and me to spend Christmas with her, and that Jane was really looking forward to seeing us. I told her it was too late to change my plans but suggested perhaps Justin and I could visit her at Easter.

The Children's Committee, on the other hand, had no objections to my trip and much to my relief made no mention of anyone visiting the family in London first to make sure they were acceptable.

When the excitement of Christmas was over, the winter doldrums set in. Anthony didn't have a job or any prospects for one, and I was constantly short of money. We didn't go out much anymore but Mrs. Desmond said it was okay for us to stay in, so mostly we just hung around the house listening to music and smoking cigarettes. I started to look forward to Easter. The Children's Committee had agreed that Justin and I should travel to Manchester together. Mum had written to say she would take us to Andover while we were with her, so that we could see our grandparents off on their trip to the States.

But Easter was still a long way away. In the meantime I had weekly shorthand speed tests and typing tests, essays to write and French to study. The pace was relentless. On the bright side, my lack of a social life gave me plenty of time to study and I was neck and neck with my friend, Di, as top student in our course.

I showed my report card to Miss Harrison during one of her visits.

"Well done, Gail. You must be very proud."

I shrugged, downplaying my achievements.

"I'm going to need good marks if I'm to find a decent job when

I'm finished," I said. "I'm a bit scared about that side of things, actually. I'll need to support myself somehow when I go out of care at eighteen, and that's only a year and a bit away. I'm worried about how I'll manage on my own."

"You have plenty of time to think about that later," Miss Harrison said, brushing aside my concerns.

I fixed her with a hard stare and wondered if she had any idea what it felt like, sitting on my side of this conversation. Could she understand how it might feel to go from having your every move watched by a committee of faceless, nameless people to being cast adrift into the void of adulthood? My file would be closed and tucked away in the basement of County Hall and I'd soon be forgotten. Just another abandoned kid passing through.

Miss Harrison sifted through the papers in my file.

"And how are things going with you and the Desmond's?"

"Okay, I guess."

"Sounds like there's a 'but' at the end of that. What is it?"

"Oh, it's nothing really. It's just that I was hoping they would think of me as a daughter, just like they do Amy. I kinda hoped that, since Amy was adopted and I'm sort of a foster child, they'd treat us both the same. But they don't. If Amy makes a smart remark to her father or answers her mother back they tell her to watch her manners, but if I try it they just look at me like I'm the rudest person they know. I'm just the lodger here, which is okay I guess, it's just that I had hoped for something more. Sometimes I think the only reason they said I could live here was to try and keep Amy happy."

"Well, when I spoke to Mrs. Desmond earlier she assured me that everything was fine with you. It just takes time sometimes, to feel like part of the family."

I hoped she was right, but in reality I had to admit there was little or no communication between Amy's parents and me. As much as I had wanted to be part of the Desmond family, the reality was that I was just a friend of Amy's who was staying with them while I went to college. The closeness I had yearned for wasn't there.

Shortly before Easter Miss Harrison came to see me again to

review the travel arrangements for my trip to Manchester with Justin. Anthony was there and offered to make tea while I talked to Miss Harrison.

"Apparently your mother wants to take you both to Andover while you're with her."

"Yes, I know. She already wrote to me about it. Oh boy, I can't wait. I haven't seen Aunty Barbara and her boys for ages, and it'll be so neat going to Southampton to see my grandparents off. They're sailing to America on the Queen Mary to see my Uncle Roger and his family. They just moved there from New Zealand. They're so lucky. I hope I get to go there one day."

"Who knows, perhaps you will one day. But in the meantime, how are things here? Are you and Amy still getting along?"

"Yes, we get along just fine but she argues with her parents a lot lately, so things get a bit tense around here sometimes."

"I'm sorry to hear that. What seems to be the problem?"

"Mostly it's about her coming home late at night and hanging around with the other students at Art School. Mr. and Mrs. Desmond think they're scruffy beatniks and they don't want Amy hanging around with them. Makes you wonder what they expected when they said she could go to Art School. It's hardly the place to meet men in suits, is it? I think Amy brings these friends home just to annoy her parents; she seems to almost enjoy shocking them. Sometimes I think she's just showing off in front of me, trying to be as outrageous as she possibly can be and seeing how far she can push her parents and how much she can get away with."

I giggled.

"Actually she's almost doing me a favour. She's giving her parents such a hard time that she's making me look good, which is quite a change for me. At Willowrey I was always considered the trouble maker."

"And how is your relationship with Mr. and Mrs. Desmond through all this?"

"Good, I guess. I just keep my head down and try to stay out of the crossfire. I always come straight home from college, mostly because I'm starving for my dinner, and then I go to my room to study or write letters. I don't have much to do with them really. If

Anthony comes over we'll hang out in the drawing room and watch TV with them if they're home, but other than that I hardly get to talk with them. It'll be good to go away for Easter though. Hopefully Amy and her parents will work things out while I'm gone."

CHAPTER FIFTEEN

Justin was waiting at the Exeter station when my train pulled in. He was standing as close to the edge of the platform as he could get, transfixed by the engine as it huffed and hissed to a stop in front of him. Mrs. Federicks, his foster mother, was clutching his arm in one hand and a well worn suitcase in the other. Justin saw me and broke free, bolting the length of the platform to where I was. Mrs. Federicks caught up with him just as he was about to board the train.

"Not so fast, young un," she said breathlessly. "Don't forget your suitcase, and you'll be needing your ticket unless you want them to put you off at the next station."

She handed me his travel warrant. Justin took his suitcase and the rolled up pound note Mrs. Federicks gave him.

"Buy yourself a little something nice while you're on your holiday," she said, "but don't go spending it all on sweets and getting holes in your teeth."

She leaned forward and kissed him on his forehead.

"See you when you get home. Someone will be here to meet the train when you get back. You'll have to ring us if there's any change in plans," she said, turning to me. Then as an afterthought she added, "It's good to see you again. You're looking very grown up these days."

"Thanks," I said, blushing slightly at the compliment.

Mum and Jane were there to meet us when we got to Manchester. By the time we got back to the house Norman had left for work already.

"Looks like you've done the place up a bit since I was here last," I said.

"It'll do until we can afford something better. They keep threatening to demolish these old row houses but nothing's happened yet."

"It's like being on Coronation Street when I come here," I said. "I keep expecting Ken Barlow to come knocking on the door, or to see Ena Sharples walking down the street. Jane's even starting to talk like them," I said, trying to mimic the Manchester accent.

"You sound more like those Beatles from Liverpool than someone from Manchester," Mum laughed. "You'll have to work on that accent if you plan on living up here."

An awkward silence fell between us.

"Well, I'll have to see what happens when I'm finished college," I said. "Shall I put the kettle on for tea?" I asked, anxious to change subjects.

We only spent a few days in Manchester before packing up for the trip to Andover to see our grandparents off. They were sailing from Southampton to America to see my Uncle Roger and his family. They had just moved there from New Zealand so that he could open another factory.

"The train fare is going to cost an arm and a leg," Mum grumbled the night before we were due to leave. "At least Justin and Jane are only half fare."

I, on the other hand, was a month away from my seventeenth birthday and would cost full fare. Mum eyed me closely.

"Don't suppose you'd pass for half fare, with all that makeup and mod clothes," she said.

"We can dress her up like a kid," Jane chimed in.

"Worth a try," said Mum. "Take off that makeup and put your hair in bunches, I bet you'd look young enough. It might save a few bob which would sure help me out. It's not like British Rail will go bankrupt over it."

I scoffed at the idea but had to admit it might work. I was slim and had a small frame which could easily belong to a younger person.

"I suppose it's worth a try," I said, frowning slightly.

When I came down to breakfast next morning I was dressed like a twelve year old school girl.

"Maybe we can say we're twins," I teased Justin, "now that we're both twelve."

"People might be inclined to believe you," Mum said, "the two of you look like peas in a pod. Always have. Now hurry up, all of you, or we'll miss the bloody train."

At the station I hung back while Mum bought our tickets. Jane had handed me one of her dolls as we were leaving the house and I clung to it as we shuffled through the gate and onto the platform.

"Don't go over doing it," Mum hissed, once we were through the gate. "People will think you're some kind of retard."

"That's exactly what I feel like," I grumbled.

When we arrived at Aunty Barbara's house in Andover there was complete bedlam. Her three young boys, Matthew, Mark and Luke, were chasing each other around the house and the free range chickens, which normally lived in the back yard, were pecking crumbs off the living room carpet. Rather than being overwhelmed by the chaos around her, Aunty Barbara was in her element. Pots of potatoes and beef stew burbled away on the stove and every inch of counter top of filled with cakes, scones, sweets, and treats.

"Hello my darlings," Aunty Barbara gushed, as she swept each of us up into her bosomy embrace. "I'm so glad you're here. I was wondering what I was going to do with all this food, but I can see you all need fattening up."

My mother, who had been tall and skinny all her life despite her healthy appetite, laughed. "Fat chance of that, but we're more than willing to let you try."

Eleven of us sat down for dinner that evening. It was almost like Christmas, only better. Uncle Sean, who had stopped at the pub on his way home just like he did every day, was in fine spirits as he took the seat at the head of the table. Aunty Barbara put a meat platter, piled high with potatoes and stew in front of him. Regular dinner plates weren't big enough for Uncle Sean's appetite. My grandfather sat at the other end of the table.

"How long will it take to get to America, Granddad?" I asked.

"We'll be on the ship for six days, and then we spend a few nights in New York with Uncle Roger before driving down to South Carolina to see the girls," Granddad said, obviously excited.

Mark held up six fingers to Matthew and made a wavy line motion with his hand, pointing towards Granddad. Matthew, the eldest boy, was completely deaf but Mark made sure he kept him involved in conversations. The two brothers communicated almost telepathically at times and even little Luke knew how to 'talk' to his big brother with his hands.

Next morning, Uncle Sean drove us in relays to the station to catch the train to Southampton. We found our way to the docks where the Queen Mary was moored at her berth, surrounded by a swirling hubbub of activity as passengers and baggage were loaded on board.

Uncle Sean took the boys on a tour of the ship while the rest of us helped Nanny and Granddad settle into their cabin. When Granddad said he was going out for some air I said I'd go with him. We stood leaning on the railing of the top deck watching the beehive of activity below us on the dock.

"I wish I was coming with you," I said wistfully. "I can't wait to finish college and travel the world. There's so much to see out there."

"You've plenty of time for that, maid. As long as you do well in college, the world will be your oyster," Granddad said. He continued watching the scene below as he talked, as if thinking out loud. "I always reckoned your mother would be a world famous pianist one day. A talent like that shouldn't have been allowed to go to waste, but she made her own bed and now she's lying in it. Don't you go making the same mistakes, maid."

"Don't worry, Granddad, I won't," I said, not really sure which mistakes he was referring to.

Was it her choice of husband? Or that she got married so young?

Or the fact that she had four babies she didn't seem to want? How do you know, without the benefit of hindsight, which mistake will be the one that maps your route through life, the one you can't gloss over and fix with an 'I'm sorry' and a smile. How often had I been on the brink of making such mistakes myself, only to be spared by good luck, or was it fate? What if the black man who had taken me back to his room in Leicester had decided to rape me, instead of sending me home to my mother with a warning not to wander the streets alone at night? What if the police hadn't found me in the back of that car before anything more serious happened? I had no illusions about how my life would have been if those 'mistakes' hadn't been avoided. And what if my mother hadn't made what my grandfather seemed to consider her biggest mistake of all, and married my father? Then my siblings and I wouldn't exist. Some mistakes weren't mistakes at all, I decided.

Shortly after my return home to Devon, Miss Harrison came to see me again. She told me she had been to visit my father earlier that day.

"Your father was very pleased to know you and Justin had been to Manchester for a holiday," she said. "He worries that Justin seems to get overlooked sometimes. He's also concerned that perhaps your mother will try to persuade you to go and work in Manchester once you're done college. I told him that you had dallied with this idea, but that you didn't feel you could really settle with your mother."

Miss Harrison raised one eyebrow as she spoke, as if looking for reassurance that she had understood my feelings correctly.

I shrugged. I wasn't even sure I understood my emotions around my mother, so how on earth could I convey them to someone else.

"We talked about it while I was there," I said, "but I told her I couldn't really think about it until I'd finished college."

"Your father was also wondering if you're happy with the Desmond's. I told him you always assured me you were."

Again she paused. When I didn't offer a response she continued.

"Your father said he felt there had been some arguments lately between you and the Desmond's, and that they had asked you to leave. I told him this was all news to me, as you had never mentioned it."

"Oh that was nothing," I said, surprised that my father had even mentioned it. "Dad came by and took me for a drive before I went to Manchester. Amy and I had just had a row about something and her mother said that if we couldn't get along maybe I should think about leaving. I was pretty upset about it at the time, but it all blew over," I offered, by way of explanation. "Whenever we have an argument Amy is always quick to point out that this is *her* house and *her* family, so I'm anxious to keep on the right side of her, which isn't always easy."

"Well, he's hoping you'll get a job in Devon so that he can still see you and you can keep in touch with your family and friends easier. He's met Anthony, I gather, and seems to like him well enough, although he was concerned about the fact that he doesn't have a job. He doesn't want you being influenced by Anthony's attitude towards working. I assured him it was unlikely. You appear to be very shrewd and independent about situations like this."

I was chuffed at the obvious compliment.

"Have you given any thought to finding a job yet?" Miss Harrison asked.

"I'm looking but I haven't found anything."

"Do you want to continue living with the Desmond's after you finish college?"

"Oh yes, I think so. I'm very comfortable here, providing of course that Mr. and Mrs. Desmond agree."

"I'll discuss it with them. I believe Mrs. Desmond wants a word with me before I leave, anyhow, to discuss her retaining fee while you were away."

"What retaining fee?" I asked.

"The County paid a portion of your room and board while you were away on holiday, so the room could be held for you. Apparently Mrs. Desmond has some concern about the amount."

"Oh, I see," I said.

I wasn't naïve enough to think the Desmond's would offer me a home without some financial consideration, but at the same time it seemed so sordid. I liked to fantasize that I was here because they wanted me here, not because I was a financially lucrative proposition. I was getting awfully tired of living on the edge of other people's lives. I wrapped a shell of arrogance around myself and pretended I didn't care. You can't hurt me. I am a rock, I am an island.

I tried to keep a low profile over the next few days, sensing that all was not well in paradise but not really understanding what the problem was. When I got home on Monday, I was surprised to find Mr. and Mrs. Desmond in the kitchen together. Mrs. Desmond looked as though she had been crying.

"Hello," I said, rather tentatively, "is everything alright?"

Mrs. Desmond turned her back to me and busied herself at the stove. Mr. Desmond turned to face me.

"No it isn't, young lady, and I've had about enough of this."

I waited for him to continue, but he didn't.

"Enough of what?" I asked, confused.

"You and your shenanigans, disrupting the whole household. You were late home again last night. We need you in by eleven. You can't expect us to wait up for you, night after night."

"But I have my own key," I said, "and I don't expect you to wait up for me. And besides, I was home before Amy, so I don't see what the problem is."

Mrs. Desmond swung around to face me. She fixed me with a bog-eyed stare, hatred and anger distorting her facial muscles almost beyond recognition.

"How dare you answer back like that, you little hussy," she hissed at me. I took a step backwards, too startled by the ferocity and suddenness of the outburst to know how to react.

Mrs. Desmond was a relatively big woman who could pack a formidable punch if she felt so inclined. Anytime I'd seen my mother this mad you could be sure she'd start hurling blows at you any minute. Tears sprang to my eyes and my body went rigid as adrenaline rushed through my veins. I prepared to do battle. But Mrs. Desmond didn't strike out. Instead, a barrage of verbal abuse spewed out of her mouth as she hurled accusations and insults at me like rocks.

"We can't even invite our own friends over for a drink these days, without having that no good boyfriend of yours sitting on the sofa night after night."

"But you said it was alright for Anthony to come over any time he liked," I protested. "I don't get it. Why didn't you say something before, instead of making me believe everything's fine when obviously it isn't?"

"And then when you do go out you stay out all hours of the night, leaving us here worrying about you. You have no consideration for other people's feelings; you only ever think about yourself."

"That's not true," I retorted, stung by her words, "and you know it."

"Watch your manners," Mr. Desmond interjected, pointing his finger at me. "Mrs. Desmond is understandably upset at the moment, so perhaps you'd better go to your room and think about how you can learn to live by the rules in this house."

Mrs. Desmond burst into tears. "I can't stand to have her in this house another minute," she wailed.

Mr. Desmond turned to console her. I was riveted to the spot, like a rabbit caught in the headlights. Was this really happening?

"Obviously I'm not welcome here any longer," I said, anger welling up in my throat like bile, "I'll go and spend the night at my girlfriend's."

Mrs. Desmond spun around and lurched towards me, her hands outstretched. For a fleeting moment I thought she was going to hug me, but instead she clutched at my arms and started shaking me violently.

"You're not going anywhere. You'll bloody well stay here and sleep in your own bed where you belong."

I broke away from her grasp and ran upstairs and locked myself in my bedroom. What had I done to bring on this onslaught? I wished Amy was home. After what seemed like an eternity, I smelled food cooking. I waited for someone to call me down to dinner, but no one did. Eventually the sounds from the kitchen were replaced by the muffled sound of the television in the sitting room. I heard the phone ring. Mr. Desmond called up to me that Anthony was on the phone. I pretended to be asleep, and didn't answer. I was afraid to leave my room.

I heard Amy come home. When she came upstairs she went straight to her own room. Usually she'd tap on my door and we'd chat about our day before going to bed. But not today. Her parents must have said something to her. I slept fitfully that night.

By morning I'd resolved to be a better person. Hunger was a great motivator. I would tell Anthony not to come over so often, and I'd make sure I was home before my curfew, not after. I would be the model lodger.

I dressed and went downstairs for breakfast. Mr. Desmond was sitting at the kitchen table drinking coffee and reading the paper. Mrs. Desmond was busy at the sink.

"Good morning," I said, careful to put a cheery note in my voice.

I presumed from the bags under her eyes that Mrs. Desmond had slept as poorly as me. She didn't speak. Mr. Desmond grunted as he quickly glanced up at me, before going back to the newspaper. I opened the fridge in search of fixings to make my lunch.

"What are you doing in there?" Mrs. Desmond asked sharply. "Cereal and milk are on the table already."

"I was just looking for something to make my lunch with," I said defensively.

"You get an allowance from the County for your lunches, so don't go taking anything from there," Mrs. Desmond said, as she reached across and pushed the fridge door shut.

"But I didn't have any dinner last night, and now I'm starving."

"You heard Mrs. Desmond," Mr. Desmond said, without lifting his eyes from the paper.

I sat down at the table and made myself a bowl of cereal. When that was done, I made myself another. I was tempted to go for a third but thought better of it. I got up to put my dish in the sink, scraping my chair across the linoleum. I hoped Amy would wake up soon and come downstairs. Something was obviously terribly wrong and I didn't know what to do next. Parents had rows with their children all the time, didn't they? And then they kissed and made up, didn't they? I hoped we'd get to the kiss and make up bit soon.

"Will you be calling Miss Harrison or shall I?" Mrs. Desmond asked, her back towards me.

My heart sank. I was hoping everything would blow over, that this was just a menopausal moment for Mrs. Desmond. But now she wanted to drag Miss Harrison into it.

"I guess I can," I said, as I rattled my dish around in the sink. "But I don't really know what to say." I put on a sing song voice. "Hello Miss Harrison, I've been a naughty girl and now Mrs. Desmond wants to talk to you about what a terrible person I am."

Out of the corner of my eye I saw Mr. Desmond rushing towards me, his hand raised.

"Don't you dare speak to us like that," he said.

I panicked and grabbed a hot water bottle which was sitting by the sink, waiting to be emptied. I hurled it at him before running around the other side of the table and out of the room.

"You better not be here when we get home tonight," I heard Mrs. Desmond screaming after me.

I slammed my bedroom door shut as hard as I could then sat on my bed and wondered what I should do next. I was shaking from head to toe.

After a while the house fell silent and I crept downstairs to use the phone. Miss Harrison said she would be right over. Next I phoned Anthony and asked him to come over too. I needed a shoulder to cry on. I went back upstairs and started packing my belongings. I had no idea where I was going; I just knew I wouldn't be staying here.

By the time Miss Harrison arrived Anthony was there already and my belongings were piled up by the front door. Anthony went into the kitchen to make some coffee while Miss Harrison and I talked in the sitting room. I chain smoked as I recounted the events of the last twelve hours.

"When I was here just a few days ago, Mrs. Desmond told me that there were several things which would have to be discussed and cleared with you, if you wanted to continue living with them. I suggested she talk to you about these. Did she do that?"

I looked at Miss Harrison through teary eyes. "No. She didn't say anything. I had no idea anything was wrong until I came home from school yesterday and she went ballistic on me. It's so unfair. One minute she makes me believe everything is just great and then this, whammo, eruption time. No warning, no nothing. I still don't really know what the problem is. Not to cause this much trouble, anyway. What kinda things did she talk about?"

"Well, she seemed to think that at times you could be very thoughtless and selfish. She mentioned an incident when you took Mr. Desmond's morning paper to school with you, without even asking."

"Oh my God, don't tell me this is all about that. That was ages ago and I've already said I'm sorry and won't do it again. What's the big deal? What's wrong with these people?"

Miss Harrison continued, ignoring my outburst.

"She also said you seemed to have difficulty getting along with Mr. Desmond. Is this true?"

"No," I said, shaking my head furiously, "I really like the man; at least I did until this morning. He's like the perfect parent that everyone wants. Amy talks back to him all the time and he doesn't seem to mind, so sometimes I did it too. But I didn't mean anything by it. I was just trying to be normal and act like I've seen other kids do with their parents."

"Well apparently anything you do seems to annoy him. Mrs. Desmond also mentioned a couple of occasions when you didn't get home until almost 2 a.m. When they tried to speak to you about it you were very rude, apparently."

Miss Harrison waited for my reply.

"I guess I was late a couple of times," I conceded, "but no later than Amy."

"And then there's the issue of Anthony being here every evening. This annoyed them very much."

"But they told me they didn't mind having Anthony here. They know he doesn't have a job at the moment. They said it was alright for us to hang out here evenings. How was I to know they were saying one thing, but meaning another, I'm not fucking psychic! I hate people like that. Why didn't Amy tell me, if her parents didn't have the guts to? She could have let me know that they were upset about things, and then none of this would have happened."

Indignation and anger boiled inside me, spilling out in wracked sobs.

"Amy breaks all her parents' rules but they don't throw her out. It's not fair."

Miss Harrison waited until my outburst had subsided.

"Well, the important thing now is to find you new accommodations. I've contacted the Southams, a foster family in Torquay. You can stay with them for now. They have four children of their own, ages twelve to six months, and two foster children, so things are a bit tight. But Mrs. Southam says two of her children can share a room until you find more permanent accommodations. You'll be finished college in three months. Once you have a job you'll probably want to find more suitable accommodations close to where you end up working."

"I suppose," I mumbled, as I slumped back in my seat. I didn't have any fight left in me.

"Well we'd better get your things into the car. Perhaps Anthony can help you while I make a phone call, to let the Southam's know we're on our way."

I swooped up armloads of bags and started towards the front door. "Come on, Anthony, let's get out of this shit hole!"

The Southam's place was a large Victorian mansion which they were in the process of renovating, apparently on funds earned by fostering children. Mrs. Southam was warm and welcoming and showed me to my room, apologizing for the childish décor.

"You can put up some posters and things to make it more comfy to your taste. Just don't go leaving holes in the walls."

She chattered on without taking a breath the whole time we were moving my belongings in. I could hear the muffled sounds of a television coming from the front room, and every so often a small child of one size or another would appear in the doorway to watch what we were doing. A baby started crying.

"Ah, there's the baby ready for his feeding. I'll leave you to settle in. Come on down to the kitchen as soon as you're ready and we'll fix you something to eat. You look like you could do with a good meal."

Miss Harrison cleared some boxes off a chair and sat down. I busied myself checking the closet and dresser drawers, half heartedly putting things away.

"Well you should be comfortable here until you find something else," she said. "We'll need to let your parents know where you're staying. And I think you should plan on going back to college tomorrow. There really isn't any need to delay it longer. And besides, it will do you good to get back to normal as soon as possible. Life goes on, you know. And it might be a good idea to contact the Desmond's soon. This was just a falling out, after all, and you did spend many happy months with them. That should count for something."

"I don't think so," I scoffed. "I wouldn't know what to say, and I wouldn't believe anything they said to me. If they'd been more honest with me from the start this wouldn't have happened. I never want to see them again."

CHAPTER SIXTEEN

I kept a low profile at the Southam's, and I made sure I obeyed all the rules. Put your dirty dishes in the sink. Be home by ten thirty. Say please and thank you. Smile. I liked the Southams and their motley crew of offspring and foster children, but I wouldn't let myself into their lives, nor them into mine. I stayed very much on the outside, referring to myself as the lodger.

My father, perhaps sensing my loneliness, became a regular visitor. Most Sundays he picked me up in his car and we'd go for a drive. If the weather was nice he'd put the roof down and we'd go exploring the back roads of Dartmoor, or head along the coast, looking for a pub where we could stop and have lunch. A pint of beer for Dad, a Babycham for me, and two ploughman's lunches with Branston pickle on the side. Dad preferred to sit at the bar so he could talk to the barmen. They all seemed to know him and wanted to know where he was playing these days.

"Your mother was your age when I met her," Dad told me one Sunday, his eyes misting over. "And you're just as pretty as she was, my beauty."

I didn't answer. I couldn't. There was a knot in the pit of my stomach. I didn't want Dad looking at me that way and thinking about my mother. He might get other thoughts. I finished my drink in silence then told Dad I had to be home early. I'd forgotten about some homework I had to do. Dad poured the rest of his beer down his throat, smacking his lips together as he always did when he finished a pint, then wiped the foam off his upper lip with the back of his hand.

"Come on then, my beauty, lets get you home," he said.

He waved goodbye to the barman then casually put his arm across my shoulders. My body stiffened involuntarily and my breath came short and shallow. I could smell the beer on his breath, just like I'd smelled it a hundred times before in Riverton, at night, when I was alone and scared.

"I just want to go home, Dad. You know, back to my lodgings."

The next time Dad came to visit, I didn't dress up or put on any makeup. I looked less like my mother that way.

My studying paid off and I was the top student in several subjects at college. Di, the girl who sat across from me, was neck and neck with me for the top spot. She was the mid-life baby of a wealthy family and was always dressed in fabulous outfits, a different pair of shoes for each of them. She wore her long bottle-assisted blond hair in a ponytail at the nape of her neck, tied with a black ribbon with long tails, just like Julie Christie in the movie Dr. Zhivago. Di had a parent-approved boyfriend, called Mike, whom she was expected to marry. He drove a new MGB convertible and sometimes picked Di up from school.

To me her life seemed perfect, but Di didn't think so. She told me her parents were overprotective and Mike was dull as dishwater, but at least he had a nice car. She yearned for more freedom and excitement in her life. Just a little, not a lot. She didn't want to fall out of the boat, just rock it a little.

Di saw my life as being free of parental interference. She believed I could do what I wanted, when I wanted. I couldn't tell her how lonely my life really was, how isolated I felt, or how much I yearned for a real home. She wouldn't understand. We started hanging around together, each yearning for what the other had.

Besides the pressure of studying and final exams there was the looming issue of my future employment. It clouded all other thoughts. What if I couldn't find a job? How would I get by? I directed my anxiety towards Anthony. I resented his lack-luster job search and berated him for being lazy. He seemed hurt and confused by my outbursts but grudgingly increased his efforts. Eventually he managed to secure 'a position with a future' as an apprentice draftsman in an architects office, but with little pay in the present.

A few weeks before the end of my course, Mr. Holden, Head of Administration at the college, announced that there would be a secretarial position opening up in his department at the beginning of July. Students from the advanced secretarial course were encouraged to apply. I threw my name into the ring and waited. Two weeks later I was summoned into Mr. Holden's office for an interview.

I was nervous, but answered his questions as best I could. I put all the interview skills I'd been taught by Mrs. Woodstock to good practice. A few days later I was summoned back to Mr. Holden's office and informed that I was the successful candidate. My joy knew no bounds.

"Can you start at the beginning of July?" he asked.

I was momentarily speechless as I grappled with the urge to crawl under the desk and kiss his feet.

"Oh yes, absolutely!" I finally managed to blurt out.

"Your salary will depend upon your exam results and the number of 'O' levels you have, which is six I believe."

I nodded and waited for him to continue.

"Unfortunately your shorthand and typing results won't be available until sometime in August, so we'll have to start you at the general clerical pay level until we know how you made out. The salary is based on the local government scale and annual pay raises will be based on performance and cost of living increases. The Devon County Education Department will send you a contract in the near future, outlining all the details of your employment here. If you have any questions when it arrives, just come and see me."

I nodded enthusiastically and waited for him to continue. When he didn't, I asked the question that had been burning on my lips.

"Can you give me an idea of how much the salary might actually be?" I asked. "It's just that I have to look for a place to live, so I need to know how much I can afford to pay in rent."

He shuffled through some papers on his desk, eventually pulling one from the pile.

"Ah, here it is. The starting salary for a general clerk is £415 per annum. Of course, this will be adjusted to the appropriate pay level once we have your exam results. Any increase will be back dated to your first day of work."

"Thank you," I said, beaming from ear to ear. "I should be able to manage very well on that, especially when my raises come through. I'm almost sure I passed at 120 words per minute in shorthand, and I'm hoping for 60 words a minute in typing."

Now that I had a job, I set about finding somewhere more permanent to live. Teresa Manley, a girl in my course, said she wanted to find a flat in Torquay at the end of the summer. She was looking for roommates and liked the idea of us sharing.

When I telephoned Miss Harrison to give her the news about my job, I launched the idea of me moving into a flat too. She didn't sound very enthusiastic but said we could discuss it during her next visit. When we met a few weeks later Miss Harrison told me the Children's Committee had not approved my request to move into a flat.

"What do you mean I can't move into a flat? Why not, for heaven's sake? I thought you people wanted me out on my own before I turned eighteen."

"We certainly hope to see you living independently by the time you're eighteen, and no longer under the care of the Children's Committee," Miss Harrison said. "But while girls in care often progress to living in a flat, this is a privilege which they have to earn. First they have to show that they can be successful living in other types of accommodation."

"But Mrs. Southam hasn't had any trouble with me, so I can't see what the problem is."

"Well, we'll have to see how things work out. You can stay at the Southam's until you've finished college, which is still a few weeks away. But we'll need to find you other lodgings after that as the Southam's need your room. Do you have any ideas where you might live, other than a flat?"

"Not really," I mumbled, "But I'll ask around."

And ask around I did. I was beginning to despair about finding anything, when Anthony came to my rescue.

Mr. Day, his new boss, said he had a room I could rent. And, if I was prepared to babysit occasionally, I could have it at a reduced rate. I arranged to move in at the end of June, just ten days away, and stay until September, by which time I hoped to convince the Children's Committee that I should be allowed to move into my own flat.

"A lady by the name of Miss Harrison will have to talk to you, to finalize all the details," I told Mrs. Day when I went to see the place. "I'll ring her and give her your number."

When I got home from college the next day, Miss Harrison was there waiting for me.

"Have you been in touch with the Days yet?" I asked as soon as I saw her.

"I've arranged to go there after I leave here. But I did meet with Mr. Holden this afternoon, to see how you were doing with your course and to discuss your future employment with him. He gave me a very glowing report and seems keen about having you as his secretary. You must be very proud to have gotten such a plum job right out of class."

"Yes I am," I conceded, "but he was a bit vague about my actual salary. Did he say anything to you about it?"

"He confirmed that your salary would be £415 per annum to start, but that it would be increased to £475 per annum if you get your stage 2 typing, and to £535 per annum if you get 120 words per minute in your shorthand exams. Once your results are in, your salary will be adjusted retroactively to the day you started."

"That's great," I said, quickly doing the math in my head, "I should be able to live very well on that. But there is a problem. Mr. Holden said I'll only get paid once a month, in arrears, which means I won't get my first pay packet until the end of July. What am I supposed to live on until then? Will the Children's Committee still pay my subsidy for July?"

"Yes, of course they will," Miss Harrison assured me, much to my relief.

"And I'll have to find somewhere permanent to live after September," I said. "My friend, Teresa, and I keep checking the papers for flats. And now we've found two other girls who are interested in sharing with us, so we can split the rent four ways."

"I've already discussed your situation with the Children's Committee and we feel you should start your job and settle in there first, before any decision can be made about you moving into a flat. You were asked to leave the Desmond's so we need to assess how you got on at the Day's in the meantime. We can discuss it again in September."

I bristled. "But that's not fair. It's not my fault Mrs. Desmond's had a spazzy fit and asked me to leave. It's not like I did anything wrong."

"I can understand that you're disappointed, but I think the Children's Committee is being very reasonable with the conditions they've set out for you. I'm sure eventually you'll come to realize just how reasonable we're all being, in trying to get you on your own two feet."

The next ten days flew by in a blur of final exams, packing and goodbyes. July 1st I moved in with the Days and the following Monday I started my new job.

Mr. Holden was a patient and enthusiastic mentor. He explained how things worked behind the scenes at the college and seemed to delight in my insatiable appetite for information.

After a very lengthy silence I finally got a letter from my mother. She congratulated me on graduating and asked when I would be moving to Manchester, now that I had finished school. She didn't comment on my job, even though I'd written to her about it. Instead she enclosed a newspaper clipping listing jobs available in Manchester. I wrote back, reminding her that I had a good job in Torquay already so didn't plan on leaving Devon at this time. As a peace offering I told her I had some holidays coming and would like to visit her for a few days at the end of July. Anthony said he would like to come with me.

We took the train to Manchester and were met at the station by my mother.

"Sleeping arrangements might be a bit awkward," Mum said as soon as we were settled in a taxi. "We only have two bedrooms so Anthony will have to sleep with you, unless he'd rather sleep in the bathtub."

"Um, I guess the bathtub will be fine," Anthony said, casting a quick glance at me to see if this was some kind of joke.

Mum looked him up and down.

"It'll be a tight fit. How tall are you anyway?"

"Just over six feet," Anthony said, as he grappled with the realization that she wasn't joking, "but I can manage. It'll be a new experience but I don't want to be any bother."

"I don't know why you don't just crawl in beside Gail. I thought you were coming for a dirty weekend but I guess I was wrong."

"I'll be fine," Anthony insisted, but I could tell from his tone of voice that he was already regretting coming. We sat in stony silence the rest of the way to Sun Street.

Anthony spent the first night trying to sleep scrunched up in the bathtub. After that it was decided that Jane and I would share a bed, and Anthony could have her bed. It meant we were all sleeping in the same room but at least we weren't sleeping in the same bed under my mother's roof. I wasn't ready for that.

When we got back to Devon Mr. Day asked if Anthony had gone to Manchester with me. I was surprised at the question, assuming that Anthony had arranged for the time off before leaving. Apparently he hadn't. When Anthony turned up for work on Monday morning Mr. Day fired him. He needed someone he could rely on, he said, and Anthony obviously wasn't that person.

"Are you crazy?" I yelled at Anthony when I saw him later that evening. "You finally get yourself a job with a future and you go and blow it by buggering off for a week without even asking for the time off. What the hell were you thinking?"

"I was afraid that if I asked for the time off he'd say no, and then I wouldn't have been able to go with you."

"I was only going for a week, for Christ's sake. You didn't have to come with me if it meant losing your job. I can't believe you were that silly! What are you going to do now?"

"Dunno," Anthony said. "I'll think of something."

"Huh," I scoffed, "it must be nice to have parents feeding you and giving you a place to live for free, and you without a care in the world. Some of us have to work for a living and take care of ourselves. Grow up, Anthony, you aren't a baby anymore."

"Why are you so angry? What's it to you?"

"I don't want a loser for a boyfriend, that's what it is to me. And what am I supposed to do about living with the Days? I'm sure they won't want me staying with them now that you've been fired. Where am I supposed to live now?"

I burst into tears, unable to explain why I felt so let down by Anthony's behaviour. I had hoped that one day he'd be in a position to take care of me, that he'd be someone I could depend on and we could build a life together, so I wouldn't feel so alone. But now I seriously doubted that. Anthony seemed more like a liability than an asset and I wasn't sure I could handle it any longer.

I wiped away my tears and asked him to take me home. I was tired and had a headache. I had to go to work next day, even if he didn't. I said I would call him in a few days, but doubted that I actually would.

Next morning I phoned Miss Harrison and explained the situation.

"Have you talked to the Day's about this?" Miss Harrison asked.

"No, not yet. I thought I'd talk to you first. I'm afraid they're going to throw me out. They only took me in 'cos I'm a friend of Anthony's."

"Is your rent paid up?"

"Yes, I gave her two weeks in advance last Friday, when I got back from Manchester. Do you think she'll give it back to me if she throws me out?"

"Well, to start with, I don't believe she will throw you out. It isn't your fault Anthony acted so irresponsibly, and I'm sure the Days know that. But you will have to talk to them about it and clear the air. They made a commitment to you that you could stay until September, so

I'm sure they'll honour that commitment. Talk it over with them and let me know what they say. If there are any problems, I'll talk to them, but I'm sure you can deal with this situation yourself."

"But what if …"

Miss Harrison cut me off.

"Don't go dreaming up a load of 'what if's' until you've talked to them. Chances are everything will be fine."

I groaned out loud. "This is so unfair. If they do throw me out because of what Anthony did, then the Children's Committee will say I screwed up and then they'll never let me go and live in a flat with my friends."

"We'll cross that bridge when, and if, we come to it." Miss Harrison replied.

When I got home from work that evening, I found Mrs. Day in the kitchen fixing tea. I asked if she needed any help, anxious for an opportunity to speak with her. The children were in the sitting room watching television with Mr. Day.

"I suppose you'll want me to move out, now that Anthony doesn't work for Mr. Day anymore," I said, as I helped set the table.

"Now why on earth would we want you to do that?" she asked, surprised.

"I dunno, it's just that you only rented me a room because I was Anthony's friend, and now, well, you know." My voice trailed off.

"We wouldn't hear of it. We like having you here, and the boys are just getting used to having you around. And besides, the money comes in handy and Lord knows there's never enough of that to go around. No, dear, don't you worry about that. Anthony has to accept responsibility for his own behaviour, not you. Now go and tell them tea's ready."

I was so happy I could have kissed her. I went to get the others for tea. It was almost like family.

Miss Harrison came to see me the following week. We met at the College after I'd finished work, and went for a coffee nearby.

"The job's going great," I told her. "I have a copy of my employment contract here which shows the terms and conditions of employment and the pay increments."

I spread the contract on the table between us so we could both study it.

"I got my first pay packet last week but it wasn't as much as I was expecting by the time they took off income tax and all that stuff. I can't wait to get my exam results so they'll put my salary up to £535 a year. I should be able to live on that, no problem."

"I'm glad to know things are going so well for you, Gail, and I'm sure you'll manage just fine once your salary gets adjusted to the full amount." Miss Harrison shifted awkwardly in her seat, avoiding eye contact. "Unfortunately, though, I have some bad news. As you know, the Children's Committee paid the July subsidy for your room and board and living expenses while you were waiting for your first pay cheque. However, at their meeting last week it was decided that you should repay half of it."

I stared at her in disbelief. "I beg your pardon? You can't be serious."

"I know it must be difficult for you to accept, Gail, but they feel you're in a position to repay half of the £27 they paid out on your behalf, that being £13-10-0."

"I don't believe this!" I said, my voice rising. "The minute I get a few quid in my hand they go and claw it back. What am I supposed to do? Don't these fucking people realize that I have to support myself from now on? I can't afford to pay back that much money. There was no mention of paying it back when you told me they'd pay for July."

"Please keep your voice down, Gail, and watch your language. I'm sorry if I misled you, but I had no way of knowing they would make this decision. Your situation is quite unique. They feel that as you've managed to secure such a well paid job you can afford to repay them, half at least."

"Oh I get it! If I was working as some low paid store clerk they wouldn't expect me to repay it. Is that it? Shit, now I'm being penalized for doing well. Doesn't that seem a little unfair to you, 'cos it sure as hell does to me!"

"They don't expect you to repay it all at once. You can make weekly payments until it's paid off."

"Well to hell with them," I snapped. "I'll show them that I can pay my bills." I pulled my new bank book out of my handbag and slammed it on the table. "Here, take a look for yourself. I got paid last Friday. I paid Mrs. Day two weeks rent in advance, took my usual one pound a week for clothing, and another pound for pocket money, and left the rest in the bank. Which isn't very much."

"You don't have to give me anything right now, but you'll need to budget some form of repayment into future pay packets. I know this is a hard pill to swallow, Gail, but there is some good news too. After discussion, the Children's Committee have given permission for you to move into a flat."

It took a moment or two for her words to sink in.

"Are you serious?" I asked, not trusting my own ears.

Miss Harrison nodded.

"Wow, I don't believe it. That's fantastic. I have a copy of the lease in my room at the Days. We can go and get it right now. The other girls have signed it already but I told them I couldn't until I got permission. We have to pay a month's rent in advance. The other girls have all put in their five pounds, now they're just waiting for mine."

I stopped short, remembering the repayment the Committee had just demanded.

"Do you think the Committee will wait until I get my rise and back pay before I repay July's subsidy?"

"I'm sure they'll understand under the circumstances, but you can't leave it too long."

When we got to the Day's I left Miss Harrison to talk with Mrs. Day while I went up to my room to get the lease. When I came back downstairs Mrs. Day excused herself, saying she was busy in the kitchen.

"Did you tell her I would be moving into my own flat?" I asked, as soon as we were alone.

"No, I thought it would be better for you to handle that, once everything is finalized."

"The lease starts the 16th September, and I'm sure the Days will let me stay here until then.

Miss Harrison reviewed the lease.

"This looks fine," she said, "you can go ahead and sign this. I'll be away on leave from 19th August until early September, but I'll come and see you when you're in your new flat."

"Oh boy," I gushed, "my life should be perfect by the time you get back."

CHAPTER SEVENTEEN

I told Mrs. Day I'd be moving into my own flat on September 16, so would be giving my notice. She seemed happy for me at first. But when I asked if she would reduce my room and board in the meantime, to make up for the fact that I never ate there on weekends, she wasn't so accommodating.

"The arrangement was for room and board, and the fact that you choose not to come home for meals is not my problem," she chided.

"But I usually eat at Anthony's on the weekend, or we go out for fish and chips. It's much easier than trying to be home at a certain time to eat."

"A deal's a deal," she said, becoming irritated. "If you remember, I gave you a reduced rent in exchange for babysitting. But you're never home to babysit, so what good is that? By rights, I should be charging you more, not less. And from now on I'd appreciate it if you didn't lock your bedroom door when you go out. How am I supposed to change your sheets?"

"You don't have to bother with that, I'll do it. I don't want you snooping around in my bedroom."

Poor choice of words I realized, as soon as they were out of my mouth. Her cheeks flushed and her eyes sparked.

"How dare you accuse me of snooping," she screamed, "after we took you in off the streets."

I scoffed. "I wasn't exactly on the streets, and you know it. I just needed a place to live until I could move into a flat, and your husband offered me a room here. Obviously it was a mistake."

"Suit yourself. You know where the door is."

"I sure as hell do. And as soon as you give me back the rent money I've paid in advance, I'll leave."

"You can forget about any refund. By rights I can keep that in lieu of notice, so you'll get nothing back from me."

"Fine, then I'll stay until the rent I've paid has run out, if that's the way you want to play it. Suits me."

The sound of the baby crying cut through the icy silence which fell between us.

"Now you've gone and woken the baby," she cried at me. "And just when I finally managed to get her down for her nap."

I stormed out of the house. I needed some fresh air and time to think. I walked down to the harbour and sat watching the seagulls. Now what was I going to do. I still had just over a month until I moved into the flat and my rent was only paid up for another week and a half at the Days. I had to work something out quickly or the Children's Committee might change their mind about letting me move into the flat.

Shazad, one of the other girls who would be sharing the flat with us, was staying in a student residence until the flat was available. She had commented that the place was half empty because of the summer holidays. I phoned her and arranged to meet with her landlady later that day. I had to show the Children's Committee that I could handle this situation myself.

"Can I move in next Saturday?" I asked the landlady when she'd finished showing me the room. "I'm already paid up where I am until then."

"That will be fine," she said, squinting at me, "but I'll need a deposit to hold the room."

I paid her two pounds and asked for a receipt.

Next morning I called Miss Harrison. I'd considered not saying anything to her, as she would be on holiday until after I moved into the flat, but I thought better of it. And a good thing too. Mrs. Day had already called to tell her side of the story.

"I just don't understand how things could go so haywire so quickly, Gail. When I was there just last week I got the impression from Mrs. Day that everything was fine. What happened?"

"We had a row, simple as that. She was being totally unreasonable and accused me of all sorts of things, so I told her I was moving out. But the stupid cow won't give me my rent money back, so I'm staying until next Saturday, and not a minute longer. But I've already found another place to stay until we move into the flat," I added, not wanting to give Miss Harrison an opportunity to interject. "Shazad's landlady has room for me. They're college approved digs, so it'll be alright, won't it? And it's only for two weeks."

It seemed to take Miss Harrison an eternity to respond.

"I'll need to at least contact the landlady by phone. But if they're college approved lodgings then I suppose it will be alright. And as you're paying your own rent there's no need to bother with a load of paperwork."

I gave Miss Harrison the details, wished her a happy holiday and hung up quickly before she could change her mind.

By the time Miss Harrison returned from her vacation I was settled into the flat. She met me at the college after work and I took her to the flat to show it off. I introduced her to Ann, the fourth member of our household, and Shazad who were home. Teresa was away on holiday with her family. After we finished touring the flat we sat in the kitchen, where we could have a little privacy. I put the kettle on and got out a jar of instant coffee.

"I got my exam results," I said, while we waited for the kettle to boil. "I passed the stage 2 typing and got 120 words per minute shorthand. I'll get that rise on my pay now, as well as the back pay they owe me. I can hardly wait to see my pay packet at the end of September. Money's a bit tight at the moment, but I think I'll be fine once my rise comes through."

I proudly set two steaming mugs of coffee on the table. Finally

I was in my own home, able to offer coffee and hospitality to my Child Care Officer. I wasn't a child anymore; I was an adult now. Or so I believed.

"How do your parents feel about your living in your own flat?" Miss Harrison asked as she sipped her coffee.

"I haven't seen my father for ages, but last time I did he was happy about the move. He seemed very proud of the fact that I was growing up and becoming independent. He's still talking about marrying his lady friend, but I've heard that before."

"And your mother, have you heard from her since you got back from Manchester?"

"Oh yes," I said, rolling my eyes. "She appeared on my doorstep out of the blue a couple of weeks ago. Didn't even write to say she was coming, just turned up with Jane in tow. Norman is away apparently, playing piano on the cruise ships, so she came back to Devon for a holiday. I had to work most of the time, so I didn't see too much of them. I think she hoped to stay with my Dad but now he's getting married again he wasn't so keen to see her, so she had to get a bed and breakfast. I don't think she even bothered to go and see Justin while she was here."

"Apparently she did ring Justin while she was in Devon, but you're right, she didn't get to see him."

"Poor Justin. Was he upset?"

"Actually, he seems very settled where he is at the moment. He's doing very well in school, and the Federicks took him to Scotland for a holiday this summer. He was very excited about it when I saw him last week."

"I hardly get to see him these days. Do you think he could come and have a visit with me, now I have my own flat?"

"It's a thought. I'll discuss it with the Federicks next time I go there."

She made a note in her file before continuing.

"There's one last thing before I go, Gail. Have you given any thought to the subsidy repayment yet?"

I groaned. "It's on my mind but it's been really expensive what with moving in here and everything. But I promise I'll give you a money order as soon as I'm able, at least for some of it."

Miss Harrison started to gather up her papers, signaling the end of our visit. I put our empty mugs in the sink along with the piles of dirty dishes already precariously stacked there. We still had a few details to work out when it came to household chores.

"And what news of Anthony; are you still dating him?"

"Not much anymore. Besides, I've met this other fellow who seems quite keen on me. His name is Robert Black and his parents own a hotel here in Torquay. He works in London but comes home most weekends. I think Anthony was a bit upset when I went for coffee with Robert, but he doesn't own me and it isn't like we did anything wrong. Anyhow, I don't know if Robert will call me again, but I'm hoping he does."

As the September sun gave way to the rains of October I saw less and less of Anthony; and more and more of Robert. Robert had a career, not an apprenticeship; and he had a car, not a scooter. He took me to fancy restaurants, not fish and chip shops; and entertained me with stories of life in London, not complaints about how he never had any money. While I once looked up to Anthony as a beacon of sophistication, I now saw him as immature and dull.

When I got paid at the end of September, I was disappointed to find that the promised pay increase wasn't included. Mr. Holden explained that these things took time to work through the system, and not to worry about it. It would be in my October pay packet, for sure.

At the beginning of October my father married his ladyfriend, Judy. It was a small wedding in a Registry Office and, as with my mother's wedding I was the only family member there. Judy had a friend from work attend as her witness, and Dad had a musician friend stand up for him. Afterwards we all went to the pub to celebrate, trailing confetti behind us. Judy, who was taller than Dad, wore a pale blue dress and matching pillbox hat. Dad wore his band suit, which had seen better days but had at least been dry cleaned for the occasion.

As always, Dad's trombone was in the boot of his car and after a few drinks he was persuaded to join with the in-house trio for a couple of tunes. He played the opening bars of Moonlight Serenade and a hush fell over the room. My heart filled with pride, as it always did whenever I heard him play.

By closing time Dad still had a line of drinks in front of him, bought by grateful patrons and well wishers. We stayed long after closing hours so he could finish them. By the time he was ready to leave it was obvious that he shouldn't be behind the wheel of a car, but he drove anyway. As we sped along the narrow country lanes Dad kept his hand on Judy's knee despite her pleas for him to keep both hands on the wheel.

I agreed to spend the night at their home rather than ask Dad to drive me home in his condition.

Dad and Judy had rented an eighteenth century cottage in South Brent, and while I had been there many times before, I had never been there at night. Judy loaned me a nightie and showed me to the spare room upstairs. The stair case was narrow and curved around an enormous fireplace which was the center of the downstairs. I was tired and said I was going straight to bed. Dad asked Judy to sit with him for a while downstairs. He cast a glance at her which turned my blood cold. I had seen that look too many times myself, in Riverton, when I lived with him.

I climbed into bed and pulled the covers tight around my ears, willing myself to fall asleep. I didn't want to be here. It felt like I was twelve again, shivering in my bed, dreading the sound of Daddy's footsteps on the stairs. Some time later I thought I heard muffled sounds on the stairs and Dad's voice, a raspy whisper, urging Judy on. I smothered my ears with the pillow. Nothing had changed. My Daddy still turned into a monster at night. He was just riding a different horse these days.

After a while the house went quiet. I lay there, rigid with fear until I fell into a fitful sleep. I was awake at first light. I got up, got dressed, and slipped downstairs. I left a note on the kitchen table saying I'd decided to take the bus back to Torquay rather than disturb them. I wished them well.

When I got paid at the end of October my pay rise still hadn't come through. When I approached Mr. Holden about the problem he suggested I call the Clerk's office to see what the delay was. The Clerk's office said they'd check into it and get back to me. I never heard back.

I'd promised Miss Harrison an installment towards the July subsidy repayment when I got my October pay. After setting money aside for rent, food, and pocket money I could only see my way clear to sending two pounds. I picked up a money order from the Post Office and mailed it, along with a letter explaining why I couldn't send more. I followed up with a phone call to ask her advice about the problem with my promised pay increase. Miss Harrison seemed as annoyed as I was about the delay, and promised to look into it.

The November rains were interspersed with sleet showers and the occasional smattering of snow. My feet got soaked every morning as I walked to work, and it took till noon to warm them up again. The mini-skirts I wore offered little or no protection from the elements and my thin raincoat provided no warmth whatsoever. I added 'winter coat' to the growing list of things I would buy as soon as my back pay arrived.

In the morning when I walked to work it was dark, and it was dark again by the time I walked home. A deep, suffocating depression began to settle over me. Nothing was working out the way I thought it would. The job wasn't paying what they'd promised; the flat was really just a place to hang out, not a home; and Robert was becoming conspicuous by his absence. I felt empty.

Even Di had stopped hanging around with me, at her boyfriend's insistence. He said I was a bad influence on her. So instead we'd meet for lunch on Wednesdays, as I had Wednesday afternoons off. But she kept our meetings very secret from Mike.

One evening, as I was waiting to cross the street on my way home from work, Di and Mike drove by in his MGB. It was pouring with rain and I was cold and wet. I waved, half expecting them to stop and offer me a ride, but instead Di quickly looked away. She pretended she hadn't seen me. She could just as easily have stabbed a knife through my heart. I stood there on the curb, fighting back tears and feeling as low as I had ever felt.

I had Wednesday afternoons off because Thursdays evenings I

worked late. It was generally quiet and I used the time to catch up on my work. But this Thursday I couldn't focus my attention on any one thing. The heavy feeling of depression which had settled over me was becoming oppressive. Tears were never far below the surface.

When Mr. Holden came in to check on his messages he seemed to sense that something was wrong.

"How's it going?" he asked, eyeing me closely. "No problems with the job, I hope."

"Oh no, Mr. Holden, everything's fine."

He looked over my shoulder at what I was reading. "Need help making sense of any of this stuff?"

"Uh, no, I don't think so, thank you. It seems pretty self-explanatory. But I do have those letters you dictated earlier ready for signature."

I handed him the signature file.

"I'll take them back to my office and review them. Perhaps you could come and get them before leaving this evening. I won't be in tomorrow morning."

When I went to his office he motioned for me to take a seat while he finished signing the letters.

"Any luck sorting out that pay issue?" he asked, glancing up briefly.

"No, not yet. I called the Clerk's office, like you suggested, but it doesn't look very promising. They never even called me back."

Much to my embarrassment my lower lip trembled and my nose started to run. I fell silent, unable to continue. Mr. Holden put his pen down and offered me a Kleenex from the box sitting on his desk. I took one with a mumbled 'thank you' and blew my nose.

"I must be coming down with a cold, what with all this rain and snow we've been having," I said with a nervous laugh. I was eager to portray myself as mature and sophisticated, not as a blubbering idiot. "If you're done signing those letters, I'd better get back to the office. No one's there in case the phone rings."

"I doubt the phone will ring at this time of night. Why don't you tell me how you're really doing? You seem to have a lot on your mind these days. Is the job getting you down?"

"Oh no," I gushed, eager to assure him I could manage the work, "it isn't that at all. I love the job and the other ladies in the office are really great to work with. It's just that …," I paused, struggling to come up with the words to describe how I was feeling.

Mr. Holden waited patiently, a look of parental concern on his face. Tears spilled down my cheeks. Life seemed so unfair. I'd worked so hard to do the right things, to look after myself, be independent. But it always seemed to backfire. And now, a simple thing like Di pretending she didn't see me had shattered my fragile ego and I wasn't sure I had the strength to put myself back together again. I was so desperately lonely. I mustered some self control and carried on.

"It's just that I'm feeling a bit homesick these days," I said, feeling a need to explain myself, yet being surprised at the words which came out.

"Homesick?" Mr. Holden said, equally surprised by my response.

The tears came burbling to the surface again, but this time I was unable to control myself. I burst into tears. Mr. Holden slid the box of Kleenex within easy reach.

"Perhaps it would be good to talk about it, get your feelings out," he said, obviously torn between embarrassment and concern.

"It's just that nothing seems to be working out the way I'd imagined it would. I thought that once I had a job and my own place that life would be perfect, but it isn't. People tell me I'm stuck up but I'm not like that really, I'm just scared. It's like I have no one to turn to. So I've been thinking lately that if I go and live with my mother and sister perhaps we can be like a family. Maybe Justin will even come and live with us one day."

"Oh, I see," Mr. Holden said, struggling to make sense of my babbling.

"It's just that I feel so disconnected, so alone. Mum keeps asking me to come and live with her in Manchester, so maybe I should give it a try."

"Well I'd be sorry to see you go, Gail. It could just be the Christmas season making you homesick, which is perfectly normal. Everybody wants family around them at Christmas. You still have some holidays coming, don't you? Perhaps take the time and visit with your mother over Christmas, and see how you're feeling in the New Year."

"Yes, I suppose so," I said, wiping away my tears and struggling to regain some composure. "My mother and sister are going to Andover for Christmas. Maybe I could join them there for a few days." I felt myself brightening at the prospect and gave Mr. Holden a watery smile. "Hopefully I'll have my back pay by then."

"If you don't hear from the Clerk's office by Monday, give them another ring. There's really no excuse for the delay. Miss Harrison rang me a few days ago, asking for some details about your contract, so I assume she's looking into it too. Let me know what comes of it." He glanced up at the wall clock. "It's getting late. I'll wait while you lock up the office, then I'll drive you home. It's on my way."

I was glad that Mr. Holden wasn't expected in next morning. In the cold light of day I regretted my emotional outburst. I had made a complete fool of myself. When he did arrive, he seemed to sense my embarrassment and suggested I leave early that day as it was the weekend. I thanked him and scurried off, eager to find some friends to lift my mood.

Ann was home when I got there. She'd slept late again and had opted for skipping work altogether. I chided her about being irresponsible and grumbled about the rent being due in less than a week.

"Don't worry, I'll come up with the money," she assured me. I somehow doubted she would. Rent days were proving to be a challenge for all of us, especially Ann.

The following Tuesday, Miss Harrison came to see me. It had been more than two months since her last visit and I actually found myself looking forward to seeing her.

"We've written to the Chief Education Officer at County Hall," she told me, "and asked him to check into the problem with your salary adjustment, Gail. There really is no excuse for it to take this long."

"Thanks for trying but I don't suppose it'll do much good, and besides, it really doesn't matter anymore," I said sulkily. "I'm thinking of handing in my notice anyway."

"Why on earth would you do a thing like that?" she asked, looking at me as if I were mad.

"I've decided to go and live with my mother in Manchester," I blurted out.

"Well," Miss Harrison said, "that would explain the letter we received from your mother this morning. She said she wanted you to come and live with her and that she had suitable accommodations for you. I didn't realize you had made up your mind to go. It's the first I hear of it; what made you decide? Has your mother been pressuring you?"

"No, not too much," I said. "It's just that I feel I need some security behind me, some family that I belong to. Living in the flat is great and all, but it isn't like a real home. But mostly I worry about next April, when I go out of care. I won't have the Children's Committee watching out for me anymore. I'll be totally on my own then, with no one to turn to. So maybe it's better if I go and live with my mother. At least she's family."

Miss Harrison frowned, obviously skeptical about this sudden and unexpected turn of events.

"I certainly can't give you an answer about this today. I'll need to discuss the matter with my senior officer and the Committee. And we'll need to contact the Manchester Children's Department, to see if they're willing to accept supervision of you. All this will take time and can't be rushed. I certainly can't give you permission to hand in your notice at work yet."

"I'll need to do it soon though," I persisted. "I talked to Mum on the phone last weekend about meeting her in Andover for Christmas. She wants me to take the train back to Manchester with her afterwards. I'll have to give in my notice soon if I'm going to do that."

Miss Harrison bristled.

"This doesn't sound like a very realistic plan, Gail. These things take time to organize, and Christmas is just over a month away. I'm not convinced you've thought this through properly. There are many other things to consider, besides making arrangements with the Manchester office. Your flat, for instance. You can't just go and leave your flat mates in the lurch. Don't forget you signed a lease and have a commitment to your landlord. We worked very hard to get the Children's Committee to agree to your moving into that flat. You can't just throw it up at a moment's notice."

"I don't think the flat's going to be a problem," I said. "We had a big talk about it last night. The other girls want to leave too, which is part of the reason why I want to go and live with Mum. Everything seems to be falling apart. Shazad has to return to Iran because of some trouble there. The Ayatollah Homenni has taken over, and he doesn't believe in educating women, so Shazad's family has told her to return home. She can't even stay and finish her courses; she has to go right away. And Teresa hasn't been able to find a job here, so she wants to go back to Riverton to be close to her boyfriend. As for Ann, she never has enough money to pay her share of the rent anyway, so she doesn't have much say in the matter. We're going to explain everything to the landlord this weekend, and see what we can do."

"This really is disappointing, Gail, especially after you had such high hopes about things working out. But I must caution you against making any rash decisions or acting recklessly, at least until I've had a chance to discuss your plans with the Committee."

CHAPTER EIGHTEEN

Miss Harrison's visit left me feeling angry and even more unsettled. Here was the Children's Committee telling me, yet again, what I could and couldn't do. When I got home Ann was watching television. I plonked myself down on the sofa beside her.

"Where's Shazad and Teresa?" I asked.

"Went out to get some fish and chips," Ann said, not taking her eyes off the television. "There's nothing in the house to eat. I'm starving too, but I don't have any money so I didn't bother going. What about you?"

"I had my usual three course lunch at work. Those catering students are getting better every week. I'll miss those gourmet lunches when I'm gone."

"Whaddaya mean, gone? Where are you going?"

"I'm thinking of going to live with my mother and sister in Manchester. My mother says there are loads of good jobs up there, and I'm tired of being screwed around by the college. They promised me a great rise if I passed my exams, but they aren't sticking to their promise. If I'd known they were going to mess me around like this, I wouldn't have taken the job, or rented a place that cost this much."

Ann turned to face me, a look of excitement on her face.

"How 'bout we go to London and look for work there. I've been thinking about going myself lately. It's a whole lot more exciting than Manchester. We could at least go and have a look," Ann urged. "Check out the job scene and see how much it costs to live there. We could even go this weekend."

"But you don't have any money, so how?"

"We'll hitch hike and surely we can stay at Robert's place. It won't cost us anything."

"We'll still need some money," I said. "I only have a few pounds left in my bank account, although I will get paid again before the rent's due."

"Can you lend me a fiver, then?" Ann asked quick as a whip. "That'll see me through the weekend, no problem. I'll pay you back as soon as I get paid."

"I dunno if going to London is such a great idea," I said, as the voice of reason took hold. "I'll have to think about it."

Next day was Wednesday, my half day. By the time I got home from work my mind was made up.

"OK Ann, if you're serious about London let's go," I told her, before I'd even taken my coat off.

"Are you serious?" she asked, jumping up from the couch, where she'd been dozing.

"You bet I am. I've just had a really shitty morning at work and I told them I wasn't feeling well. I acted like I was getting the 'flu or something. I said I probably wouldn't be in tomorrow or Friday. That gives up four whole days in London, if we leave this afternoon."

Ann let out a yelp of excitement and bounded off the couch. We threw some things in an overnight bag and left a note for Teresa and Shazad. I said we had gone to London for a few days, back Sunday evening. I tried to telephone Robert to say we were on our way, but he was out.

We had no trouble getting rides and by early evening we were on the outskirts of London. I telephoned Robert again and was relieved to hear his voice on the other end of the phone. I told him where we were and once he'd gotten over his surprise, he agreed to come and pick us up. I wasn't completely sure he was glad to see me, but it was too late to worry about that now.

When Robert left for work next morning Ann and I went with

him as far as Oxford Street. There were several temp employment agencies there, all advertising for secretaries with my skills. I went into one to enquire. After testing my typing and shorthand skills they assured me I wouldn't have any trouble finding work in London. We spent the rest of the day checking out the shops. When our feet could stand it no more, we made our way back to Robert's. We were waiting on his doorstep when he got home from work.

Robert looked tired and grumpy, a side of him that I'd never seen during his weekends at home in Devon. He changed out of his business suit into jeans and a sweater, his mood relaxing along with his clothing. He started packing his overnight bag. He said he was going to Devon for the weekend and would leave straight from work next day. I felt a stabbing pain in the gut of my belly.

"I didn't know you were planning on going home this weekend," I said, fighting to keep the tone of accusation out of my voice. "I wouldn't have come all this way, had I known."

I wondered why he hadn't told me about it. I thought we were dating, but apparently not.

"I have some things to take care of down there. I probably wouldn't have had time to see you anyhow, that's why I didn't tell you I was coming."

"Oh," was all I could manage to say.

Ann slipped her arm through mine, sensing my dejection.

"Actually, Gail and I were planning on going to Manchester tomorrow, so it's no big deal," she said.

I could have hugged her for sparing me any further anguish.

Next morning Robert took his car so that he could get an early start to Devon after work. He dropped Ann and me off at Waterloo station, ostensibly so we could catch the train to Manchester. However, as soon as he was out of sight we slipped around the corner and started hitchhiking. It seemed to take forever to get out of London but eventually we found ourselves on the side of the motorway. A cold drizzle had started to fall. We stuck out our thumbs and waited for a ride. Within minutes a lorry stopped and we were on our way.

By the time we got to Manchester it was almost dark, and the place looked as dreary as I remembered. When we knocked on the door of Sun Street, Jane answered. It took her a minute or two to register who we were and I, in turn, hardly recognized her. She had grown by several inches and had put on a lot of weight. Her long brown hair had been cut into a modern bob, accentuating her big brown eyes.

"Hey little sister, how ya doing?"

"Gail," she squealed, finally finding her tongue. "What are you doing here?"

"Come to see my little sister, of course. Are you going to let us in, or do we have to stand out here all night?"

"Mum isn't home yet," Jane said, as she led us through to the dining room, "but she shouldn't be much longer. She goes grocery shopping on her way home on Fridays."

"Oh good," I said, rubbing my tummy, "I'm starving."

By the time Mum got home we were all settled in front of the television drinking tea and eating biscuits. She seemed pleased to see me, albeit a little surprised.

"What the dickens are you doing here?" she said, struggling to put the grocery bags on the table. "You're the last person I expected to see sitting here when I got home."

"I took a couple of days off work, so Ann and I decided to come up here and see you. This is Ann, by the way. She shares the flat with me in Torquay."

"Nice to meet you Ann, I'm sure. Gail's mentioned you in a couple of her letters. You're the one who never seems to have the rent money on time, aren't you."

"Mum!" I howled.

Ann seemed unruffled by my mother's revelations of my letter-writing gossip. Mum started unpacking the groceries.

"My parents live in Durham, or at least they did last time I heard," Ann said, as she grabbed a bag of groceries and followed Mum into the kitchen.

"Doesn't sound like you have much to do with your family," Mum said, obviously curious.

"Not if I can help it," Ann said. "My dad's a drunk. I got fed up with him slapping us around every time he'd had one too many, so I left. I don't understand why my mother stays but she does, more fool her. I told her anytime she wants to leave she can come and stay with me, but I never heard from her again. And now I've moved so many times she probably wouldn't be able to find me anyhow. She's made her choice, and I made mine. Where shall I put this bag?"

I was surprised by Ann's revelations. In all the months we'd lived together she'd never mentioned her family and I'd never thought to ask. I was amazed at how easily she was able to shrug them off. It was something I had been unable to do.

The four of us laughed and giggled our way through dinner, trading stories and secrets like long lost girlfriends. We were just clearing the dishes off the table when there was a knock at the door.

"Jane, can you get that," Mum said, "it's probably one of your friends."

Ann and I carried the dirty dishes into the kitchen, followed by Mum. A moment later Jane appeared in the kitchen doorway looking wide eyed.

"Mum, there's a copper at the front door. Says he wants to talk to you."

Mum cast a quick glance at Ann and me. "You two better lay low while I go and see what's up. I've a hunch this is to do with you."

The three of us huddled in the kitchen, straining to hear what was being said. When Mum came back she looked like a schoolgirl with a naughty secret.

"Yup, just like I thought. They're looking for you, missy," she said, a mischievous twinkle in her eyes.

"Oh my God, what did you tell them?"

"Said I hadn't seen or heard from you since I got a postcard last week, saying you wanted to come and live with me."

"But why on earth are they looking for me?"

A sense of foreboding washed over me.

"Well no point worrying about it," Mum said. "You're here now, so you might as well stay and enjoy yourself. I said I'd let them know if I heard from you, so they won't be back. Relax. You only just got here. If I told them you were here they'd probably send you back to Devon right away. We're having so much fun you might as well stay for the weekend at least."

"I suppose," I said.

We spent the whole weekend in the house drinking tea, smoking cigarettes and playing cards. Jane was sent on a couple of errands to restock our cigarette supply or pick up fish and chips, but other than that the front door was never opened. Norman was away playing piano on the cruise ships and wouldn't be home until the end of January.

Monday morning, Mum put us on the bus back to Torquay. I had wanted to go home on Sunday but the fare was half price on Mondays, so Mum persuaded us to stay the extra day. 'In for a penny, in for a pound' she had said. And as she was the one paying our bus fare home, we couldn't really argue. She told me she'd go to the police station on her way to work, and let them know we'd spent the weekend with her. They were going to find out sooner or later so better to hear it from her, she reasoned. I supposed there was some logic in that.

"Better to ask forgiveness than permission," she said, laughing.

It wasn't until we were well on our way back to Devon that the excitement and camaraderie of the weekend gave way to a gnawing dread of what was waiting for me back home. Who had sounded the alarm, and why had the police come looking for me? Couldn't I do anything without being hunted down like a criminal? I was almost eighteen and thought I was through with having my every move watched, but I was obviously wrong.

When we got back to the flat, Shazad and Teresa pounced on us.

"Where on earth have you been?" they asked us, sounding more like angry parents than flat mates. "Everybody's been looking for you."

"Who's 'everybody' exactly," I asked, immediately on the defensive.

"Mr. Holden, the police, even your grandparents."

"What! I don't get it, what's the big deal?" I asked, mystified, "All I did was go to London and Manchester for a few days. It isn't like I was kidnapped or anything. And who told them we were gone in the first place? I told Mr. Holden I had the flu and probably wouldn't be in till Monday. How did they even find out we were gone?"

"I didn't know what was happening," Shazad said, sounding defensive in her turn. "Mr. Holden saw me at school and asked how you were feeling. I said you'd gone to London for a few days, like you said in your note. I didn't know you were supposed to be sick. Then next day, he came around to see if you were home yet but I told him you weren't. How was I supposed to know what to say?"

"I know, I know," I said, realizing Shazad wasn't to blame. "Christ, why can't they just leave me alone and let me live my own life."

"And another thing," Teresa chimed in. "We talked to the landlord while you two were gone. We told him that Shazad and I would be moving out at the end of this month, so he's going to give you and Ann your notice to move out too. He said he couldn't see how the two of you could manage here on your own."

"Oh great," I groaned, "that's just what I need. Couldn't we at least keep the place until Christmas? Miss Harrison's gonna have a shit fit over this, I just know it. Now I'll have to move to Manchester, whether they like it or not. It looks like everything's screwed up here."

The depression which had been nipping at my heels for the last few weeks now threatened to consume me. How had everything gone so wrong, so fast? I thought I had it all, a flat, a boyfriend and a well paid job–but everything was crumbling to dust. It was just an illusion.

Now I had to face Mr. Holden and explain my actions to him. While taking a few days off sick wasn't the end of the world, being caught out in a lie was a different matter. I didn't like the feeling it left in the pit of my stomach.

When I got to work the next day there was an icy chill in the air, and it had nothing to do with the weather. Mr. Holden summoned me to his office.

"I hope you're feeling better," he said.

"Much, thank you."

"I came around to your flat, to see how you were doing."

"Yes, so I heard."

"And how were you doing?"

"Alright, I guess."

"And what are your plans now?"

"I'll have to give my notice, I guess, unless I'm fired already."

"You're not fired, although I must express, in the strongest terms possible, my disappointment with your behaviour."

Silence.

"What have you to say for yourself?"

"I just wasn't thinking I guess. Now I've let everyone down, so I've decided to give in my notice and start over in Manchester, with my mother."

"Are you sure about this?"

"Yes, quite sure. I really appreciate you giving me the job and all that, but I can't stay. Not now."

"We all make mistakes, Gail. You don't have to throw in the towel just because of this."

"Thanks, but it's not just this, it's everything," I said, taking a deep breath. "When I took this job I was led to believe that my salary would go up if I passed my exams. Well I did pass them, but my salary still hasn't been adjusted and it's been five months now. Without the pay rise I was promised, I can't really afford to live in a flat on my own. The other girls are moving out, so I have to go too. Besides, I've promised my Mum already so I have to move to Manchester now. She's counting on me, and I've let enough people down already. I'll give you my notice in writing, if you need it. I know I'm supposed to give a month's notice, but I want to leave by December 22nd which isn't quite a month away. I hope that's alright. I'm sorry it didn't work out, Mr. Holden."

"Me too, Gail."

The following week we moved out of the flat. I found myself a bed-sitter which was close to the college and on the approved accommodations list. It was so meager in its offerings that no student had taken it. My room was on the third floor and I had to haul my pared-down belongings up two sets of dark, narrow stairs with peeling linoleum.

The room was so small I could turn on the hot plate for my morning tea without even getting out of bed. Which was a good thing as the room was always freezing cold in the morning and only slightly warmer by evening. The single bed was lumpy, the sheets scratchy and the lone blanket paper thin. I asked for another blanket, but it wasn't forthcoming. There was a small dresser with drawers which sat askew and had to be shaken violently to make them open. A mirror hung precariously by one nail above it. The shared bathroom was one floor below and stank of urine. On the wall outside the bathroom was a sign up sheet where you wrote your name for the nights you wanted a bath. It took two shillings in the meter to get the water up to a tepid temperature which passed for bath water.

The landlady lived at the back of the house on the ground floor. Every time I came or went I heard the squeak of her door opening as she peaked out to see who was there. She never spoke, but would nod her head curtly and clutch her cardigan close to her chest, as if warding off attack. I wondered why she didn't turn the heat up but didn't dare ask. People had a way of taking offense when I asked questions like that. I could put up with the cold for the three weeks I planned on being there.

Miss Harrison came to see me the week before I was due to leave Devon. I could tell she was more than a little frustrated with me.

"You really should have consulted with us before handing in your notice, Gail. I told you last time I was here that you weren't to do anything until the Children's Committee had had an opportunity to consider your request."

I sipped my tea, and measured my response carefully.

"Well, it wasn't exactly a request that I was making, it was more a statement of fact," I said, struggling to keep my voice even. "After messing things up so badly here, I felt I had no choice but to quit, before they fired me. Mum's been on at me for years about moving to Manchester, so now seems like a good time. And besides, if I'd waited until after the Children's Committee had met, it would have been too late to hand in my notice in time for me to go to Andover for Christmas."

"I don't need to remind you that you are still a ward of the court, and as such you need the permission of the Children's Committee before you can go and live with your mother. You were taken out of her care for good reason, and a lot of consideration needs to be given to your returning to live with her."

"I thought you'd be glad that I'd finally agreed to go home to live," I said defensively, "so what's the big deal?"

"Our concern is what's best for you, Gail, and that has to be carefully weighed against your mother's ability to provide an appropriate home environment for you."

"Well you let Jane go and live with her, so why not me. I just don't get it, what's the problem?"

"A prime example would be what happened when you ran away to Manchester last month. Your mother lied to the police about your whereabouts, I understand, and doesn't seem very concerned about it."

I slumped back in my seat. I knew in my heart that Miss Harrison was right. My mother was irresponsible and a poor role model, but she was all I had. I felt a need to defend her.

"She didn't see what the big deal was. I am almost eighteen after all. She was married with a baby at my age."

"Be that as it may, your actions were irresponsible. You're an intelligent girl, Gail, and you should learn to face up to your responsibilities. As you say, you are almost eighteen and as such will be on your own."

I fell silent, disturbed by the reminder of my eighteenth birthday and all that that would entail. The plank I was walking along was getting awfully short. I watched a lone tealeaf floating in circles in my teacup, and wondered if it was a harbinger of my future.

Miss Harrison changed tacks.

"How are your new accommodations?"

"Pretty grim, but it's only for a couple of weeks so I can manage till then. It's about all I can afford anyhow. I never did get that rise they promised me."

"We're seeing what we can do on your behalf, Gail. As you know, we wrote to the Chief Education Officer outlining the terms of your contract and asking him to look into it. His office called back and said that apparently there was a mistake in your original contract, and that they'll issue a new one. Now they're saying it depends on what you verbally agreed to, when you accepted the position."

"Mr. Holden told me what the starting salary was and then said it would be adjusted according to my qualifications. He didn't know exactly how much, but he was very clear about the fact that it would be considerably more than the starting salary, if I passed my exams." I flushed with anger. "And the contract they sent me was pretty damn clear about the pay scale."

"We explained that to them, and sent another letter yesterday expressing our concern. Here's a copy for you."

She handed me a sheet of paper.

Chief Education Officer
County Hall,
Exeter
18th December, 1967

KMH/MD/7952/2

Gail Elizabeth Puddicombe 19.4.50

Thank you for Memo of the 27th November, the contents of which have been noted by the Honiton Case Sub Committee. I have been asked to put their view very strongly to you. They feel that as they act in place of parents to many young people, whom they encourage to honour agreements entered into – it makes their position extremely difficult when the employing body which is part of the same Council does not in its turn honour its agreement.

My Committee feels that the original contract must be adhered to and that Miss Puddicombe should receive the back salary due to her.

I am sending a copy of this memo to the Clerks Department for their information as you may wish to consult with them.

County Children's Officer

I handed the letter back.

"Well thanks for trying, but I'm not holding my breath."

"Can you tell me what made you finally decide to move to Manchester?" she asked, obviously still bothered by my decision. "You seem to have come to this decision quite suddenly. Has your mother been pressuring you?"

"Not really, although every time she writes she says how she hates being in Manchester on her own, now that Norman is away on the cruise ships. But that didn't make me decide. It's just that now I'm nearly eighteen I got to wondering how I'd get on in life without a family or roots. It would probably be better to be with my mother, rather than on my own."

"Well, for what it's worth, the Children's Committee discussed your move to Manchester at their meeting last week. They've given approval for you to live with your mother, on a trial basis."

"That's a relief," I said. "I'd hate to think I'd chucked up my job and flat and then they wouldn't let me go."

"Miss Fielding, from the Manchester Children's Department, has been assigned your supervision until your eighteenth birthday. She'll come and see you soon after you get there. We feel this is very much a trial situation, Gail. If at any time you're in difficulty or need help or advice of any kind, don't hesitate to contact the Manchester Children's Department. They are there to help."

"Thank you, but there shouldn't be any problems. Mum already has a few irons in the fire for me and I don't think I'll have any trouble finding a good job."

"Well Gail, I wish you the best of luck on your move to Manchester. I hope you'll settle down and be happy there. And good luck on your eighteenth birthday and going out of care. I'm sure you'll do fine."

I felt a sudden rush of emotion and busied myself with gathering up my jacket before responding.

"Thank you for everything you've done for me. I really appreciate it. I hope I haven't let you down too badly. It's hard to imagine that I've been in care for almost six years now. If you ever see Miss Stinson, would you tell her thanks for everything, from me? And thanks to the Children's Committee too, whoever they are."

"They're just people, like you and me, trying the best they can to do a good job."

"Well, I'll miss Devon and all the people I know here, but it will be good to be with family. At least Mum won't ever kick me out for no reason."

CHAPTER NINETEEN

Christmas in Andover was just what I needed to boost my sagging spirits - family, food and laughter. Surrounded by family, I felt secure again and the anxiety and depression of the last few months lifted. On January 1st, Mum, Jane and I boarded the train from Andover to Manchester headed for my new home.

Two days after arriving in Manchester I signed up with an employment agency as a temp. My first assignment was with an export company. I reported to work promptly at 8 o'clock next morning and was taken to the typing pool. There I was introduced to Miss Beecham, the supervisor. She peered at me over her pinch nez glasses. She seemed to have a smell under her nose which caused her face to twitch.

"Well, I certainly hope you're better than the last girl that agency sent. Here, take this and type it up then bring it back to me. We need an original and two carbon copies. Put your initials at the bottom of each page"

She waved her hand towards the empty desk at the back of the room, indicating that I was dismissed.

As I walked past the other typists I tried to make eye contact with them, but no one dared to stop typing and say hello. I took my seat. The typewriter had probably been salvaged from the local museum and the desk wobbled precariously. I pushed my knee against one leg to steady it and started typing.

Every so often one or other of the typists would get up from their desk and take their completed assignment up to Miss Beecham for review. They'd place the sheets in her inbox and wait to be handed another assignment. Occasionally Miss Beecham would extricate herself from her seat and waddle towards one of us, flapping sheets of paper above her head as she went. I soon realized that this was to be avoided at all costs. She would berate some poor typist for sloppy work, in a voice which carried over our clattering typewriters with alarming clarity.

When I picked up my first pay packet at the end of the week, I went to the Post Office and bought a money order for ten shillings. I mailed it to Miss Harrison at the Devon County Council, along with a covering letter saying that I had found work. I said I would send more towards my subsidy repayment whenever I could.

When I got paid the following week I decided to take the train back to Devon to visit Robert for the weekend. My mother got angry when I told her what my plans were, accusing me of squandering my money.

"Well it must be nice to have no one to worry about but yourself," she snapped. I thought that was funny, coming from her.

It felt good to be back in Devon and smell the ocean air, if only for the weekend. Robert took me to the Hot Spot Disco on Saturday night and on Sunday afternoon we went to Macario's for coffee, still the in place to see and be seen, before taking me to the train station. It was hard to leave Devon again.

At the beginning of my third week in the typing pool of the export agency, I made what turned out to be a terminal error - I corrected the grammar in one of the documents I'd been given to type. Miss Beecham waddled the length of the room, rustling the offending document above her head as she went.

"What's the meaning of this?" she asked, her shrill voice cutting through the air like a knife. "Can't you read? Is it so hard to type what's written?"

I studied the sentence which her scarlet-painted fingernail was jabbing at.

"It says the same thing," I mumbled, horrified at the attention her outburst was attracting. "It's just that the English wasn't right the way they had it written, so I corrected it."

I heard gasps from several of the ladies within earshot.

"You corrected it?" Miss Beecham said, her voice rising an octave. "You corrected it! Let me remind you, missey, that your job is to type what's written. My job is to correct it."

"But," I started to argue, then thought better of it. "Sorry," I mumbled, "I didn't realize."

"Well you'd better start realizing it. Now re-type this, the way it was written."

"Yes, Miss Beecham," I said, lowering my eyes to hide the hatred smoldering there. The agency wasn't paying me enough to put up with this shit. I wondered how Mr. Holden was making out with his new secretary.

At the end of my third week, my career in the typing pool ended abruptly. Miss Beecham called me up to the front of the room and said I would probably be happier working some place else. She said I didn't seem to be fitting me.

"I couldn't agree with you more," I said. "I quit."

When I called the agency Monday morning, they said they had another assignment for me at a factory not far from where I lived. I was to go there at ten for an interview. If they liked me I could start work right away. The regular secretary had been in an accident and wouldn't be back for weeks, maybe even months. I was ten minutes late for my interview but the woman who interviewed me didn't seem to mind.

"Everyone gets lost coming here for the first time," she said. "It can be a bit of a maze finding your way around in here, but now you know where we are you shouldn't have any trouble tomorrow."

I took her comment to mean that I was hired.

When I got home from work on Thursday, Norman was there. He was very surprised to find me living there. I wondered why Mum hadn't mentioned it to him in any of her letters.

With Norman home, Mum had little or no time for anyone or

anything else. Norman went back to playing at his usual club, coming home in the early hours of the morning and sleeping until well past noon. The only time I really saw him was at supper time. He would eat with us before going to work, leaving Mum, Jane and I to carry on our lives much as we had before he came home. On the surface nothing had changed, and yet I felt a subtle shifting.

Before Norman came home, Mum and I had behaved more like room mates than mother and daughter. But now it seemed I was in the way. Mum grumbled about my things lying around the house, my radio being too loud, and how often I washed my hair. I wondered why these things hadn't bothered her before.

Just over three weeks after Norman returned home, I woke up to find a note from my mother on the dining room table. She had left for work already. Her note berated me for leaving my makeup on the dining room table every morning. She said Norman was fed up with having to clear my stuff out the way before he could even sit down to his breakfast. She said the house seemed very crowded with all of us there. Perhaps I would be happier in my own place.

I stared at the note, dumbfounded. I read it over, three, four times, trying to make sense of it. Mum and I always sat at the dining table together to put on our make up before leaving for work. We'd eat our breakfast and chat while we were doing it. It was one of the few things we actually did together, and I enjoyed it. I thought she did too. Or at least she had, until Norman came home.

I screwed up the note and threw it across the room, cursing the day I'd agreed to come and live in this hell hole. I gathered up my make-up bag and mirror and every other thing which was mine, and put them in the bedroom I shared with Jane.

Before leaving for work, I picked up Mum's make-up bag which was neatly stashed on the table against the wall, and threw it across the room. The contents spilled out across the lino. 'Fuck you!' I screamed, before storming out the door to work.

I didn't come home from work that evening until after I knew Norman would be gone. I felt betrayed and directed the full force of my resentment towards him. We had been doing just fine until he came home. And I hated my mother for siding with him. Why hadn't she just said something to me, instead of leaving a note and sneaking off early to work? I remembered her letters to me in Devon, telling me how great life would be if only I'd come and live with her in Manchester. How everything would be perfect, we'd be a family again. But now the winds had changed. Now I was in the way. Norman was home now and she didn't need me for company any more, or my money to help with her hire purchase payments.

When I finally went home, Mum had gone to the club to hear Norman play. Jane was home alone, watching television. I plonked myself down beside her, and put my arm around her shoulder. She looked lost and alone, with only the flicker of the television for light.

"Why are you sitting here in the dark?" I asked.

"There's only a couple of shillings left for the meter, and I don't want to waste electricity on the lights. I'd rather have the telly on."

I rummaged in my handbag and pulled out the half dozen shilling coins I'd collected during the week.

"Here, put a couple of bob in the meter and let's get some light on in here, cheer the place up."

"Mum left your dinner in the oven. She didn't know where you were."

I took the plate of congealed bangers and mash out of the oven and ate it in front of the television. I had been walking around aimlessly for hours, trying to decide what to do with my life, and had worked up quite an appetite. But now my mind was made up. I was going back to Devon. This whole thing had obviously been a terrible mistake.

Mum slept late next morning. When she did eventually get up she made no mention of her note. It was as if nothing had happened. As soon as Norman left for work I told her I'd decided to go back to Devon. She feigned horror.

"But this is what you wanted, isn't it, now that your precious Norman is home? How did you expect me to react, after that note you left?" I asked. "You as good as told me to get out, so I'm going. I hope you and Norman will be very happy together. I only wish I didn't have to leave Jane here with you."

"If that's your bloody attitude you can just clear off, the sooner the better."

"Suit yourself! I don't know why you asked me to come here in the first place. Everything was fine till Norman got back. Was it his idea to chuck me out?"

"Just for the record, missey, no one is chucking you out."

"Well you hardly laid down the welcome mat in your note, did you? What did you expect me to think? It doesn't take a brain surgeon to work out that I'm not wanted here anymore, not now Norman's home."

Now that my mind was made up, I felt as if a great weight had been lifted off my shoulders. Even Mum seemed relieved, once she'd calmed down. She had obviously given some thought to my departure.

"Do you remember Jack Thornton, from Nestleton?" she asked, next morning.

"Yes, I think so. He's the saxophone player isn't he? I was kind of friendly with his daughter, Jamie. Why?"

"Norman said he's playing on the cruise ships too these days, so Jamie is at home alone while he's away. Perhaps you could stay with her for a couple of weeks, until you find something. Why don't you drop her a line?"

"I suppose it might be worth a try," I said.

I mailed a letter to Jamie on my way to work Monday morning, asking if she could put me up for a couple of weeks while I got settled in Devon again. Meanwhile Mum phoned Miss Fielding, the Child Care Officer with the Manchester Children's Department, and asked her to come and visit us as soon as possible. She came to see us the next evening.

It was Norman's night off and we were just finishing supper when she arrived. Norman got up, cleared the table and offered to make tea. As soon as we were settled, Miss Fielding asked what the problem was.

"I want to move back to Devon," I blurted out, seeing no point in beating around the bush.

"I see," Miss Fielding said, looking at each of us in turn to gauge the reaction. "And what brought this on?"

Before I could answer Mum spoke up. "She just announced it out of the blue last Saturday. I've been beside myself ever since. I can't talk any sense into her. That's why I called you."

"It wasn't exactly 'out of the blue', Mum, and you know it. You said in your note that I was in the way here, and that I was causing problems between you and Norman, and that you didn't want me coming between the two of you."

"That's not what I meant at all," Mum said, feigning horror once more.

"Well that's what you said!" I snapped. I wished I still had the offending note to show Miss Fielding but there was no sign of it. I assumed Mum had destroyed it when she found it crumpled on the floor where I'd thrown it.

Mum ignored me and carried on with her sugar coated version of what had transpired. According to her she had done everything possible to make me happy in Manchester. When Mum had finished, Miss Fielding asked me if I had anything to add.

"Not really," I said. I didn't see any point in getting into a 'he said/she said' banter. My mind was made up; I was going back to Devon, so what did I care what they said or thought. A feeling of total rejection was tainting all my thought processes and I just wanted out of there, the quicker the better.

"I really don't feel you've given Manchester enough of a chance, Gail. It hasn't even been two months yet. How can you be so sure you want to go back to Devon after such a short time?"

"I just know," I said, a look of determination on my face.

Miss Fielding sighed heavily. "I'm sure I don't need to remind you how insistent you were about wanting to come and live with you mother in the first place. You can't just run away every time you encounter a problem, Gail. I really think you need to give this arrangement more time, before making any decisions."

I didn't respond. I was unable to offer any defense. How could I explain the pain I was feeling at being rejected once again by my mother; or the sorrow I felt as my hopes for the future lay in crumbled ruins? For years I had dreamed of going home to be with my mother, to be part of a family again with a place where I belonged and was unconditionally loved and accepted. There were no words to describe these feelings, this sense of loss, of anger. How had I been so gullible to believe any of it might come true?

"I don't see any point her staying here and making everyone miserable," Norman said, speaking for the first time.

I wanted to tell him to mind his own bloody business; that this was nothing to do with him, except it was all his fault in the first place. If my mother had never met him, maybe she would have stayed at home with us in Riverton, and been a wife to my father and a mother to her children. But instead I bit my tongue. It was all water under the bridge now and nothing I could do or say would change any of it.

"Well, at the very least, you'll need to stay here until I've had an opportunity to talk to my supervisor. And of course I'll have to contact Miss Harrison in Devon. They'll need to know that you're planning on coming back."

It was a week before we heard from Miss Fielding again. I had spent the time going through my boxes of belongings, sifting through the remnants of my life. Letters and birthday cards which I had cherished before now seemed like painful reminders of my shattered family. I scoffed as I reread Mum's eloquent prose in countless letters, telling me how everything would be wonderful if only I came and lived with her in Manchester. Letters dating back to my days at grammar school, painting pretty pictures of a fictional family life. I kicked myself for believing them, for buying into the fantasy. It was time to let go of my dream for a 'normal' family life. It was never going to happen. I had to accept the fact that I could never go home. There was no home for me to go to, not in the way I wanted. My mother was devoid of any maternal instinct and seemed incapable of loving me in the way I needed to be loved. I had to stop looking backwards – I could only look forward from now on. I realized I could never regain the family life I had lost. I had to focus on my future.

Miss Fielding was hardly in the door when I asked what news she had.

"I've spoken to Miss Harrison. Needless to say, she was very disappointed to hear that things haven't worked out as you'd hoped, Gail."

I shrugged. I was disappointed too.

"She's discussed the matter with her Area Children's Officer and, to be honest with you, they believe it will be a backward step for you to return to Devon so soon. I told them I'd discussed this with you very fully, but that you seemed determined to return. Are you still feeling that way, now that you've had a week to think about it?"

"Definitely," I said tersely, not wanting to rehash all the pros and cons again.

"If that's the case, the Devon Children's Committee feels that you will have to accept full responsibility for finding your own accommodation and job when you get there. The Committee also said you'll have to pay all your own moving expenses."

"That's no big deal. I have enough in my bank for the train fare and something to live on for a week or two, until I find a job. And I've heard back from Jamie and she says I'm welcome to stay with her until her Dad gets back at the end of March."

"Have you given any thought to when you might go?"

"I warned them at work that I'd probably be handing in my notice on Monday. I'm hoping to leave for Devon next Saturday, March 9, but I was waiting to hear what you had to say first."

"Are you sure you've given it enough of a chance here? Can you give me some idea what sort of difficulties you've had here, Gail? What makes you so determined to leave? Were you unhappy in your job?"

"No, not really, although I don't enjoy it as much as I enjoyed my job at the college."

"Were there problems between you and Jane?"

"No, that's not it at all. She can be a brat at times but she's growing up and getting better. We got along great most of the time."

"Were you able to make any new friends while you were here?"

"Yes, some, although I didn't really get to know anyone particularly well. I don't feel like I have anything in common with them, like I do with my friends in Devon."

"And how do you get along with Norman?"

I felt my mother's piercing stare, daring me to say anything negative about her dearly beloved.

"Fine, I guess. I hardly see him and when I do he's either watching television or telling us jokes. He can be quite funny at times. Things are just different with him home. We all got along great when it was just Mum and Jane and me, but we seem to be tripping over each other all the time now. The house probably just isn't big enough for all of us."

"Your eighteenth birthday is less than two months away. Have you considered staying here, at least until then?"

"No," I said curtly, "absolutely not, although I suppose it would save everyone a ton of paperwork if I did."

Miss Fielding ignored my comment and I immediately regretted it. Her concern seemed genuine and she was only trying to get a better understanding of what had gone wrong.

"If you're determined to go then perhaps it's better that you go now, while you're still in care. At least that way you'll have the support of the Children's Committee should you encounter any problems settling back down."

"I suppose," I said, somewhat confused. Hadn't she just told me that I would have to accept full responsibility for finding my own accommodations, a job and the train fare back?

"And something else you need to consider, Gail, is the fact that your mother may not be so willing to accept you back, should you decided to return to Manchester in the future."

I nodded. "I understand that perfectly, but I don't anticipate wanting to come back."

There was no way I was going to open myself up to this type of rejection again. I wouldn't be back. No thank you.

CHAPTER TWENTY

Mum and Jane came to the station to see me off. There were no tears in my eyes, just an unspeakable sadness. A sense of betrayal, so strong I was numbed by it. My farewells were superficial, even light hearted, as I struggled to hide the hurt inside. Or was it anger? Anger at being fool enough to think that I could ever go back to that elusive family life I craved. I thought I'd feel complete if I came 'home' to what was left of my family. But any illusions I had embraced about putting my family back together were now shattered forever.

It was time to get on with my own life, face up to reality. In forty days I was going to turn eighteen, and then I'd be completely on my own. Forty days to find myself a job and somewhere to live and put my life back together. The Children's Committee would have finished their job; my file could be closed.

As the train hurtled me home towards Devon, I turned my thoughts to my future. No point in looking back. I assessed what I had and developed a game plan. I had a few pounds in my pocket but they wouldn't last long. Finding a job was priority number one. And even though I had a place to stay while I looked around, Jamie's father would be home in less than three weeks. After that I'd be out on the street. There was no time to waste.

I'd written to Robert to let him know I was returning to Devon. He met me at Nestleton station and drove me to Jamie's.

"These suitcases weigh a ton," he grumbled, as he lugged them up the two flights of stairs to the bedroom I'd be using.

"You can leave the small bags down here," I said. "I'll carry them up later. Come and meet Jamie, she's made some tea for us."

"I'd love to but I don't have much time, so I'll have to pass. Sorry. But maybe next time, eh beautiful? I'm sure you and Jamie have lots to talk about. I'll see you in a few days, once you're settled in."

So much for the romantic re-union I'd been looking forward to. Instead, Jamie and I settled in for an evening of girl talk. Although Jamie was only a couple of years older than me she seemed so much more mature. She too had taken the secretarial course at Torquay and was now working as a secretary in one of the largest law firms in the area. She told me her boyfriend worked as a chef in one of the big hotels. They had been going steady for over a year and were beginning to talk about marriage.

By the end of the evening I felt I had known Jamie all my life. She seemed so complete. There were no parts of her psyche missing, no anger burbling to the surface every chance it got, like there was with me.

"Nobody ever said that life was fair," she laughed, when I grumbled about coming from a broken home. "Life is what you make it, it's up to you. Who's to say you would have been better off if your parents hadn't divorced? No point in letting it ruin your life is there?"

"I guess I'm probably better off. If they hadn't divorced I'd still be living in Riverton. Probably knocked up with a couple of kids by now."

An involuntary shudder ran through me.

"It's just that I feel so empty inside all the time, like part of me is missing. I thought that going home to live with my Mum and sister would make that feeling go away. But it didn't, it just made it worse. It's like I chucked everything up chasing this fantasy. Before I always told myself I could go home to Mum if things got really bad, but now I know that isn't true."

Jamie jumped up and retrieved a pile of newspapers from the table.

"Here, don't let yourself get down in the dumps worrying about it. You'll feel much better once you have a job and some place to live. I've been saving the newspapers for you so you can go through them."

I flipped open the newspaper to the Help Wanted section. It wasn't very long. Jamie saw me frowning.

"There aren't a lot of jobs around at the moment, but I've mentioned you to the ladies at work so if anyone hears of anything we'll let you know. And you're welcome to stay here for a couple of weeks until my dad gets back. I'm sure you'll find something by then."

The countdown on my forty days had begun.

With a week of job hunting under my belt, I had nothing to show for it. Not even an interview. I phoned Robert in London to see if he was coming to Devon for the weekend. He said he hadn't decided what he was doing yet. Once again, not the response I was looking for. I had to admit, if only to myself, that I had hoped for more enthusiasm from Robert upon my return to Devon. But instead he seemed to be slipping away. I hardly had time to worry about it now though.

Next I phoned Miss Harrison to give her an update on my progress. She was annoyed that it had taken me a week to contact her.

"But I've been busy job hunting all week. I wanted to wait until I had some news before calling. I was hoping to have a job by now. There isn't much around and I don't have that much money left so I'll have to find one soon. Have you heard of anything?"

It took Miss Harrison a few moments to respond. I interpreted her silence as a positive sign, thinking she was trying to come up with ideas. I was wrong.

"Gail," she said, in a clipped tone of voice which barely concealed her frustration, " I believe Miss Fielding made it perfectly clear to you that if you came back to Devon, you, and you alone, would be responsible for finding a job and accommodations. I'm afraid I can't help you."

I was stunned by her coolness.

"I just thought you might know of something, so thought I'd

ask. No need to get your knickers in a knot. I'll work something out, don't worry."

"I wish you the best of luck. Let me know when you do."

"When should I expect a visit from you?" I asked.

"Not for a while. I'm very busy at the moment. I really don't see a need to visit with you until you're settled somewhere. Let me know when you find something more permanent."

I said goodbye and quickly hung up the phone.

I phoned my dad, to let him know I was back in Devon. He invited me over for dinner on Sunday and said he would pick me up from Jamie's. At least he seemed pleased that I was back in Devon, even if Robert and Miss Harrison weren't.

On Saturday night I went out with some friends, determined not to sit at home waiting for Robert to call. There was a new disco opened in Nestleton which was supposedly all the rave. We decided to check it out.

When we got there the place was hopping. The miniscule dance floor was packed with sweaty bodies gyrating to the sounds of Motown. As I elbowed my way in, I spotted Robert standing by the bar. He didn't see me, but as I made my way towards him a pretty blond girl snuggled up close to him. I didn't know her but she obviously knew Robert very well. I stopped dead in my tracks, not sure what to do next. Robert put his arm around her waist, and pulled her close. These people were definitely not strangers to each other. I felt a stabbing pain in heart. I had been blind to his indifference towards me, but now it hit me full force. I was a fool for believing that Robert and I had something going. He had obviously found other things to occupy his mind during my absence. I turned to leave and bumped full force into John, one of the boys I had had a crush on during my college days.

"Hey, Gail, fancy seeing you here. I heard you'd moved up north."

I felt a flutter of excitement in my belly, to think he remembered me.

"Yeah well I thought better of it," I yelled over the music, "so I'm back."

"Great! Let's dance," he said, as he grabbed my arm and made a path for us through the crowd. I made sure that Robert saw me dancing with John. When the song ended, Robert motioned for me to follow him outside. I hesitated then followed.

"I was going to call you," he said, rubbing his hand up and down my arm.

"Yeah well you didn't, did you? And I can see why," I said jerking my head towards where he'd been standing at the bar.

"She's just a friend from London. Said she wanted to come down for the weekend, get away from the city. It's no big deal."

"Sure looks like it is," I said, fighting back tears.

"You don't own me, Gail," he said, suddenly on the defensive.

"Obviously not," I hissed. "See ya!" I spun around and went back inside. John was standing just inside the door. I grabbed his arm and pulled him towards the dance floor.

I felt lost without Robert, or at least the illusion of Robert, in my life. Not that he was ever really in my life, in the way I had imagined. I hadn't been without a steady boyfriend since I'd started dating Thomas back in grammar school, and now I felt lost without one. I hadn't realized what a void they filled in me, and how empty I was inside when I had no one to lean on.

Monday morning I took the bus to Nestleton to continue job hunting. Now there were only thirty days left until I went out of care. Not that being in care was proving to be of much use, given Miss Harrison's snot-nosed attitude, but it was the only safety net I had, and even that would be gone soon.

When Jamie got home from work that evening she was brimming with excitement.

"One of our estate agent clients was in today," she said, before she'd even taken her coat off. "They're looking for a secretary to work with a new partner who's joining their firm. I mentioned your name to them. They said for you to drop by."

When the estate agent's office opened next morning I was waiting outside, resume clutched in my hand. I told the receptionist why I was there and she asked me to take a seat. A few minutes later an elderly gentleman appeared. He introduced himself as Mr. Weir senior and invited me into his office. I handed him my resume and watched anxiously as he reviewed it.

"You seem to have jumped around a bit," he said frowning, "although I see your qualifications are impeccable. Why so many job changes?"

"I went to live in Manchester with my mother for a while but I missed being in Devon, so I came back. My father still lives here," I added, eager to give the impression of being a person of substance, the sort of person who would stick around for a while, despite what my resume indicated. I didn't want him mistaking me for one of the hundreds of young women who came down to Devon every spring looking for a summer job close to the beach, only to disappear like the summer sunshine in September.

"Well the position pays eleven pounds a week, with two weeks paid vacation a year, three weeks after five years. The office hours are nine to five. My son-in-law has just joined the firm and needs a secretary. Of course, we'll need to check your references before we can make you a firm offer."

I gave him Mr. Holden's name and phone number as a reference.

"We'll be in touch," he said. "If you are the successful applicant, how soon can you start?"

"This afternoon," I said with a smile.

I left Weir & Weir Estate Agents and went in search of a phone box. Now that I'd given Mr. Holden's name as a reference, I'd better let him know I was back in town. Besides, he had asked me to stay in touch and I saw no reason not to.

"What a coincidence that you should call today," he said, after we'd exchanged pleasantries. "I've just received a cheque for you from the Clerk's Office. It's for your back pay. Seems they felt duty bound to honour your contract after Miss Harrison gave them an earful for the way they were handling things. She wouldn't let it drop until they did the right thing by you, and paid you what they had promised. Where can I send the cheque?"

"Just hold on to it for me, please. I'll come and pick it up this afternoon. Oh boy, you can't imagine how much I need this right now. The timing couldn't be better. I had no idea Miss Harrison was still working on it. She didn't even mention it when I called her, and I'd given it up."

It occurred to me that perhaps I'd been a little hasty in my judgment of Miss Harrison.

When I got back to Jamie's after picking up my cheque, there was a message waiting for me from Mr. Weir senior. He asked me to call him as soon as I got in.

"Well Mr. Holden certainly gave you a glowing reference, Gail, so I'd like to offer you the position. Would you be able to start in the morning?"

"Absolutely!" I said, "Thank you so much. I'll see you then."

One hurdle down, one to go.

Now that I had a job, I busied myself with finding somewhere to live. It would have to be within walking distance of my new job or on a bus route. Jamie used her father's car to drive me around looking at places for rent, but they were all either taken already, too expensive, or too grungy. I had to put my search on hold until the weekend and focus my attention on learning the ropes at my new job. But time was running out. I began to worry that perhaps I wouldn't be able to find something before Jamie's father came home. Then what would I do?

I phoned Miss Harrison again.

"I thought you'd like to know that I found myself a job. I started on Wednesday at an Estate Agent's office in Torquay."

"Congratulations, Gail. I didn't think you'd have too much trouble finding something. Are the wages good?"

"They're paying me more than the college ended up paying me. And by the way, I finally got my back pay from them. It couldn't have come at a better time. I was almost out of money and won't get paid until the end of next week. Thanks for talking to them like you did. I don't think they would have paid me the money if you hadn't gone to bat for me."

"I'm glad I was able to help, Gail. And what about your accommodations, have you had any luck with them yet?"

"No, not yet. I can't find anything I can afford close to work. I'm still at Jamie's but her dad will be home in a week or so and

I promised her I'd have my own place by then. Do you have any ideas?"

Miss Harrison's tone changed abruptly.

"As I've explained to you before, Gail, you have to sort this out for yourself. I'm sorry, but I can't help you. It was your decision to go to Manchester, against my best advice, and your decision to come back to Devon. It's time for you to start taking responsibility for your own actions, and not expect other people to run around behind you cleaning up the chaos you create. You aren't a child anymore. Maybe in future you'll think twice before chucking up everything you've worked so hard to get. You just don't seem to appreciate how hard everyone worked to try and make things right for you. You'll have to handle this on your own. Let me know when you find something."

I slammed the phone down without saying goodbye. I wasn't in the mood for lectures today. I had too many other things on my mind. I stood in the phone box shivering and wondered what to do next. I had no one to turn to. It was dark and cold and rain pellets slashed against the glass of the phone box. I realized I was crying, but there was no sound. What was the point, there was no one to hear.

I wiped away my tears and set off in the rain, not knowing where I was going. I wandered down along the harbour, checking for 'accommodations to rent' signs. I wasn't sure which hurt most, the cold rain stabbing at my face or Miss Harrison's cold attitude. As I passed a pub door I heard Mary Poppins singing *Those were the days my friend.* I saw John sitting at a table with a group of friends, and was tempted to go in and join them. But instead I kept walking. I was in no mood for company and I didn't want my friends to see me this way.

The weekend newspaper had a new batch of rental advertisements. One place sounded particularly promising: it was cheap, close to a bus route, and available immediately. Jamie drove me to look at it. I sensed that she was getting as anxious as me about her father's imminent return, and was eager to do whatever she could to facilitate my departure. I tried not to take it personally.

We found the place without too much trouble. A lady by the name of Jill answered the door and invited us in. She was very attractive and looked to be in her late twenties. She showed us the room for rent and explained that she and her husband had split up shortly after moving in. She needed help managing her bills and was renting out the master bedroom. She had two young boys under the age of three and said she would appreciate some help babysitting occasionally. The house was bright and airy though sparsely furnished, and had a comfortable feel about it.

"The rent's four pounds a week, but that doesn't include food. You'll have to buy your own but you get full use of the kitchen."

"That'll be fine," I said, a little nervous about my complete lack of culinary skills. "When can I move in?"

"Any time you're ready. The room's available now."

First thing Monday morning I telephoned Miss Harrison to let her know I'd found somewhere to live. Now that the pieces were falling into place I began to relax. Despite all my worries I had managed to find myself a job and somewhere to live without any help from Miss Harrison or the ubiquitous Children's Committee. I began to believe I would make it on my own.

"I'll be moving in this weekend. It's a great place and my room is enormous so I'm sure I'll be very happy there."

"I hope so, Gail," Miss Harrison said, without too much enthusiasm. "Let's hope you can settle. I'll make arrangements to come and visit you there soon."

That evening I wrote a long letter to my mother telling her how well things were working out for me in Devon. I tried to sound as upbeat as possible, determined not to let her know how frightened I'd been about finding a job and somewhere to live. I didn't hear back from her for several weeks, by which time I was settled in at Jill's.

Jill and I got along well even though I nearly drove her crazy checking to see if it was alright if I did this, or alright if I did that. She told me to relax, settle down. This was my home too. She saw us as equals and treated me as such. But it didn't take her long to realize I was a total loss in the kitchen. She teased me about my ability to open tin cans and boil water, and not much else. I took it in stride, knowing she was right, but told her I was a willing student.

Some evenings when I got home from work she would have a hot meal waiting for me. I, in turn, helped with the boys and picked up groceries on my way home, to save her the trouble of having to go out.

As the chill of winter gave way to the warmth of spring I felt the bleak shroud of depression which had been my mantle for so long beginning to lift. I was settled at Jill's and my job was going well. I didn't have a boyfriend but perhaps that was a blessing. I realized I needed time to get to know myself, to learn to love myself, before I could ever truly love anyone else.

Miss Harrison eventually came to see me two days before my eighteenth birthday. She picked me up from work and we drove to Jill's. I was pleased to be able to show off my new home, and she was obviously impressed. I made us coffee which we took up to my room. I told her all about my job and how much I enjoyed it.

"I clear nine pounds a week, so I'm managing alright. After paying Jill four pounds for lodging, I'm left with five pounds in my pocket for food and spending money. I'm even managing to save a little," I said proudly.

"So it sounds like you feel you made the right decision, by coming back to Devon."

"Absolutely!" I gushed. "I couldn't believe how much I missed the countryside and the ocean. I guess I'm just not a city girl."

"Do you think Norman's return home had anything to do with your departure?"

"I suppose that's what clinched it, although it wasn't just that. Mum and I got on well enough as friends, but I guess what I was really looking for in Manchester was a mother, you know, someone who'd be there for me and love me, no matter what. But I guess I'm not a baby anymore, so it's just as well that I stand on my own two feet and get on with my own life. At least I know I tried. It just didn't work out. Now I can let go of my fantasy of going home to mummy. I'm not even sure why she was so keen to have me move up there anyhow, unless it's because I was old enough to work and could help out with the bills."

"Well it really is too bad things didn't work out for you up there, especially after giving up what you'd worked so hard for here in Devon. But it seems you managed to put your life back together again, what with your job and this lovely place to live. You must be feeling good about that, especially knowing you did it all yourself. I think you're going to be just fine, Gail. I know you've worried a lot about turning eighteen and being on your own, but you've proved that you can take care of yourself very well. I must admit it was hard, having to sit by and not help, but we all felt it was important that you learn to deal with these things on your own."

"Well I'll be eighteen in a couple of days and it doesn't seem so scary anymore. At least here in Devon I have friends and some family. Dad's really pleased to have me back in Devon. I've been seeing him and his wife, Judy, just about every Sunday since I got back. We usually go for a drive on the moors and stop at some pub for a couple of drinks before going back to their place for a yummy roast beef dinner. And I get together with my friends a lot and go dancing any chance I get."

Miss Harrison shuffled through her papers.

"I'm sorry to have to bring this up," she said, pulling a sheet of paper out of the file, "but have you given any thought to the money you owe the Children's Committee?"

"Oh yes, I nearly forgot," I said, jumping up to fetch my handbag from the dresser. "When I knew you were coming I went to the bank and drew out the money I owe."

I handed Miss Harrison a wad of one pound notes. She carefully counted them before slipping them inside the file.

"The Children's Committee will be very pleased indeed that you've been able to repay this loan, Gail. I'm proud of you."

"Thanks," I said, "but I'm still really annoyed about having to repay it in the first place. If it wasn't for the fact that I got my back pay from the college, I don't know what I would have done."

"I've got a hunch you would have managed somehow," she said, smiling.

"I guess you're right. I was bound and determined to pay off that debt before going out of care. It was a matter of pride."

"Going out of care isn't as final as it may seem. Under Section 58 of the Child Care Act we can offer voluntary assistance to boys and girls going out of our care, if they ask for it."

"That's good to know, but I think I'll be alright now. I feel I've grown up a lot in the last few months. It's like something clicked inside and I suddenly realized that the only person I was hurting by being so angry all the time was me. I spent all those years fighting the Children's Committee and resenting their interference but deep down inside I know they were only doing what was best for me. Or at least trying to. I don't think I made it very easy on any of you," I said, smiling sheepishly. "But now I realize I have to take care of myself. And that's okay. It doesn't scare me as much anymore and I can stand on my own two feet. I used to worry about turning eighteen and falling off the end of a plank into a shark infested ocean, if you know what I mean. But now I think I'll be alright. I've learnt how to swim. Jamie, the girl I stayed with, is on her own mostly too, but she manages just fine. It's just a question of getting used to it, and then getting on with it, is what she said."

"Well, I'll still be visiting Justin until he turns eighteen, so I'm sure I'll continue to get news of you. I hope you stay in touch with him. He always asks after you and tells me all about your letters and visits."

"Maybe he can have that visit with me that we talked about before, now that I'm back in Devon. I'm sure Jill wouldn't mind if he came and stayed here one weekend. Perhaps I'll write and suggest it to him."

Miss Harrison scribbled a note in her file, and I waited for her to finish.

"By the way," I said, "my friends are organizing a party for me this weekend to celebrate my birthday. Would you like to come? I'd love it if you could."

"That's very sweet of you, Gail, but unfortunately I'll be away on holiday then. But you know, even if I was available I'm not sure it would be a good idea for me to attend. You'd only have to explain to everybody who I was. I know you've been upset in the past about having to explain to your friends that you were in the care of the Children's Committee so perhaps it's just as well that I'm busy."

"I suppose you have a point," I said, "but nonetheless I would like to have you there. You've been a big part of my life for several years, and by Saturday I won't be in care anymore so I wouldn't have to explain anything to anybody."

"Thanks for inviting me, I really do appreciate it, but I must decline. You go and have fun with your friends. I'll be thinking of you. I believe Nurse will be thinking of you too. I was at Willowrey recently and she asked after you. I told her you were back in Devon and I'm sure she'd be delighted to hear from you."

"Maybe now that I'm settled I'll give her a ring," I said, feeling slightly guilty that I hadn't been in touch before.

"Well, Gail, I think that just about covers everything. Unless you have any questions, that is."

"No, at least nothing that comes to mind at the moment. Oh, I think Jill's just come home," I said, eager for something to distract us from the awkward moment of goodbye. "Would you like to come and meet her?"

Jill was busy unpacking groceries in the kitchen. The boys were sitting on the floor enjoying a snack.

"Jill, I'd like you to meet Miss Harrison, my Child Care Officer. We've just been having a visit upstairs but I wanted her to meet you before she leaves."

"Nice to meet you," Jill said, "Gail has told me about you, so it's nice to be able to put a face to the name."

"Likewise," Miss Harrison said, smiling and extending her hand.

"I'm really enjoying having Gail here," Jill said. "She's a great help with the children, which I really appreciate. It's hard, being on my own, but at least this way I get to go out once in a while."

The baby let out a squeal as his older brother tried to grapple something from his hand. Jill rushed to intervene.

"Nice meeting you," Miss Harrison said, as we made our way towards the front door.

"Well, Gail, I want to wish you the very best of luck in the future. And please remember, if any difficulties arise you can still contact the Children's Department. There will always be someone available to help or advise you, should you ever feel you need it."

"Thank you," I said, fighting back tears. I could hardly believe that such a major part of my life was over. I was truly and finally about to be on my own, but I wasn't frightened anymore. I knew I would survive.

On April 19, 1968 I received a letter from the Devon County Council. Enclosed was a receipt for the subsidy refund which I had struggled so hard to repay, stamped 'Paid in full', along with a letter.

> *Dear Gail,*
>
> *I am writing to send you my best wishes for your eighteenth birthday. As Miss Harrison will have explained to you, you will no longer be in the care of the Children's Committee under the Court Order. However if you wish for advice at any time in the future, Miss Harrison will be glad to help if you would like to get in touch with her.*
>
> *The Children's Committee is sending you separately a cheque for £2 and hope you will buy yourself a nice present.*
>
> *With every good wish to you for the future.*
> *Yours sincerely,*
>
> *Children's Officer.*

God bless the child who has her own ....

Meeting adjourned.

EPILOGUE

In September, 1968 I moved to London with a group of friends where I worked as a secretary on Fleet Street, among other places. In 1970 I decided to emmigrate to Canada on my own. During my trips home to England I would occasionally visit with Nurse but eventually lost touch.

In 2004, when I started doing the research for this book, I was unable to find any trace of Nurse in Devon. I assumed she had passed away as she would have been well into her nineties. I was however able to locate Aunty Dawn. When I contacted her she informed me that Nurse was in fact still alive and well and living in Poole. She gave me the phone number and I called.

"Hello, Nurse," I said rather tentatively into the phone. "I don't know if you remember me but my name was Gail."

"Oh yes, dear, I remember you," Nurse said with a chuckle. "You're the one who called me a witch."

What could I say?!

A few weeks later Jim and I boarded a plane for England to visit Nurse and Aunty Dawn. At 95 Nurse was still as sharp as a whip and able to get around on her own. She told me tales of her youth, of love unrequited, and of the countless children she had raised. We talked about the other girls who had been at Willowrey [not the true name] and what they were up to now. Nurse remembered them all and was still in touch with many of them. Her 'family' is spread far and wide and I am proud to be a part of it.

During that trip I obtained a copy of my file from the Devon County Council and had an opportunity to read, first hand, the accounts of my turbulent adolescence. I'd like to say that none of it was true, but unfortunately it is.

LaVergne, TN USA
28 January 2010
171347LV00010B/64/P